WEST ACADEMIC EMERITUS ADVISORY BOARD

ADVOCACY ON APPEAL

Fourth Edition

■ ■ ■

Randall P. Ryder
Director of Appellate Advocacy
University of Minnesota Law School
Minneapolis, Minnesota

Bradley G. Clary
Emeritus Clinical Professor
University of Minnesota Law School
Minneapolis, Minnesota

Sharon Reich Paulsen
Vice President for Legal Affairs and General Counsel
University of Vermont
Burlington, Vermont

Michael J. Vanselow
Former Adjunct Professor
University of Minnesota Law School
Minneapolis, Minnesota

WEST
ACADEMIC
PUBLISHING

COPYRIGHT © 2000 By WEST GROUP
© West, a Thomson business, 2004
© 2008 Thomson/West
© 2021 LEG, Inc. d/b/a West Academic
      444 Cedar Street, Suite 700
      St. Paul, MN 55101
      1-877-888-1330

ISBN: 978-1-64708-653-4

To Katie, Mason, Mia, and Lochlan; thanks Mom & Dad.

R.P.R.

To Mary-Louise, Cheryl, Ben, Caroline, Margot,
Sam, Rich, Mom and Dad.

B.G.C.

To Jeff and Katherine.

S.R.P.

To Joni, Michelle, Jason and Jesse.

M.J.V.

PREFACE

This handbook on appellate advocacy is set out in three parts. Part One lays out a basic advocacy recipe (i.e., decide where you are going; give the court a reason to want to go there; and give the court a permissible legal route), and then discusses theme selection, argument balancing, roadmapping, and analytical processing as devices to help you prepare the recipe. Part Two and Part Three apply the recipe to brief writing and oral argument, respectively, and give you further how-to-do-it advice. There are sample exercises throughout.

The handbook also includes an Appendix, containing six items. The first is a case problem containing two substantial issues. The second is a case problem containing three substantive issues. One or more of these issues may form the basis for a law school appellate advocacy course, enabling readers to practice their skills. Practitioners will be more interested simply in the substantive text for insights to inform their argument techniques in "real" cases. The third and fourth items in the Appendix are a sample appellate brief and a sample oral argument. The fifth item is a fact-description exercise for the Goldilocks hypothetical in the text. The final appendix contains information about the use of unpublished opinions.

We also have prepared for teachers a separate supplement, discussing potential pedagogical issues and containing two bench memoranda relating to the mock case problems. We hope you find these materials helpful.

R.P.R.
B.G.C.
S.R.P.
M.J.V.

May 2021

ACKNOWLEDGMENTS

There are far too many persons who have influenced us and our work over the years to thank all of them here. We do wish to recognize especially certain individuals and organizations, however.

We extend our thanks to West Group, and particularly Pamela Siege Chandler, who encouraged us to write this handbook, and who made it possible.

We are grateful to Susan Miller, who spent countless hours formatting and re-formatting the original document through the preparation process, and to Michelle Tillman, who assisted with the third edition.

We also thank the American Bar Association, for its permission to model the equal protection problem in this handbook upon one of its National Appellate Advocacy Competition problems from many years ago.

We thank the following University of Minnesota faculty and law students: Director of Legal Writing Christopher Soper, who helped create the underlying problem for the Model Brief and also provided feedback on the *Smith* problem; Janelle Ibeling, who was our research assistant and prepared the initial draft of the bench memorandum for the *Lane* problem in the teacher's supplement for the book; David Hansen, who assisted with citation updates in the third edition; Brooke Hokana and Alex Duffine, who helped re-write the *Lane* case record and bench memo in light of legal developments for the third edition; Andrew Prunty, who helped create the underlying problem for the Model Brief; Jonas Persson, who helped write the *Smith* problem and the initial draft of the bench memorandum; Linnea VanPilsum-Bloom, who helped rewrite the *Lane* problem and bench memorandum, and also assisted in reviewing the book; and Evan Nelson, who provided an earlier version of the model brief.

We want to acknowledge the inspiration we received from the complaints, dockets, orders, and appeals in *Thompson, et al. v. Merrill, et al.*, No. 2:16-cv-783-ECM, 2020 WL 7080308 (M.D. Ala. Dec. 3, 2020) and *Jones v. DeSantis*, 462 F. Supp. 3d 1196 (N.D. Fla. 2020).

We also thank various judges and teachers whose thoughts have in one way or another shaped the way we think about argument in this handbook. These include Justice Paul H. Anderson of the Minnesota Supreme Court and Richard S. Slowes, Commissioner of the Minnesota Supreme Court, whom we thank for their generous reviews of a draft of the first edition of our book; Eighth Circuit Court of Appeals Judge James B. Loken and Federal District Court Judge Joan N. Ericksen, whose advice on oral argument helped shape some of the recommendations found in these pages;

Professor C. Robert Morris, whom we thank for ideas about argument recipes; former Adjunct Professor Mark S. Olson, whom we thank for ideas about caricature; and Professor David McGowan, whom we thank for thoughts on the nature of common law analysis.

Finally, we extend our thanks to the judges, colleagues, and clients who have read our briefs and heard our oral arguments over our collective one hundred and thirty years of experience, and from whom we have learned so much in both victory and defeat.

Of course, the views expressed are those of the authors, and we take responsibility for any failings readers may perceive in this book.

SUMMARY OF CONTENTS

———————

TABLE OF CONTENTS

ADVOCACY ON APPEAL

Fourth Edition

INTRODUCTION

■ ■ ■

This is a handbook on appellate advocacy. Webster's dictionary defines a handbook first as "a book capable of being conveniently carried as a ready reference: manual," and second as a "concise reference book covering a particular subject."[1] We intend this text to be convenient, concise, and a ready reference.

In addition, this is a particular kind of handbook—a cookbook. We intend you to use the formula in this text to take the ingredients you have to work with (the facts and legal rules that govern your case), and to make an argument which (like a good meal) your audience will eagerly consume. Like any chef, we expect that you will modify the formula to create a masterpiece that reflects your best work.

We start by focusing on our audience. Legal writing is audience-based. An advocate does not make appellate arguments for the sheer fun of it. The advocate's audience is a particular court that must resolve a particular problem in a manner the advocate hopes will benefit a particular client.

Our audience consists of teachers, students, and practitioners of appellate advocacy. We assume that you, like most legal audiences, are busy people. You have to teach and learn appellate advocacy. You also have too much to do, and too little time in which to do it.

Thus, we write this handbook mindful of the key ingredient in all good legal argument—First, have a point to make. Then make it, and get out! In this book, we will:

- Set out two challenging legal problems, both of which involve multiple issues, any one or combination of which is suitable for a moot court or appellate advocacy course;

- Provide a set of exercises in each chapter where students may work through the problems;

- Explain how to argue effectively on behalf of a client for a beneficial resolution of the client's problem.

We do not intend this handbook to be a comprehensive text on all facets of appellate practice. We do not separately analyze, for example, how to preserve issues for appeal or the important threshold question whether an advocate should even file an appeal in a given litigation matter. We also

---

[1] "Manual." *Merriam-Webster.com Dictionary*, Merriam-Webster, https://www.merriam-webster.com/dictionary/manual. Accessed 14 Dec. 2020.

do not analyze in detail the many different local rules of appellate practice in the nation's jurisdictions. Nor do we debate technical rules exhaustively.

We instead limit our mission. We give you a basic advocacy recipe. Use it. Cook with it. Make it your own. Then, as an experienced chef, modify the recipe to suit your own needs on specific occasions with specific audiences.

PART ONE

AN APPROACH TO ADVOCACY

■ ■ ■

I.   THE BASIC RECIPE

> - **Decide where you are going.**
> - **Give the court a reason to want to go there.**
> - **Give the court a permissible legal route.**

Forty-six years ago, Professor C. Robert Morris of the University of Minnesota Law School gave one of the authors the following advice:

A lawyer making a persuasive argument first has to give the audience a reason to want to get to a particular result. Then the lawyer has to give the audience a legal route to get there.

We precede this advice with only one additional premise for a persuasive appellate argument recipe: Before an advocate can persuade an audience to go anywhere, the advocate must first decide upon the desired destination.

Based upon our own observations as lawyers and teachers over a combined one hundred and thirty years of experience, we suggest that the single biggest defect in ineffective arguments is that the advocate never fully decided what to say; so ultimately the advocate did not say it. This defect appears in numerous variations. For example:

- The advocate really has only one point to make, but has not determined what that is.

- The advocate really has only one point to make, and has determined what that is, but then makes additional points and causes the court to lose direction.

- The advocate really has one point to make, and is determined to make it, but then changes course in response to the other advocate's argument or the court's questions.

- The advocate really has three points to make, but has not determined what they are.

- The advocate really has three points to make, and has determined what they are, but then makes only one and causes the court to lose direction.

Consider a simple illustration involving a case presenting a personal jurisdiction issue. Assume that State A has a statute which says that an act committed outside of State A by a non-resident appellee subjects that appellee to personal jurisdiction in State A. The act does so when it causes injury to an appellant in State A. Now assume that a nonresident actor blows up a car just across the state line in neighboring State B. The force of the explosion pushes debris across the state line, thereby injuring an appellant in State A.

If these facts are stipulated, or "found" for purposes of appeal, appellant's argument should be: "All of the elements of the statute are satisfied. There is an act. The act occurred outside of State A. The actor is a nonresident. The act caused injury to the appellant. The injury occurred in State A. So the only personal jurisdiction issue is whether the statute satisfies constitutional due process. The statute does satisfy due process because it is fair to make the appellee take responsibility to defend his conduct in State A, for the following reasons . . . ."

How could advocates go wrong in this argument? They could go wrong by exploring unnecessary intricacies, thereby creating potential issues where none otherwise exist. They could go wrong by leaving out a step in the sequence. They could go wrong by applying the law out of sequence. They could go wrong by addressing the statute only, and not due process. They could go wrong by highlighting what *didn't* happen, instead of making it clear what *did* happen. They could go wrong by not explaining the "because" at the appropriate time. They could go wrong by not focusing on the fundamental fairness of making the appellee take responsibility for his actions. They could go wrong by not thinking through the problem and determining exactly where they need to go with their audience to get to a desired result. And, if these are the ways in which advocates do go wrong, the errors will significantly, and perhaps fatally, damage their argument.

So how can an advocate avoid going wrong? The basic recipe identifies the three things to do, but it does not identify how to do them. We offer in the following sections of Part One four thoughts on the how-to-do them question: first, select a theme by creating a caricature of your case; second, create a balancing chart to use in comparing and selecting potential arguments; third, create a road map for your selected argument to the court; and fourth, keep in mind the processes for working with two fundamental sources for rules (case law and statutory law), one or both of which you will use, depending on your case.

II. THE IMPORTANCE OF A THEME

> - **Identify your theme.**
> - **To help yourself do that, draw a one-frame cartoon of your case with a one-sentence caption.**

Effective advocates organize their arguments around a central theme.[1] Selection of a theme is at the heart of the first two pieces of the model argument paradigm, i.e., *deciding* where you are going and causing the court to *want* to go there with you. A theme is a core value that the advocate wants the court to embrace or recoil from. A theme is the preservation of a "good," such as stability, trust, freedom, responsibility, and loyalty, or the prevention of a "bad," such as abuse, laziness, recklessness, slippery slopes, and open floodgates.

A theme is not in itself a legal rule. A theme anchors the advocate's argument in support or rejection of a legal rule. A theme is an opportunity for an advocate to connect with their audience. Your audience knows the law, studies the law, and interprets the law. Your audience, however, is also a group of people who care about making a moral and just decision. Put another way: your theme informs the audience what the case is about and why it matters. If a point materially bears upon the theme, the advocate considers including the point in the argument for adoption of a specific rule. If a point does not materially bear upon the theme, the advocate considers discarding the point when arguing for adoption of the specific rule.

Notice that we refer to "theme" in the singular. Focus is important. If an advocate cannot articulate *any* theme, the advocate has not identified the problem involved in the case. Similarly, *too many* themes are a sign of the same concern.

So, what are examples of themes in practice? The following are three illustrations that revolve around a possible prevention of abuse theme in different contexts:

> Assume the United States files an environmental lawsuit under the Resource Conservation and Recovery Act, 42 U.S.C. § 6973 (RCRA) to pursue responsible parties for toxic waste. Congress enacted RCRA to protect the environment. When the government enforces the Act, it argues that the Act should be construed broadly to prevent environmental abuse. *See generally United*

---

[1] Carole C. Berry, Effective Appellate Advocacy: Brief Writing and Oral Argument 50–51, 77, 139 (3d ed. 2003); Bradley G. Clary, Primer on the Analysis and Presentation of Legal Argument 16–19 (1992).

States v. Reilly Tar & Chemical Corp., 546 F. Supp. 1100, 1107 (D. Minn. 1982).

Assume local authorities proceed against a parent for extreme physical discipline of a child. The parent defends on the basis of the need for parents to have freedom to enforce particular rules for the benefit of the child. When the authorities proceed against the parent, the authorities argue that their mission is to prevent child abuse. *See generally Cobble v. Commissioner of the Dep't of Social Services,* 719 N.E.2d 500, 507 (Mass. 1999).

Assume prosecutors charge a suspected criminal with burglary. The police interrogate the suspect for hours. They do not give him *Miranda* warnings.[2] He eventually confesses. The police say the confession is voluntary. When defense counsel moves to suppress the confession, she argues that the *Miranda* warnings are vital to prevent police abuse of suspects. *See generally Dickerson v. United States,* 530 U.S. 428, 442, 120 S. Ct. 2326, 2335 (2000).

You may not immediately identify your precise theme. Your first attempt may be too broad, or too narrow. Your theme also may evolve as you write your brief, or when you prepare for oral argument. However, because of the importance of your theme, it is critical to have at least a general understanding of your theme before you start crafting your arguments.

How do you pick the theme? One answer is: Draw a one-frame cartoon of your case. Fill the frame with a picture. Write a one-line caption. If you have to see the case in a single frame picture, with one caption, what do you see?

The following are three simple illustrations of this technique:

- Three bears are suing Goldilocks for converting their porridge. You are defense counsel for Goldilocks. As you picture your case, what do you see?

  You picture a pretty cottage in the woods. You picture an open front porch, with boxes containing colorful flowers hanging from the railings. You picture a big mat in front of the door. On the mat, embroidered in large capital letters, is the word "WELCOME." Standing on the porch is a forlorn little girl with golden hair. She is staring at the mat. Underneath the cartoon frame you see a possible caption, "They didn't mean it." The theme—caring.

  If you represent the three bears, you see a very different picture. A modest house in disarray; broken chair,

---

[2]   Miranda v. Arizona, 384 U.S. 436, 86 S. Ct. 1602 (1966).

refrigerator door open, half-eaten bowls of porridge strewn about the kitchen table. Three despondent bears with open paws look at a smug girl sleeping on their couch. Underneath the cartoon frame: "the front door was locked." The theme—stealing.

• An emperor is suing a little boy for defamation for having the audacity to tell the emperor in front of his advisors that he is wearing no clothes. You are defense counsel for the boy. As you picture your case, what do you see?

You picture a road in the city. There is a big crowd. The emperor is walking among the throng with his advisors. He is stark naked except for a t-shirt and undershorts. The entire crowd is raving about the ruler's fine clothes, but they are also staring at the emperor behind his back, and smirking. Underneath the cartoon frame you see a possible caption, "Dissemblers." The theme—honesty.

• A landowner is suing a girl for trespass. She has wandered onto his property and stuck her thumb in a hole in his wall. You are defense counsel for the little girl. As you picture your case, what do you see?

You picture a wall. On one side is the open sea—an angry, stormy sea. On the other side are green pastures, cows, colorful flowers, windmills, and farms. There are cracks in the wall and a large hole. A little girl is racing along the wall to put her thumb in the hole to keep the water from rushing through. Underneath the cartoon frame you see a possible caption, "Saved." The theme—heroism.

These are not the only cartoons an advocate might draw in the hypothetical. Reasonable advocates might picture their cases differently, with different captions. One of the themes of this book is the importance of trusting your instincts. You will know the facts of your case, the relevant law, and the applicable arguments, better than anyone else. Craft a theme based on your vision of the case.

Our purpose is not to decree one correct set of themes for the illustrations or for any other appellate cases. We merely suggest that legal problems all arise from some kind of story. Stories can be pictured. Stories have themes. Those themes anchor the relevant legal rules which will resolve the problems in the stories. Picture your story. Find your theme. Then mold your argument around it.

EXERCISES

1. Review the three bears example from above. Change the facts to alter the narrative. For example, suppose Goldilocks had

been wandering in the woods for days. Or, it was baby bear's birthday, and Goldilocks not only ate his porridge, she broke a handmade chair made by grandma bear. Picture the cartoon, write the caption, and identify the theme based on these new facts. *See* Appendix E.

2. Review the emperor has no clothes example from above. Picture the cartoon, write the caption, and identify the theme from the emperor's perspective.

3. Review the hole in the wall example from above. Picture the cartoon, write the caption, and identify the theme from the landowner's perspective.

Turn to Appendix A, and read the case record.

1. Picture the cartoon, write the caption, and identify the theme for the appellant in *Lane v. Moot State University Law School* on the question whether the law school's admissions policy violates the equal protection clause of the Constitution.

    Picture the cartoon, write the caption, and identify the theme for the appellees on the question whether the law school's admissions policy violates the equal protection clause of the Constitution.

    Picture the cartoon, write the caption, and identify the theme for the appellant in *Lane* on the question whether Attachment A to the Lisa Packer Affidavit should remain under seal.

    Picture the cartoon, write the caption, and identify the theme for the appellees in *Lane* on the question whether Attachment A to the Lisa Packer Affidavit should remain under seal.

2. Question for counsel to consider: Is it possible to pick a single theme that covers both issues?

3. After you have identified a theme for both sides of an issue, consider which side has the stronger theme. Determine if you can equalize the themes. If you are unable to do so, consider how that may impact the arguments on both sides.

Turn to Appendix B, and read the case record.

1. Picture the cartoon, write the caption, and identify the theme for the appellants in *Smith et al. v. Willis, et al.* on the question whether Moot State's disenfranchisement provision is racially discriminatory and violates the equal protection clause of the Constitution.

Picture the cartoon, write the caption, and identify the theme for the appellees on the question whether Moot State's disenfranchisement provision is racially discriminatory and violates the equal protection clause of the Constitution.

2.   Picture the cartoon, write the caption, and identify the theme for the appellants in *Smith* on the question whether Moot State's re-enfranchisement statute discriminates on the basis of wealth and violates the equal protection clause of the Constitution.

Picture the cartoon, write the caption, and identify the theme for the appellees on the question whether Moot State's re-enfranchisement statute discriminates on the basis of wealth and violates the equal protection clause of the Constitution.

3.   Picture the cartoon, write the caption, and identify the theme for the appellants in *Smith* on the question whether Moot State's re-enfranchisement statute is an illegal poll or other tax and violates the Twenty-Fourth Amendment of the Constitution.

Picture the cartoon, write the caption, and identify the theme for the appellees in *Smith* on the question whether Moot State's re-enfranchisement statute is an illegal poll or other tax and violates the Twenty-Fourth Amendment of the Constitution.

4.   Question for counsel to consider: Is it possible to pick a single theme that covers two of the three issues? All three of the issues?

5.   After you have identified a theme for both sides of an issue, consider which side has the stronger theme. Determine if you can equalize the themes. If you are unable to do so, consider how that may impact the arguments for both sides.

III.   THE IMPORTANCE OF BALANCE

> ▪ **Solutions to legal problems involve balancing.**

Courts decide legal problems through balancing equations.[3] The advocates present competing themes and competing rule choices based upon those themes. The advocates explain why their proposed themes and rules will preserve "goods" and prevent "bads." The courts, as neutral

---

[3]   *See* CLARY, *supra* note 1, at 22–25.

decisionmakers, decide how to resolve the problems by weighing the choices in light of the facts and the law.

Good advocates will take this balancing process into account in giving a court a reason to want to find in their favor and a permissible legal route to get there, two of the three ingredients of the basic argument recipe. Good advocates will actually prepare a balance sheet, as explained below, for their own use in preparing the argument because they know that, since the court consciously or unconsciously will do the same thing, there is no point in making their argument in a vacuum. It is not enough for advocates merely to tell the court why their theme and legal rule will achieve a good result; they have to convince the court that their theme and legal rule will achieve a good result that is *better* than the one their adversaries propose. Similarly, it is not enough for advocates merely to tell the court why their theme and legal rule will prevent a bad result; they have to convince the court that their adversaries propose a theme and rule that will produce a *worse* result.

In other words, the formation of legal arguments is a process of "compare and contrast." A court is always thinking about the balances it already has struck to resolve similar problems in the past, and the balances it will have to strike in the future if it adopts specific themes and related rules. And there is seldom only one "right" answer. There usually is a spectrum of potentially "right" answers. The question is which answer is *more* right on the facts of the specific case. If there were only one right answer, then the case should not be on appeal in the first place.[4]

This sometimes comes as a shock to beginning advocates. They assume that there is an agreed upon rule for any given problem. Everybody just needs to learn the rule. It will then provide the solution to whatever dilemma confronts the parties and the court. If the facts do not neatly fit the rule, the rule remains rigid and inflexible. But the law does not work that way. Appellate courts get cases from trial courts that have made decisions based upon the facts advocates identified and developed, and based upon themes and legal rules that lawyers advocated. Cases are like meals—depending upon the ingredients at hand and the way chefs assemble them, the resulting food tastes good or bad. There are lots of chocolate chip cookies in the world. They may all have some common ingredients. But they do not all turn out the same.

---

[4]   The United States Supreme Court, for example, takes cases precisely because different courts disagree over the proper resolution of problems. SUP. CT. R. 10. The Supreme Court itself also may be divided. In the October Term 2018, the Court issued 5–4 split decisions in 21 of 72 cases. Adam Feldman, *Final Stat Pack for October Term 2018*, SCOTUSblog, (June 28, 2019, 5:59 PM), https://www.scotusblog.com/2019/06/final-stat-pack-for-october-term-2018/.

So how should an advocate prepare a balancing chart? The following is one format. First, list all of the categories that will comprise components of your argument and your adversary's anticipated argument:

RECITATION OF ADVOCATE'S POTENTIAL ARGUMENT LIST	PREDICTION OF ADVERSARY'S POTENTIAL ARGUMENT LIST
• Problem to resolve	• Problem to resolve
• Potential "goods" to preserve	• Potential "goods" to preserve
• Potential "bads" to prevent	• Potential "bads" to prevent
• Material facts of dispute	• Material facts of dispute
• Material policy facts to consider	• Material policy facts to consider
• Potential legal rules to apply	• Potential legal rules to apply
• Proposed resolution of problem	• Proposed resolution of problem

Second, fill in each of the categories with the specifics of your controversy. Let your mind roam. Just because you put something on the chart does not mean you ultimately will use it. The chart exists to help you determine what is important. You are brainstorming the argument ingredients.

Third, determine what is important on the lists. Which theme is *best* on your list? On your adversary's predicted list? Which five facts relating to the specific dispute are *best* on your list? On your adversary's predicted list? Which five policy facts on your list will help *best* inform the court as to the overall implications of the dispute? On your adversary's predicted list? Which legal rule is *best* on your list? On your adversary's predicted list? Why are the argument components on your side of the balancing chart *better* than the components on your adversary's predicted side? Now you are evaluating the ingredients you actually will use.

Fourth, prepare the argument from your side of the chart. In other words, cook the meal you want to serve, based on the ingredients you evaluated. Out of all of the elements, comparatively, what is most important to your argument? As you prepare your argument, be mindful of all of the factors, and choose what you will highlight. Do you have a comparatively stronger theme based on policy facts? Do you have the best potential legal rule? Are you protecting important "goods?"

You are mindful, of course, of the likely meal your adversary will prepare. But cook your own first, and then compare and contrast it to the other. This will provide an opportunity to incorporate new ingredients into your own meal and make it even more appetizing.

Consider the following hypothetical balancing chart which could have been used in preparing the arguments in *Wyoming v. Houghton,* 526 U.S. 295, 119 S. Ct. 1297 (1999). The facts in *Houghton* were these: A Wyoming Highway Patrol officer stopped a car for speeding and brake light violations. The officer noticed a hypodermic syringe in the shirt pocket of the driver. When the driver admitted he used it to take drugs, the officer searched the car. He found a purse, concededly belonging to one of the passengers, Houghton. The purse contained a brown pouch, which Houghton claimed not to recognize, and a black container. Both contained syringes with methamphetamine in them, although only the brown pouch contained enough of that substance to justify the relevant felony charge. A jury convicted Houghton of a drug possession felony. The legal issue became whether the search of the purse was legal.

Assume you are counsel for the State of Wyoming on appeal. Your balancing chart might look like this:

Problem to resolve (Wyoming's view)	*Problem to resolve (Houghton's predicted view)*
Can a police officer search all containers in a car for evidence when the officer has probable cause to believe that the car's driver is involved in illegal activity?	Can a police officer search the belongings of a car passenger for evidence when the officer only has probable cause to believe that the car's driver, but not the passenger, is involved in illegal activity?
Potential "goods" to preserve Preservation of evidence Preservation of safety of police officers Preservation of stability of precedent interpreting reasonableness of searches under the Fourth Amendment	*Potential "goods" to preserve* Preservation of personal privacy rights Preservation of personal property rights
Potential "bads" to prevent Prevent drug abuse Prevent suspects from using containers belonging to passengers to escape detection, i.e. prevent impairment of law enforcement	*Potential "bads" to prevent* Prevent police harassment of suspects and non-suspects Prevent diminished expectation of personal privacy rights

Prevent a flood of mini-trials in already overloaded courts as to ownership of containers in cars	***Material facts of dispute for which to account***
Material facts of dispute for which to account	No indication that passenger had used drugs
Car involved—mobile	Contraband involved—no danger to officer
Contraband involved—easily disposed	Passenger did not concede all contents of purse were hers
Container in car	No specific probable cause to search the passenger or the passenger's personal effects
Container not on the person of the passenger	
Search of car, but not of the passenger personally	
Specific probable cause to search the driver and the driver's personal effects	***Material policy facts to consider***
Material policy facts to consider	Statistics regarding number of warrantless car stops and related searches in United States
Statistics regarding methamphetamine epidemic and the social and economic impacts	Facts regarding expectations of privacy in automobiles
Facts regarding reduced expectations of privacy in automobiles on public roads (likelihood of thefts, car accidents, rides given to friends, etc.)	Statistics regarding non-likelihood of "common enterprise" among driver and passengers
Statistics regarding likelihood of "common enterprise" among driver and passengers in drug cases	Statistics regarding police overreaching
Statistics regarding logjam of criminal cases in the courts involving potential unreasonable search arguments	
Potential legal rules to apply	***Potential legal rules to apply***
Bright line test—a police officer may search any containers in a car for possible evidence/ contraband, regardless of the	Alternative test—a police officer may search any containers in a car for possible evidence/ contraband, when the containers belong to the driver of the car, if the officer has probable cause to

ownership of the containers, whenever the officer has probable cause to believe evidence of a crime is present	believe the driver is engaged in illegal activity
Proposed resolution of problem	***Proposed resolution of problem***
A police officer should be able to search containers found in a car, regardless of the containers' ownership, when the officer has probable cause to believe the driver is engaged in criminal activity. The state's interest in effective law enforcement outweighs the limited personal privacy interest of a passenger, at least when the containers are not physically located on the person of the passenger at the time of the search.	If a police officer only has specific probable cause to believe that a car's driver is engaged in criminal activity, then the police officer should only be able to search containers belonging to that driver and found in the car. Any other rule is unreasonable and subjects passengers who are presumptively innocent to invasion of privacy.

In fact, the chart might look even more detailed. The point is not that the above is the only way to prepare. The point is rather that completing such a chart is a good way of making sure that an advocate understands where she is going. That makes it more likely the court also will understand the advocate's destination.

EXERCISES

1. Draft a balancing chart for the equal protection argument relating to the law school's admissions process in *Lane v. Moot State University Law School*.

2. Draft a balancing chart for the public access argument relating to the sealing of Attachments A and B to the Lisa Packer Affidavit in *Lane*.

3. Question for counsel to consider: When you prepare the balancing charts for more than one of these arguments, are you being consistent?

4. Draft a balancing chart for the equal protection argument relating to Moot State's felon disenfranchisement provision in *Smith et al. v. Willis et al.*

5. Draft a balancing chart for the wealth discrimination argument relating to Moot State's re-enfranchisement statute in *Smith et al. v. Willis et al.*

6.   Draft a balancing chart for the poll tax argument relating to Moot State's re-enfranchisement statute in *Smith et al. v. Willis et al.*

7.   Question for counsel to consider: are there elements on the opposite side that you did not previously consider? If so, will you incorporate those elements into your own argument? In the alternative, how will you address those elements in your argument?

IV. THE IMPORTANCE OF ROADMAPPING

> - **Think first about who, what, when, where, why and how.**
>
> - **Then set out a road map for the court that tells it what you want it to do, why, and how.**

An advocate must give the court a permissible legal route to the result she wants. First, of course, this means actually analyzing the relevant facts and potential legal rules to find such a route. But merely finding the route is not enough. The advocate also must take the court through the route step by step in a logical sequence.

As you begin to consider your roadmap, there are two critical components. One, the destination. Where do you want to take your passengers (audience) at the end of this journey? Two, how to get there; the journey is arguably as important as the destination. Your roadmap should involve careful consideration of what you want your passengers to see, what order they see things, and the perspective from which you want them to view landmarks along the way. There is more than one roadmap for each argument. Well-designed roadmaps, however, lead to the same destination: success.

To do that, an advocate first needs to ask herself various *What, Why, Who, When* and *How* questions:[5]

- *What* exactly is this case all about? What do I want the court to do? What does the court need to know to properly decide the case? What is my theme? What legal rule should the court select to solve my client's problem, consistent with the theme? Upon what facts should the court focus to support that choice of legal rule? What are my strongest arguments, or facts? In

---

[5]   A version of this what, why, who, when and how structure, in the form of a legal writing lesson exercise, appears in Bradley G. Clary and Deborah N. Behles, *Roadmapping and Legal Writing*, 8 PERSPECTIVES: TEACHING LEGAL RES. & WRITING 134 (2000).

other words, look at the balancing chart. It is not just an exercise to complete and then ignore.

- *Why* is that my theme? Why should the court want to adopt it? Why should the court conclude that my proposed choice of legal rule is the best choice to support that theme? Why do the facts support a favorable, and just, outcome for my client? Why should the court decide that my argument is more persuasive than the opposing party?

- *Who* are the members of the court? Do they already have views in my problem area? Have I taken those into account? If they do not already have views in my problem area, have I taken that into account?

- *When* did the relevant events in the story of my client's problem occur? When am I appealing in the context of the case? Am I on appeal from an interlocutory ruling or a final judgment? Am I on appeal from summary judgment or a jury verdict? In other words, does the story chronology matter? Does the procedural posture affect the standard of review on appeal?

- *How* will the court best follow my argument? How can I best convey the picture of my theme? How can I convey the proposed resolution in a way that will allow the court to adopt the same mindset? Is one sequence of rules and facts more logical and compelling than another? How will I answer the court's challenging questions? How will I address the opposing party's arguments?

Having thought about those questions, the advocate must create a road map to help the court understand how to reach a correct result. The court should be able to follow the advocate's road map to the proper destination. The road map will do the following:

- *State the theme*: This case is about [courage, responsibility, slippery slopes, etc.]

- *State what you want the court to do*: We ask the court to [affirm, reverse, remand the trial court's ruling on . . .]

- *Tell the court why it should want to do that*: You should [affirm, reverse, remand because . . .]

- *Tell the court the facts*: The material facts in this story are . . . [Tell the story.]

- *Tell the court what legal rule it should apply to give it a permissible route to the result it wants to reach*: The rule you should adopt in this case is [state rule.] Its elements are [state elements.] They are found in [identify source.]

- *Tell the court how it should apply the relevant legal rule to the relevant material facts to resolve the case in the proper way*: When you apply this rule, the result is . . .

All appellate argument is a form of road map. Briefs are simply road maps in written form. Oral arguments are simply road maps in spoken form. Road map well and you are on your way to effective advocacy.

EXERCISES

1. Prepare the road map for the appellant on the equal protection issue in *Lane*.

   Prepare the road map for the appellees on the equal protection issue in *Lane*.

2. Prepare the road map for the appellant on the issue of the propriety of sealing Attachments A and B to the Affidavit of Lisa Packer in *Lane*.

   Prepare the road map for the appellees on the issue of the propriety of sealing Attachments A and B to the Affidavit of Lisa Packer in *Lane*.

3. Prepare the road map for the appellants on the equal protection issue regarding the disenfranchisement provision in *Smith, et al. v. Willis, et al.*

   Prepare the road map for the appellees on the equal protection issue regarding the disenfranchisement provision in *Smith, et al. v. Willis, et al.*

4. Prepare the road map for the appellants on the wealth discrimination issue in *Smith, et al. v. Willis, et al.*

   Prepare the road map for the appellees on the wealth discrimination issue in *Smith, et al. v. Willis, et al.*

5. Prepare the road map for the appellants on the poll tax issue in *Smith, et al. v. Willis, et al.*

   Prepare the road map for the appellees on the poll tax issue in *Smith, et al. v. Willis, et al.*

V. TWO FUNDAMENTAL SOURCES OF LEGAL RULES: CASE LAW AND STATUTORY LAW

In this day and age, few legal problems are of entirely first impression. Thus, courts often select permissible legal routes to get to preferred results by reference to legal rules already articulated by constitutions, statutes, administrative regulations, and prior court decisions. Because courts do this, advocates also should do this. References to established sources of legal rules tend to give an advocate and her audience—the appellate court—confidence in choosing the *best* route to resolve a legal problem among the potentially competing choices.

Depending upon the type of authority potentially applicable to the advocate's case, there are essentially two ways in which to select a route by reference to previously articulated authority, and then to road map a legal argument for an appellate court. Understanding these two ways will give an advocate a method for proceeding to implement the three-part basic recipe for appellate argument. The chart on the next page sets out the two possibilities, focusing on case law and statutory interpretation.[6]

Before looking at case law and statutory analysis, notice that each column in the chart always starts with the problem confronting your client. Notice also that the problem always arises from facts. Facts drive legal analysis, and legal rules exist to apply to facts to resolve disputes. The question of what rule to apply always follows consideration of what problem has to be solved. Note also in the case law column that the cases are not entirely linear. Some will have different facts that will cause different rule choices.

CASE LAW Court decision	LEGISLATIVE LAW Status	
Problem to solve	Problem to solve	Problem to solve
Facts	Facts	Facts
Distill rule of law from Previous decisions:	Plain language [Intent clear]	Ambiguous language [Intent unclear]
	Determine intent of Legislature from:	Determine intent of Legislature from:
	Language	Language
	Purpose	Purpose

---

[6] Although we outline below a general approach to statutory interpretation, there is much modern debate over the proper methodology for analysis of statutes. For an extensive and informative discussion of the nuances, see the Symposium on Statutory Interpretation found beginning at 53 SMU L. REV. 3 (2000). Also, although we will focus on the development of the law through court decisions and the interpretation of statutes, the two methods of analysis also can apply generally to interpretations of constitutional language and administrative agency rules and decisions.

Case # 5 / Case # 4 \ Case # 3 \ Case # 2 / Case # 1		Canons of construction Legislative history [Committee reports, debates, sponsor remarks] Agency Interpretation Court interpretations (see Case Law side)
	Distill rule of law from language	Distill rule of law from all of above
Apply rule of law to present case by comparing case with previous similar and dissimilar cases.	Apply rule of law to present case by reference to intent of legislature, as shown by purpose and language.	Apply rule of law to present case by reference to intent of legislature, as shown by all of above.
Speak to sense of justice, common sense, sense of stability.	Speak to sense of justice, common sense, sense of stability.	Speak to sense of justice, common sense, sense of stability.

There are two primary sources of legal rules—case law and statutes:

Case Law.

Assume that an advocate is arguing a case in which the solution to the relevant legal problem will be governed entirely by a rule that flows solely from the decisions of the jurisdiction's relevant courts. In that event, a primary role of the advocate in selecting and describing a permissible legal route for the court is to identify how the present problem is like or unlike problems the court has resolved in particular ways in prior cases. The process is one of compare and contrast. "The common law is developed through patterns of cases, decided with reference to their facts, which come to stand for general propositions consistent with the patterns and holdings. It is an inductive method . . . ."[7] The advocate's job is to look carefully at what courts did in the past with problems involving similar and dissimilar facts, and then to reason from those individualized comparisons to a more general rule that appropriately will resolve the relevant problem. While

---

[7] Michael Stokes Paulsen, *Dead Man's Privilege: Vince Foster and the Demise of Legal Ethics*, 68 FORDHAM L. REV. 807, 845 (1999).

facts drive the analysis, skilled advocates also focus on the court's reasoning in every case. Even if a case has similar facts, but a different outcome, effective advocates can use strong reasoning to their advantage.

Case Analysis Example.

The Minnesota Supreme Court's opinion in *Pine River State Bank v. Mettille,* 333 N.W.2d 622 (Minn. 1983), illustrates the type of analysis involved.

The facts of the case were these (in relevant part): Pine River State Bank hired Richard Mettille as a loan officer in 1978. There was no written employment agreement. Later in 1978 the bank issued an employee handbook containing, among other things, sections on "job security" and "disciplinary policy." The bank fired Mettille in 1979. In subsequent litigation between the parties, the bank argued that Mettille was an at-will employee whom the bank was free to terminate at any time with or without cause. Mettille counter-argued that the handbook became part of his employment contract, and that the bank could not terminate him without complying with the handbook terms.

The court looked at the dispute, and laid out its analysis:

First, it identified the relevant problem: When can an employee handbook become part of an employment contract, and what are the implications of that?

Second, it identified the context for the problem: An employer, to save the transactional costs of negotiating written contract provisions with every employee in the organization, might opt to issue a personnel handbook as a form of unilateral contract offer, which each employee might then accept by continuing to work for the employer.

Third, it looked at its own treatment of other employee handbook cases. It looked at *Cederstrand v. Lutheran Brotherhood,* 117 N.W.2d 213 (Minn. 1962). There, "a 'control copy' of the employer's personnel policies contained a provision that employees would not be dismissed without good cause. We held, however, that since this dismissal provision did not appear in the separate manuals given to employees it was not a contractual offer to employees but merely a policy guide for supervisors." *Pine River State Bank,* 333 N.W.2d at 627, n.4. Then, the court looked at *Degen v. Investors Diversified Services, Inc.,* 110 N.W.2d 863 (Minn. 1961). There, "the employer's personnel policy provided for a preliminary discussion between the employee and his immediate supervisor and for a dismissal interview with a member of the personnel department present before termination. We held that the employer's failure to follow this procedure did not create a contract for either lifetime or definite term employment." *Pine River State Bank,* 333 N.W.2d at 627, n.4.

Fourth, the court concluded that these prior cases were different from the *Pine River State Bank* case in that the bank distributed its personnel policy to employees, and Mettille (in relevant part) was not contending he was entitled to lifetime or definite term employment, but merely compliance with specific termination procedures.

As a result, the court concluded that the disciplinary policy section of the handbook was part of the parties' employment contract, which was breached when Pine River State Bank failed to follow it.

Statutory Law.

Now assume that an advocate is arguing a case in which the solution to the relevant legal problem will be governed by a rule that flows from a statute passed by the legislature in the relevant jurisdiction. In that event, a primary role of the advocate in selecting and describing a permissible legal route for the court is to identify how the statute applies to the case at hand. The process is essentially deductive, rather than inductive.[8] The advocate starts with the general rule given by the text of the statute to cover a class of problems, and then imposes it on current facts.[9]

Statutory Analysis Example.

The United States Supreme Court's opinion in *Abbott Laboratories v. Portland Retail Druggists Ass'n*, 425 U.S. 1, 96 S. Ct. 1305 (1976), illustrates the type of analysis involved.

The facts of the case were these: Manufacturers of pharmaceutical products were selling them in Oregon both to commercial pharmacies and to nonprofit hospitals. The commercial pharmacies were dispensing the drugs to customers at their retail outlets. The hospitals' pharmacies were dispensing the drugs to inpatients, outpatients, employees, and doctors. The manufacturers were selling the drugs to commercial pharmacies at higher prices than to the nonprofit hospitals. The commercial pharmacies sued the manufacturers, claiming that the higher prices violated the federal Robinson-Patman Price Discrimination Act, 15 U.S.C. § 13(a). The Act makes it unlawful for a seller in commerce to discriminate in price between purchasers of like commodities, when "the effect of such discrimination may be substantially to lessen competition." There also is a Nonprofit Institutions Act, however, which exempts from Robinson-Patman "purchases of their supplies for their own use by schools, . . . hospitals, and charitable institutions not operated for profit." 15 U.S.C. § 13c. Thus, the case turned on whether hospitals are purchasing drugs

---

[8]   Paulsen, *supra* note 7, at 845.

[9]   There also are hybrid circumstances: There is a statute that applies to a legal problem. The courts believe the statute is ambiguous. The courts have adopted a case-by-case look at specific fact scenarios to determine how to apply the statute. The process is both deductive and inductive.

"for their own use" when their pharmacies dispense the drugs to inpatients, outpatients, employees, and doctors.

The Supreme Court divided the facts into categories, and announced that it was "concerned with line drawing."[10] Then the Court laid out its analysis:

First, it looked at the language of the two statutes, and compared them. [Always start with the language of the statute.]

Second, it examined the context of the dispute involving the tension between supporting charitable work, and yet not giving charities unfair advantage over other businesses when the charities engage in commercial activities.

Third, it decided whether the Robinson-Patman Act was the kind of statute that is remedial and should be interpreted broadly to protect small businesses, like retail pharmacies. [Always look at the type of statute, and its purpose.]

Fourth, it examined the legislative history of the Nonprofit Institutions Act, to try to ascertain its intent (and identified competing possibilities) relating to protection of charities. [If a statute is ambiguous, examine the committee reports, legislative debates, and statements of sponsors for insight into the legislature's intent.]

Fifth, it determined to establish a test for what constitutes "for [hospitals'] own use" that would make sense, would not be arbitrary, and would comply with congressional intent. [Always distill a relevant legal test.]

Finally, it ruled that certain drug purchases by nonprofit hospitals would be exempt from Robinson-Patman as being "for their own use," and others would not. [Always apply the test to solve the problem.][11]

When you have a case to argue, think about the problem involved. Identify clearly the material facts. Then ask yourself whether the solution to the problem is governed by common law or statute, or both. Next, make sure that you go through the analysis in the chart above as you try to

---

[10] Abbott Labs., 425 U.S. at 10.

[11] Other particularly informative statutory interpretation cases are Exxon Mobil Corp. v. Allapattah Servs., Inc., 545 U.S. 546, 558, 125 S. Ct. 2611, 2620 (2005) (suggesting examination of a statute's text "in light of context, structure, and related statutory provisions"); Koons Buick Pontiac GMC, Inc. v. Nigh, 543 U.S. 50, 60, 125 S. Ct. 460, 466 (2004) (stating that "[statutory construction is a holistic endeavor"); Gen. Dynamics Land Sys., Inc. v. Cline, 540 U.S. 581, 600, 124 S. Ct. 1236, 1248 (2004) (relying on "text, structure, purpose, and history" to determine a statute's meaning); Barnhart v. Sigmon Coal Co., 534 U.S. 438, 450, 122 S. Ct. 941, 950 (2002) (seeking a "coherent and consistent" statutory scheme first from plain language, then context); FDA v. Brown & Williamson Tobacco Co., 529 U.S. 120, 133, 120 S. Ct. 1291, 1301 (2000) (remarking that "it is a fundamental canon of statutory construction that the words of a statute must be read in their context and with a view to their place in the overall statutory scheme"); and Kokoszka v. Belford, 417 U.S. 642, 650, 94 S. Ct. 2431, 2436 (1974) (analyzing statutes by considering their "language and purpose").

identify what you will tell the court. In that way, you will help the court understand the permissible legal route to resolve the problem in the manner you wish.

EXERCISES

1. Determine the type of analysis you need to do for the equal protection issue relating to the admissions policy in *Lane v. Moot State University Law School.*

2. Determine the type of analysis you need to do for the protective order issue in *Lane.*

3. Is the type of analysis the same for each issue?

4. Determine the type of analysis you need to do for the racial discrimination issue in *Smith, et al. v. Willis, et al.*

5. Determine the type of analysis you need to do for the wealth discrimination issue in *Smith, et al. v. Willis, et al.*

6. Determine the type of analysis you need to do for the poll tax issue in *Smith, et al. v. Willis, et al.*

7. Is the type of analysis the same for each issue?

PART TWO

THE BRIEF

∎ ∎ ∎

I. IN GENERAL

The most important part of an appeal is the appellate brief.[1] This part includes general remarks regarding appellate briefs, a more detailed discussion of the different components of a typical appellate brief, and a discussion of various writing style considerations in the preparation of a brief. Finally, this part concludes with some comments specific to reply briefs.

A. IMPORTANCE OF THE BRIEF

Most appellate judges and attorneys would agree that the brief is the most important part of an appeal.[2] There are several reasons for this. First, the brief is the first opportunity for you to create a favorable, or unfavorable, impression with the appellate court. Appellate judges and their law clerks usually will have read your brief before the oral argument and often will have formed some strong impressions regarding the merits of your case. Often, such initial impressions are nearly impossible to alter in a relatively short oral argument.

Second, and perhaps most importantly, the brief is your opportunity to lay out your analysis of the case in detail with supporting citations to case law and other authorities and to the factual record on appeal. It is impossible to articulate your detailed and comprehensive legal analysis in the short time available for oral argument. Because questions from the court frequently dictate the content of an oral argument, many oral arguments jump around to different topics in a very disjointed fashion. The brief, on the other hand, allows you to articulate your analysis in a logical and organized structure.

---

[1]   This part of the handbook deals with appellate briefs on the merits of an appeal. There are other types of briefs submitted in connection with appeals, including, for example, briefs in support of motions directed to the appellate court and amicus briefs.

[2]   Although judges and practitioners may disagree about the relative importance of oral argument in the appellate process, no one disagrees with the fundamental proposition that the brief is by far and away the most important feature of the appeal. . . . [M]ost cases are won or lost on the briefs. If you file a good brief, you will probably be okay, no matter how ineffective your oral argument. If you file an ineffective brief, however, you are almost certainly in deep trouble, regardless of your oratorical skills." William J. Bauer & William C. Bryson, *The Appeal,* THE DOCKET, Spring 1987, at 12.

Finally, the brief is not only your first, but often your last, opportunity to persuade the court. This is especially the case where a long time has expired between the oral argument and the final preparation of the court's opinion. While appellate judges and their law clerks may have difficulty recalling what you said at an oral argument months earlier, they will always have your written brief to read and reread to remind them of your arguments. In fact, in some appeals, in which no oral argument is permitted, the brief is not only your first and last, but your *only,* opportunity to persuade the court.[3] In other words, think of your brief as your written road map designed to guide the appellate court to the destination you seek. Just as you may consult a road map several times during the course of a complicated journey, so may the court consult your brief several times as it determines the direction it wants to take on your appeal.

B. PURPOSES OF THE BRIEF

The paramount goal of the appellate brief is to persuade. An appellate brief is an opportunity to showcase your advocacy skills on every page. An objective legal analysis, appropriate for an internal memorandum a law firm associate might write for a partner, is not persuasive to an appellate court. Neither is an overly comprehensive analysis stuffed full of lengthy string cites and scholarly citations such as one often sees in a law review article. Counsel sometimes lose track of this goal and their briefs end up reading more like law firm memoranda or law journal articles. As such, the briefs lose their persuasive force.

As explained in Part One, your mission in an appeal is to identify the result you want, to convince the court to desire the same result, and to provide the court with a sound legal analysis that enables it to reach that result. In order to prevail, you need all three ingredients. It is not enough to persuade the court that you should prevail (the why), and then fail to give it some reasoned way to rule in your favor (the how). Likewise, it is not enough to give the court a technically viable means to rule in your favor consistent with precedent, but fail to provide an analysis of the equities and public policy reasons that compel the court to want to rule your way.

Because the central goal of the brief is to persuade, advance this goal throughout your brief and not just in your argument section. You should draft your entire brief in a manner calculated to persuade, including, for example, the statement of the issues and the statement of the facts.

---

[3] "[T]he brief speaks from the time it is filed and continues through oral argument, conference, and opinion writing. Sometimes a brief will be read and reread, no one knows how many times except the judge and his law clerk." H. Goodrich, *A Case on Appeal—A Judge's View, in* A CASE ON APPEAL 10–11 (ALI-ABA 1967), *quoted in* ROBERT L. STERN, APPELLATE PRACTICE IN THE UNITED STATES 227 (2d ed. 1989).

Another goal of the brief is to maximize your personal credibility as counsel. Appellate judges are more likely to rule in favor of counsel they trust and respect. Conversely, they are likely to distrust counsel who fail to follow the court's rules, who miscite cases and the record, who employ faulty logic, who fail to proofread their briefs, or who fail to cite directly contrary authority. This part discusses ways in which you as counsel can maximize your credibility with an appellate court as well as ways in which you can lose credibility.

C. COURT RULES REGARDING BRIEFS

Every appellate court has rules relating to appeals and the preparation of briefs.[4] Read these rules and follow them. Your failure to follow these rules can undermine your credibility and even prove fatal to your client's position on appeal.

These appellate rules typically govern such things as the color of the cover of the brief, contents of the brief, typeface and margins, maximum page length, word count, number of footnotes, permissible types of bindings, content of the appendix, service and filing deadlines, and the number of copies to be served and filed. Some of these rules are extremely detailed. If you do not understand a particular rule, you sometimes can get clarification by calling the office of the clerk of court. Do not, however, get lazy and use the clerk's office as a substitute for your own legal research. Your reliance on the clerk will not prevail in the face of contrary judicial interpretation of the rules that you could have uncovered through your own research. In the final analysis, it remains your obligation to comply with the rules.[5]

It is imperative that you as counsel familiarize yourself with these rules and follow them. You may have a very persuasive brief, but it will do you no good if the court refuses to read it because you failed to follow the court's rules. Appellate judges get particularly annoyed when counsel deliberately circumvent the court's rules. For example, counsel who try to get around page limitation rules for briefs by creative manipulations of margins, lines per page and typeface risk having their briefs thrown out or not read past a certain page. While you can sometimes cure mistakes made from non-compliance with the court's rules, this can be time-consuming and very costly. You also risk the fact that the court may never read your late, "corrected" submission. In some instances, you can even expose

---

[4] The United States Supreme Court has such rules. Appeals in the federal circuits are governed by the Federal Rules of Appellate Procedure. In addition, many of the federal circuit courts have additional or supplemental rules. *See, e.g.,* 8TH CIR. R. APP. P. Likewise, state appellate courts have their own appellate rules.

[5] It may be helpful to reference other briefs filed with the same court. Be careful, however, in relying on other previously filed briefs. Some of these briefs may not have been in compliance with the rules when they were filed. Moreover, it is possible that the court's rules changed since the filing of these briefs.

yourself to sanctions and/or a professional malpractice claim if your failure to follow the court's rules prejudices your client's case. At the very least, you will certainly undermine your credibility before the court has even had a chance to consider and evaluate your brief. If you are arguing that the trial court should be reversed because it did not follow the law or rules, your own failure to do so will cast your appeal in a poor light.

II. COMPONENTS OF THE BRIEF

While appellate court rules differ somewhat in regard to the required contents of an appellate brief on the merits, most require that such briefs include the basic components described below.

A. STATEMENT OF THE ISSUES

An articulation of the issues on appeal is an absolutely critical part of an appellate brief. In many briefs, this statement is the first thing the appellate judges will read and your first opportunity to create the impression that your case presents interesting and important issues for the court to decide. Judges often form strong initial impressions about the seriousness of the appeal from counsel's threshold articulation of the issues.[6] The statement of the issues is especially critical when you are seeking discretionary review on appeal. If you do not include a well-articulated statement of interesting and important issues in your petition for review, there is little chance the appellate court even will accept your appeal to review from among the many other competing petitions the court receives.[7] Following are several principles to keep in mind when preparing your statement of the issues.

> **FRAMING THE ISSUES**
> - Reflect your theme
> - Suggest the result you desire
> - Be specific—highlight and incorporate your key favorable facts
> - Follow the court's rules re: format of issues
> - Lead with strength
> - Incorporate standard or review/burden of proof if helpful
> - State issues as narrowly as necessary to win the case

---

[6] Albert Tate, Jr., *The Art of Brief Writing: What a Judge Wants to Read, in* THE LITIGATION MANUAL 230, 234 (John G. Koeltl & John Kiernan eds., 1999).

[7] The United States Supreme Court receives approximately 8,000 certiorari petitions each term and accepts only about 130 of these petitions to review. Telephone call with United States Supreme Court Clerk's Office (Sept. 14, 2000). Given these odds, it is absolutely vital that the appellate litigant prepare a strong statement of the issues that will pique the Court's interest.

1. Number of Issues—Do Not Shotgun

While there is some temptation as counsel for an appellant to include every single alleged error the lower court made as a distinct issue in your statement of the issues, such a strategy is destined to fail. Almost all appellate judges and commentators strongly advise counsel to limit the number of issues raised on appeal to the very small, select number of issues that present a genuine question whether the lower court committed reversible error. This means that in all but the most extraordinary cases you ought not include more than a few issues in your statement of the issues. An appellate brief is not a law school exam answer for which you get extra points for spotting collateral and obscure issues. To the contrary, your inclusion of too many issues will only weaken and dilute your brief and the legitimate issues you raise by conveying the impression that you are desperate and that all of your issues are as weak as the weakest you include. Quite simply, throwing as much mud at the wall as you can with the hope that some of it will stick is a doomed strategy in an appeal.

You also should not include multiple iterations of the same issue in your statement of the issues. This will tend to weaken your brief and likely annoy the busy appellate judges who will read your brief and decide your appeal. There is nothing improper about a brief that presents a single issue on appeal. In fact, the court will likely appreciate your focus and your brief will be even more powerful. If you have a case that has inter-related issues, you should consider presenting them as subparts of a single issue rather than distinct issues.

> **Example:** *Should certification of a class be denied under Fed. R. Civ. P. 23 if:*
>
>   *a. the interests of the class representatives conflict with the interests of the majority of the class members; or*
>
>   *b. relief in the action would inure to the benefit of all of the proposed class members even in the absence of certification?*

Do not, however, try to make a lengthy list of issues appear to be a shorter list through the use of subparts.

Having said all this, you should still engage in the exercise of cataloguing all possible issues when you are initially preparing your appeal. Simply make sure you do not just dump this laundry list into your brief. Once you have the list of possible appellate issues, you should critically review it, select one or a few of the strongest issues and set the rest of the list aside. Keep in mind when you are identifying possible issues that issues not raised below usually are not appealable.

2. Order of the Issues—Lead with Your Strongest Issue Unless Logic Dictates Otherwise

In setting forth the order of your issues, you should lead with strength. That is, set forth your strongest issues first. This will create an immediate impression of the strength of your appeal that will likely affect the court's attitude toward the remaining issues and the rest of your brief. Many judges expect that you will include your strongest issues first and may, therefore, tend to discount other issues left to the bottom of your list.

In some cases, you may want to alter this principle and put one or more of your weaker issues first if this logically makes sense. For example, you may raise a threshold jurisdictional issue that the court should appropriately consider before it decides the issues going to the merits of the case. In other instances, based on the issues you raise, it may make sense to present them in a particular sequence even though you will end up deferring some of your stronger issues. This is especially the case when the issues are inter-related and logically build upon one another.

3. Form of the Issues—Read the Court's Rules Regarding the Form and Style of the Issues

Be sure to read the appellate court rules regarding the form of the statement of the issues. Typically, these rules require that the issues be stated succinctly, without unnecessary detail and in a non-argumentative manner. The rules may or may not require that you set forth immediately after each issue how the court or courts below decided the issue. The rules also may require you to identify the cases or statutes most germane to each issue.

It is common, although typically not required by court rules, for issues to be stated in the form of a question. The issue may be stated in the form of a simple declaratory question such as:

Example: *Are school districts required to realign their staff to reinstate the most senior teachers on unrequested leave just as they are required to realign their staff to retain their most senior teachers when they place teachers on unrequested leave?*

Alternatively, some attorneys prefer to frame the issue in a statement beginning with the word "Whether." The same issue above can be converted to this form as follows:

Example: *Whether school districts are required to realign their staff to reinstate the most senior teachers on unrequested leave just as they are required to realign their staff to retain their most senior teachers when they place teachers on unrequested leave.*

Some judges and commentators prefer that the issue be set forth in several sentences that provide some additional factual and/or procedural context for the legal question.[8] An example of an issue in this format is:

Example: *School districts in the State of Moot are required to realign their staffs when they place teachers on unrequested leave in order to try to retain the districts' most senior teachers. The Pine Tree School District placed the plaintiff on unrequested leave and subsequently reinstated a teacher less senior than the plaintiff. Was the District obligated to realign its staff to reinstate its most senior teacher on leave?*

Any of these forms may be acceptable depending upon the rules and practice of the court.

4. Draft the Issues in a Way That Suggests Your Theme and the Result You Desire but Do Not Overdo It

Just as the brief in general is intended to persuade, the statement of the issues should also be drafted if possible in a manner intended to persuade the court to adopt the result you seek. You can do this by drafting your issues in a manner that suggests your theme and the desired outcome. For example, following are two issue statements that are presented in an objective and neutral manner.

Examples: *Did the trial court err in refusing to tell the jury of plaintiff's settlement agreement with the settling defendant physicians?*

Did the trial court improperly deny plaintiff's motion for leave to amend his complaint?

You can redraft these issues in a manner that presents the same basic issues but is calculated to start to condition the court to favor your side of the case:

Examples: *Did the trial court err in refusing to disclose to the jury the terms of the plaintiff's settlement agreement with the defendant physicians when the physicians had a direct financial stake in the outcome of the trial and testified as witnesses?*

Did the trial court abuse its discretion in refusing to allow plaintiff to amend her complaint on the eve of trial, and seven years after the action was commenced, to add two entirely new claims based on

---

[8]   *See, e.g.,* BRYAN A. GARNER, THE WINNING BRIEF 77–79 (1999); Jordan B. Cherrick, *Issues, Facts, and Appellate Strategy, in* THE LITIGATION MANUAL, *supra* note 6, at 96, 101.

facts known to plaintiff at the time the suit was first commenced?

As these examples demonstrate, you can often make a neutral issue statement more persuasive by identifying and referencing a few of the key facts that support your case. These facts create some additional context for an otherwise neutral legal question that can suggest that the court ought to decide the question in your favor.

While you should try to prepare your issue statement in such a way that it conveys your theme and suggests the result you desire, be careful not to overdo this. In an effort to be persuasive, attorneys sometimes draft issues that are so grossly one-sided that they no longer accurately set forth the questions for the court to decide. The Wyoming Supreme Court noted an example of such overly argumentative and melodramatic issue statements in a banking case it decided. Following are the first two issues as framed by the appellants in that case:

1. Is dishonesty within the banking industry acceptable?

2. Do banks have a right to be dishonest—so long as they only cheat or defraud other banks?[9]

A court is not going to find such issue statements useful and is only likely to conclude that counsel is over-reaching. While you want to persuade, you also need to be fair to preserve your credibility. It is better to draft a neutral issue statement than an overly one-sided and argumentative one that undermines your credibility.

5. Consider Incorporating the Burden of Proof and/or Standard of Review in Your Issue Statement

In some instances, you may want to include in your issue statement a reference to a party's burden of proof or the applicable standard of review if it helps you. For example, in representing an appellee, you may want the court to focus on the fact that the appellant must show not simply that the trial court made an error, but that the court clearly abused its discretion. Following is an example of a statement that incorporates the standard of review in this fashion.

Example: *Did the district court clearly abuse its discretion in enjoining the plaintiffs from prosecuting a duplicative and later-filed lawsuit challenging the administration of a trust over which the district court has had primary jurisdiction the last forty years?*

Similarly, you may want to highlight the burden of proof if it is something other than a mere preponderance of the evidence.

---

[9] First Bank of Wheatland v. Am. Nat'l Bank, 808 P.2d 804, 805 (Wyo. 1991).

Example: *Did the district court correctly award summary judgment for the defendant newspaper because no reasonable jury could have concluded that the newspaper's failure to investigate the veracity of a source established, by clear and convincing evidence, that the newspaper acted with actual malice?*

Including such a reference to the standard of review and/or burden of proof may help condition the court early on in its review of your brief that your opponent has an especially high hurdle to overcome to prevail on the appeal.

6.   State the Issues as Narrowly as Possible to Win Your Case

When preparing your issues, be careful to not unnecessarily broaden the issues on appeal and thereby lessen your client's chances of prevailing. As counsel, your role is to prevail on the case for your client. Your role is not to champion some grand cause and change the world. You may be tempted to articulate the issues in a manner that might indeed advance some broader personal or societal interests. In doing so, however, you may jeopardize your client's interests by expanding the breadth of the issues and the possible ramifications of the court's ruling. While a broad, new expansion of the law may be desirable, it may be necessary for you only to show that your client meets an already recognized exception to the accepted rule. Do not serve the court Baked Alaska when a simple apple pie will suffice for your client. Keep in mind what your client needs to win the case and draft your statement of the issues accordingly.

7.   Do Not Frame Your Issues Too Generally

All too often, counsel prepare issues that are far too general. Examples of such issues are the following:

Examples: *Did the trial court err in granting defendant's summary judgment motion?*

Does the complaint fail to state a claim upon which relief can be granted?

Such issue statements are of little, if any, value to the court. They communicate almost nothing about the legal and factual questions presented on the appeal and "why" the court below committed reversible error. Moreover, there is little chance that an appellate court would decide to exercise discretionary review of a case based on such poorly drafted issue statements in a petition for review. For example, the issue statements in Case Record #2, are fairly general, for pedagogical reasons. Compare that to the issue statement from the Model Brief, discussed below.

In drafting your statement of the issues, identify the key legal principles and facts that you intend to address and try to weave these into your issues.

Examples: *Whether Moot Health and Safety Code § 159 is a reasonable exercise of the State of Moot's inherent police power to protect the health and safety of its citizens under the Tenth Amendment?*

[In this issue statement, the state of Moot wanted to highlight the deference owed to the state's exercise of its police powers (inherent) and their importance (protect health and safety)]

Does a school district violate the Establishment Clause if it allows its students to perform a religious song, that the student body selected, at its high school graduation ceremony?

[In this issue statement, the school district wanted to highlight the fact that the students selected the song of their own volition.]

Is a school district liable for the tortious conduct of one of its teachers if the district had no actual or constructive knowledge of any prior torts committed by the teacher?

[In this issue statement, the school district wanted the court to focus on the district's lack of prior knowledge of torts committed by its employee.]

This is not to say that your issues should be overly-lengthy and include extraneous details. Your goal is to try to strike a reasonable balance—to give the court enough detail so that it has an accurate sense of what it needs to decide without inundating the court with confusing and unnecessary verbiage. Highlight only a few of the most critical facts that should affect the resolution of the issue.

8.   Test of a Good Issue Statement

The authors of **Supreme Court Practice** advocate a test to use to evaluate an issue statement in a brief. After you have drafted your issue statement, take the statement and turn it into a holding by adding the words "We, therefore, hold that" to the start of the statement. Then ask yourself whether your statement in the form of the court's holding presents an intelligent and important ruling that would have some applicability beyond the confines of your particular case. If it does, your issue statement is probably a good one.[10]

> **Examples:** **Issue:** *Does the National Labor Relations Act preempt a state statute that prohibits employers from hiring permanent replacements for striking employees?*
>
> **Revised:** *We, therefore, hold that the National Labor Relations Act preempts a state statute that prohibits employers from hiring permanent replacements for striking employees.*
>
> **Issue:** *Whether Moot Health and Safety Code § 159 is a reasonable exercise of the State of Moot's inherent power police to protect the health and safety of its citizens under the Tenth Amendment?*
>
> **Revised:** *We, therefore, hold that Moot Health and Safety Code § 159 is a reasonable exercise of the State of Moot's inherent power police to protect the health and safety of its citizens under the Tenth Amendment.*

This test can help you see whether your issue statement is too general, and whether it suggests an answer that would have some relevance outside your case.

9. Review and Revise Your Issue Statement as You Draft the Rest of Your Brief

While you need to have a good command of the issues you plan to argue before you start drafting your arguments relating to these issues, you may find that you need to revise your issue statement as or after you prepare the rest of your brief. You may find, as you draft your arguments, that you are emphasizing certain points or referencing certain facts that could be incorporated in your issue statement. The tone and theme of your brief may also evolve in your drafting and redrafting and this may cause you to want to go back and conform your issue statement accordingly.

B. STATEMENT OF THE CASE

The statement of the case is the part of the appellate brief where the parties identify who they are, the general nature of the case and how the case got to the court on appeal.[11] This is the one part of the appellate brief

---

[10] ROBERT L. STERN, EUGENE GRESSMAN, STEPHEN M. SHAPIRO & KENNETH S. GELLER, SUPREME COURT PRACTICE 343 n.90 (7th ed. 1993).

[11] In some courts, such as the United States Supreme Court, the statement of the case also is intended to include a statement of the facts. This part of the handbook discusses the statement of the case and the statement of the facts separately.

that may be the same for both sides. In fact, sometimes an appellee will simply adopt the statement of the case from the appellant's brief if the appellee believes it accurately describes the parties, the general nature of the case and what happened below. Following are a few principles to keep in mind in preparing the statement of the case in your appellate briefs.

1. Succinctly Identify the Parties and the Nature of the Action

The statement of the case should begin with an identification of the parties and the type of action brought.

> **Example:** *Appellant Sherry Schiller brought this negligence action against her employer, Appellee Ace Trucking ("Ace"), and Appellee Viking Enterprises ("Viking"). Schiller claims that as a result of the negligence of Ace and Viking, she was sexually harassed on Viking's work premises by one of Viking's employees.*

Usually such a general description of the action will suffice. Remember that you will discuss the pertinent legal claims and defenses in much greater detail later in your brief. Do not laundry list every count of the complaint or every affirmative defense in the answer.

Appellate court rules often state that counsel should refer to the parties in the text of their briefs by their actual names or their designations in the lower court (e.g., plaintiff, defendant) and avoid references to party descriptions such as "appellant" and "appellee." The statement of the case is where you should designate how you will identify the parties throughout your brief. In the above example, the brief would use the parties' shorthand name designations identified in the first sentence and avoid further references to the appellant and appellee labels.

2. Describe the Procedural Posture—How the Case Got to the Court on Appeal

Your statement of the case should also succinctly identify the procedural posture of the case—how the case got to the appellate court.

> **Example:** *[This would come immediately after the identification of the parties and description of the nature of the case in the above example.] Following the close of discovery, Ace and Viking moved for summary judgment, claiming that Schiller's complaint failed to state a legally cognizable claim against either of them. In an order dated May 15, 2000, Prosper County District Court Judge James Garry granted the motions of Ace and Viking. The district court reasoned that Schiller's exclusive remedy against her employer, Ace, was a claim for*

> *workers' compensation benefits, and that Viking owed no legal duty to protect Schiller from sexual harassment because she was not Viking's employee. Schiller brought this appeal from the adverse judgment below.*

In drafting your statement of the case, avoid references to unimportant dates and other extraneous details. For example, the dates of answers, discovery requests and responses, the filing of motions, hearings, etc. typically are wholly unimportant.[12]

It may be helpful to include a short explanation of how the court below resolved the case in your statement of the case. Sometimes, however, counsel prefer to delay this recitation until after the statement of the facts has been set forth so that this explanation has some additional context and is more understandable.

If, in representing an appellee, you believe that the lower court judge is especially well-respected, you may want to refer to the judge by name (e.g., "Judge Genius reasoned that . . .) This is a subtle way of reminding the appellate court that the judge who ruled in your client's favor was not just any judge, but an especially well-respected trial court judge.

C. STATEMENT OF THE FACTS

Like the statement of the issues, the statement of the facts is a critical part of your appellate brief. Appellate judges often say that cases are usually won or lost on the facts. There are several principles to keep in mind when preparing the statement of the facts in your briefs.

STATEMENT OF THE FACTS

- **Tell an interesting story**

- **Develop your theme**

- **Organize chronologically or topically**

- **Use subheadings**

- **Be fair**

- **Exclude extraneous facts**

- **Cite to the record for each fact stated**

- **Omit argument**

---

1. Tell Your Client's Story—Develop Your Theme

Your statement of the facts should tell your client's story in a way that conveys your theme on appeal. While the facts may be less than riveting in your appeal, your job is to weave them into a clear and interesting story that conveys a message about why your client should prevail.

For example, consider Goldilocks and the Three Bears. At first glance, the story seems straightforward and

---

[12] As one commentator noted: "The indiscriminate use of dates is another Linus blanket for the writer, but cruel and unusual punishment for the reader." John C. Godbold, *Twenty Pages and Twenty Minutes, in* THE LITIGATION MANUAL, *supra* note 6, at 107, 115.

not easy to manipulate into two different versions of the same story. With creative framing and reorganization, however, advocates can create two distinct stories based on the same facts.

Examples: *This is the story of a young girl, lost and isolated in an unknown place, who took necessary measures to protect her well-being.*

Contrast that with:

A family's home was invaded by an unwelcome trespasser who thoughtlessly damaged their property and ate their only source of food.

2.   Be Organized—Use Subheadings if Appropriate

Because your statement of the facts should tell a story, it usually is best to organize the statement in a way a story is organized—chronologically. There may be some instances in which you will want to deviate from this structure and organize the facts by some other manner (e.g., topically). Again, think of Goldilocks. If you are telling the story from her perspective, you could start at the beginning to justify her actions. If you are telling the story from the bears' perspective, you could start at the end to maximize the impact of Goldilocks actions.

Most often, however, what happened below is best understood by reciting the facts chronologically. In so doing, your recitation should highlight the half dozen or so facts that really matter in the appeal. You should avoid a witness-by-witness or document-by-document account of the facts that simply mirrors the presentation in the trial below. Such an organizational structure often is boring and repetitive and can result in a disjointed story. Your statement of the facts should sound more like an opening statement at trial than a serial regurgitation of all of the trial testimony and exhibits.

It also is helpful to include subheadings in your statement of the facts to provide transitions and to help the reader follow your organizational structure. While you should not introduce arguments in the facts, you should effectively use your headings. Headings are the only part of the fact section that do not contain citations, which provides an opportunity for advocacy.

Examples: **Effective heading:**

Goldilocks is Lured Into the Bears' Home by an Enticing Smell and Open Door

Too argumentative:

Goldilocks Commits Trespass and Breaks Into the Bears' House

In preparing the statement of the facts, try to keep your story simple. Remember that the appellate court judges have not been immersed in the facts to the extent you have and may not appreciate or track every subtle plot twist and nuance you uncovered in handling the case at the trial level. They may get confused or bored with overly-complex recitations of what happened below.

3.   Be Fair—Do Not Misstate the Record

Although you want to start to persuade and develop your theme in your statement of the facts, you also must be fair. This not only means that you cannot misstate the facts, but you must include in your statement significant facts that are unfavorable, including, for example, adverse findings of the trial court. Use your statement as an opportunity to frame those facts favorably, or as favorably as possible. You want to create the narrative, not be forced to change your opponent's narrative.

Do not try to slip facts into your statement that are not part of the record on appeal. While you generally are required to stick to the "adjudicative" facts in the record in your appellate brief—those facts relating to the particular case on appeal—you also may call the court's attention to "legislative" facts of the type presented in so-called Brandeis briefs. These facts generally inform the court's judgment as to the policy implications of choosing a particular legal rule. The facts relate to the type of information considered in the legislative process including, for example, social science and economic data, and information about how the court's decision may affect others outside the parties to the litigation.[13] Although not all cases lend themselves to this kind of brief, some appellate briefs make very effective use of such legislative facts to buttress the more technical legal arguments.

Even if there is no substantial dispute over the basic facts, the way in which the facts are arranged and emphasized can create significantly different impressions of what transpired. Appellate judges understand that and expect that the parties' factual accounts usually will differ in arrangement and emphasis to reflect their respective themes.

Although it is permissible to organize and emphasize the facts to support your theme, it is not permissible to state the facts inaccurately or omit significant unfavorable facts. Such misstatements will seriously undermine your personal credibility. If you are unsure about whether your characterizations are fair, we recommend a simple test. Pretend you are in court orally relaying the facts to the judge. If you are hesitant about a characterization, change it. If you could state the fact in open court without hesitation, keep it in your brief. Judges often are accepting of counsel who

---

[13] *See* Ellie Margolis, *Beyond Brandeis: Exploring the Uses of Non-Legal Materials in Appellate Briefs,* 34 U.S.F. L. REV. 197 (Winter 2000).

espouse a differing view of the meaning or significance of a court decision, they are far less tolerant of counsel who misstate the facts. It is far better to acknowledge and frame the facts from your client's perspective than to omit them and hope that the judges, their law clerks and opposing counsel will all overlook your omission. Your omission of unfavorable facts will only imply to the court that you realize and fear that you will lose the case if all the facts are on the table. Your job is to convince the court that you should prevail irrespective of the bad facts.

4. Include in Your Statement of the Facts Only Those Facts Necessary to Present Your Issues on Appeal—Omit Extraneous Facts

The statement of the facts should include only those facts needed to discuss the issues on appeal. This means that the statement of the facts should not include *all* the facts in the case, especially if the appeal only raises issues pertaining to some smaller subset of the facts. Appellate judges greatly appreciate brevity; the inclusion of extraneous facts is likely only to confuse or irritate them.

Your statement of the facts should include all facts that you reference later in the argument section of your brief. Once you complete your argument, you should go back and edit your original statement of the facts with this in mind.

Remember that the court has access to the entire record on appeal. You also can reproduce certain parts of the record in the appendix to your brief for the court's convenient reference. If, however, there are certain critical facts that you want to make sure the court will read, you should include them in your brief in the statement of the facts and not assume that the judges will go elsewhere to find them.

5. Include Citations to the Record for All Facts in Your Statement

Most appellate court rules require counsel to provide a citation to the place in the record where a particular fact appears that is referenced in the statement of the facts. This may be a citation to a factual finding of the trial court, a pleading, a stipulation of facts, or a trial or deposition transcript or exhibit. The citation should pinpoint a precise page, paragraph, or line. You can use certain common abbreviations to shorten the length of such citations. Identify the abbreviation you will use the first time you refer to a particular type of source.

Example: *Carrie Swanson entered the clinic at 1:05 p.m. on the afternoon of June 3, 1997. Transcript ("Tr.") at 53. According to her clinic medical record, Carrie complained of severe abdominal pain when she*

> *arrived at the clinic. Plaintiff's Exhibit ("Pl. Ex.") 4.*
> *Carrie continued to experience severe pain for over*
> *two hours. Tr. at 56–57.*

Be sure to double-check the accuracy of your citations to make sure that the underlying sources do, in fact, establish the referenced facts. You can be sure that the judges and their law clerks will check many, if not all, of these sources. If a fact does not have a citation, the court will presume it is not part of the record. If your citations are inaccurate, and if you require the court to hunt in the record for the sources of the facts you allege, you will seriously undermine your credibility and your chances of prevailing on appeal.

6. Do Not Interject Arguments in Your Statement of the Facts

Your statement of the facts should not include your arguments based on the facts. Save your characterizations of the facts, the credibility of the witnesses and your legal claims for your argument. The challenge is to tell a story that starts to condition the court to rule in your favor without leaping into your legal argument. For example, assume you represent on appeal a plaintiff in a medical malpractice case. You claim that the defendant doctor and his clinic failed to diagnose your client's placental abruption and to provide her appropriate care when she appeared at the clinic in labor. Your statement of the facts in such a case should not refer to the doctor's "negligence" or "malpractice" or expressly impugn his credibility at trial. Rather, you can convey a powerful sense of what happened by sticking to the facts and reserving your argument for later. Part of your statement of the facts might look something like the following (with appropriate record cites omitted from this example):

Example: *Carrie Swanson appeared at Dr. Scum's clinic at 1:05 p.m. in labor on the afternoon of Tuesday, June 3, 1999. Carrie was accompanied by her husband, a co-worker, and three of her sisters. Carrie was in extreme pain when she entered the clinic and talked to the attending nurse. She was pale and could not stand upright from the intense abdominal pain she felt.*

                     Carrie and her husband talked to the clinic nurse and explained her condition immediately after they entered the clinic. Dr. Scum then stopped by and talked to Carrie for about 15 seconds. He said he would be "right back" to examine her. In fact, neither he nor anyone else at the clinic ever returned to check on Carrie until an hour and a half later when she slipped into unconsciousness and was rushed into surgery.

Despite her condition upon entering the clinic, Dr. Scum and his clinic never took a history from Carrie. They never did a physical examination of her. They never placed a fetal monitor on her. Rather, Dr. Scum left Carrie alone while he went to play racquetball with a colleague. While Dr. Scum testified at trial that he "believes" he did an examination of Carrie when he first saw her and did not believe her to be in distress, Carrie, her husband, her co-worker and her three sisters all testified unequivocally that Dr. Scum never came within 10 feet of Carrie in the few moments he rushed through her room that afternoon on his way to his racquetball game.

There are a number of effective techniques in the above example. We encourage you to use these techniques, and others, to craft a compelling version of your client's story.

First, notice the effective use, but not over-use, of adjectives and adverbs—*extreme* pain, *intense* abdominal pain, explained her condition *immediately*, *never* came within 10 feet.

Second, the quotes highlight key components in a simple and effective manner—"right back" and "believes."

Third, the last paragraph does an excellent job of saying what the record *does not* reflect: never did a physical examination, never placed a fetal monitor on her, etc.

Fourth, notice the limited, but important usage of specific details. The doctor stopped by and talked to Carrie for *10 seconds*. The doctor *never came within 10 feet* of Carrie.

Each technique is effective on its own. Used together, they allow an advocate to create a compelling version of their client's story. You can tell a very powerful story, convey your theme and generate some significant pathos for your client with a simple recounting of the facts devoid of argument and conclusory legal characterizations.

Fact Development Exercise

Review the Goldilocks exercise in Appendix E. Try applying one or more of the techniques described above as part of that exercise.

D. STANDARD OF REVIEW

The standard of review is critical in any appeal. The standard of review reflects the degree of deference afforded to the findings or decisions in the lower court. Various metaphors are used to describe it—the lens through which the court will view your appeal or the hurdle over which the

appellant must jump. Appeals flow
from alleged errors by the lower
court. Only some of these errors are
grounds for reversal. Some
decisions are left to the sound
discretion of the lower court. Other
findings cannot be overturned on
anything less than clear and
convincing evidence. These highly
deferential standards can make
certain appeals essentially futile.
Appellate courts often state that
while they might have decided some
matter differently than the lower

> **STANDARD OF REVIEW**
>
> - Identify applicable standard(s) of review
> - Define the standard(s)
> - Remember that there may be different standards for different issues
> - Incorporate the standard(s) in your argument

court, they are compelled to affirm because of the deference owed to the
lower court pursuant to the applicable standard of review. Following are
comments regarding the standard of review as it pertains to appellate brief
writing.

1. Identify and Analyze the Applicable Standard of Review

It is imperative that you understand and deal with the standard of
review in your appeal. In order to do so, you need to identify the applicable
standard of review and understand exactly what it means for your appeal.
While a detailed discussion of the different standards of review is beyond
the purview of this handbook, following is a brief discussion of the general
standards of appellate review.[14]

a.   Questions of Law

The standard of review on appeal for questions of law is *de novo*.[15] This
is the most favorable standard for the appellant inasmuch as the appellate
court does not owe any deference to the unfavorable decision of the lower
court. The appellate court reviews the question as if the lower court never
decided it. Examples of such pure questions of law include the issue of
whether a particular cause of action may be asserted, the issue of whether
a particular defense exists, and the issue of what elements must be proven
under a statutory or constitutional claim.

---

[14] A more extended discussion of these standards of review is found in George A.
Sommerville, *Standards of Appellate Review, in* THE LITIGATION MANUAL, *supra* note 6;
EIGHTH CIRCUIT APPELLATE PRACTICE MANUAL 12–26 (2d ed. 2003); and RUGGERO J.
ALDISERT, WINNING ON APPEAL 57 (rev. 1st ed. 1996).

[15] Bose Corp. v. Consumers Union of United States, Inc., 466 U.S. 485, 498, 501, 104 S. Ct.
1949 (1984).

b. Questions of Fact

There are three general standards of review for questions of fact depending upon whether the fact-finder was a judge, a jury, or an agency. Appellate courts review facts found by a judge under the standard set forth in Rule 52(a) of the Federal Rules of Civil Procedure. They will not overturn the factual findings in a bench trial unless they are "clearly erroneous."[16] This refers to a definite and firm conclusion that a mistake has been committed even though there is evidence to support the finding. This standard does not permit an appellate court to reverse a finding simply because it would have decided the matter differently.

The standard of review of jury findings of fact is reasonable basis.[17] This means that a jury's factual finding will not be disturbed if there is a reasonable basis in the record for its conclusion. The entire record is reviewed and all reasonable inferences are drawn in favor of the jury's finding. The appellate court also cannot reweigh conflicting evidence and substitute its judgment for that of the jury.

The standard of review of agency findings of fact is substantial evidence. An agency fact finding will not be overturned if there is substantial evidence in the record to support it.[18]

c. Mixed Questions of Law and Fact

Some questions, of course, are not clearly legal or factual but rather a hybrid between the two. These questions often intertwine the application of a legal test or standard and some set of facts.[19] As counsel for an appellant, you may want to highlight how a particular question on appeal involves a legal component and argue that the lower court erred in its determination of the applicable law. As counsel for a respondent, you may want to highlight the factual aspects of the relevant question.

d. Rulings Re: The Conduct of the Trial

The trial judge is entrusted with making numerous procedural and evidentiary decisions affecting the conduct of a trial, such as ruling on the conduct of voir dire and evidentiary objections. Judges also resolve discovery disputes, rule regarding class certification motions, and impose sanctions against parties and lawyers. Generally, appellate courts look to whether the lower court abused its discretion if it is alleged that the court

---

[16] *Id.* at 499; United States v. United States Gypsum Co., 333 U.S. 364, 395, 68 S. Ct. 525 (1948).

[17] Lavender v. Kurn, 327 U.S. 645, 652–53, 66 S. Ct. 740 (1946).

[18] F.T.C. v. Ind. Fed'n of Dentists, 476 U.S. 447, 454, 465, 106 S. Ct. 2009 (1986).

[19] *Compare* Ornelas v. United States, 517 U.S. 690, 695–99, 116 S. Ct. 1657 (1996) *and* Cooper Indus., Inc. v. Leatherman Tool Group, Inc., 532 U.S. 424, 435, 121 S. Ct. 1678 (2001) *with* Anderson v. Bessemer City, 470 U.S. 564, 573, 105 S. Ct. 1504 (1985).

erred in making one of these types of rulings.[20] Appellate courts usually will assume that the lower court did not abuse its discretion unless the record clearly shows otherwise. This is generally regarded as the highest standard of review. In other words, the greatest deference is afforded to such lower court rulings. Your client is entitled to a fair trial—not a perfect trial.

What does it mean to say that a lower court abused its discretion? The answer is not entirely clear. In some situations, a lower court's exercise of discretion involves the application of legal standards to a set of facts. For example, a court exercises its discretion in granting or denying a motion for a temporary restraining order. An appellant may argue that the court considered impermissible factors in deciding such a motion and/or failed to consider the appropriate factors.

An opinion of the lower court that gives no explanation whatsoever may be worth attacking on appeal. You might argue that the court at least has to exercise some discretion and that its opinion leaves doubt over whether that ever happened. You may also object if the lower court impermissibly delegated some of its discretion to others. Be prepared, however, that the outcome of such arguments may merely be a remand to the lower court to exercise its discretion and to explain its ruling.[21]

2. Clearly Identify the Standard of Review in Your Brief

The parties should clearly identify the applicable standard of review in their respective briefs. Some appellate court rules expressly require that the standard of review be discussed in a separately identified section of the brief. Others are silent, leaving it up to counsel to decide where to include this discussion. Whether required or not, this discussion should be included. If an appellant fails even to mention a demanding standard of review on an appeal, the appellee will most assuredly pounce on this omission in its brief and the court will no doubt wonder why the appellant omitted something this important.

If the standard of review is generally favorable to you, you may want to elaborate at greater length, with appropriate citations, exactly what that standard means and what narrow, or wide, latitude it gives the appellate court. This usually can be done in a couple of paragraphs because appellate courts are quite familiar with these general standards of review and usually do not need a treatise or string cites to explain them.

The standard of review also will influence how you shape your arguments on appeal. For example, if your appeal concerns alleged errors in the factual findings of the trial court, which are only overturned if they

---

[20] *E.g.*, Gen. Elec. Co. v. Joiner, 522 U.S. 136, 141, 118 S. Ct. 512 (1997).

[21] Some attorneys believe that the more a court explains the reasoning for its decision, the better off the appellant because there is more to criticize and a greater likelihood of some error.

are clearly erroneous, you may want to try to cast the issue as more of a legal question than a factual one.

3. There May Be Different Standards of Review for Different Issues in an Appeal

Sometimes an appeal presents multiple issues for which there are differing standards of review. A legal ruling regarding the construction of a statute may be reviewed *de novo* by the appellate court while an evidentiary ruling in the same case may be subject to an abuse of discretion or clear error standard. In such a case, you should clearly identify the different standards of review for the different issues.

4. You May Need to Argue Regarding the Appropriate Standard of Review if It Is in Dispute

While the standard of review often is undisputed, the parties disagree regarding the applicable standard in some appeals. In such a case, you will need to include an argument in your brief addressing why the standard is as you advocate. In some appeals, the standard of review is essentially case dispositive and requires a substantial, detailed argument.

E. SUMMARY OF THE ARGUMENT

The summary is an important first impression or "snapshot" of your overall argument. In fact, some appellate courts require counsel to include such a summary. The court should be able to read your summary and know where you are going, why the court should want to go there and the basic route to get there. The summary also provides an excellent opportunity to develop your theme. Judges may reread your argument summary several times over the course of an appeal to refresh their recollections.[22] Following are a few guidelines to consider when drafting your argument summary.

1. Write a Concise Summary—One to Three Pages

The summary should be just that—a summary. Generally, one to three pages should suffice. If the summary is much longer than that, it is no longer a true summary. Some appellate courts dictate the length of the summary by court rule. You may include citations to a controlling or highly persuasive case or other authority in your summary but should avoid lengthy and numerous citations.

---

[22] One former appellate judge stated that: "I think the most important portion of the brief is the summary. I invariably read it first. It is almost like the opening statement in a trial. From a clear and plausible argument summary, I often get an inclination to affirm or reverse that rises almost to the dignity of a (psychologically) rebuttable presumption." James L. Robertson, *Reality on Appeal, in* THE LITIGATION MANUAL, *supra* note 6, at 142, 147.

2. Do Not Merely Repeat Your Argument Headings in the Summary

The summary should be more than a mere regurgitation of the argument headings in your brief. These headings are already pulled together for the court in your table of contents. The summary should be your distillation of the main points in your argument in an interesting and persuasive narrative. One way to think of it is that you have sixty seconds to tell the court why the case is important, your desired outcome, and the legal route the court should take to get there. You should not include every subsidiary argument. Your summary should be tightly focused on your most important points.

3. The Summary Should Track the Organization of Your Argument

Your summary should have the same organizational structure and order as your argument. Although it is usually not required, you can use Roman numerals in your summary that correspond to the respective arguments summarized. You may want to begin your summary with an introductory paragraph that sets forth the overall theme of your appeal.

4. Consider Writing Your Summary After You Have Drafted Your Argument

You should write the final version of your summary after you have written your argument section. By doing so, you can determine whether you are able to distill the essence of your arguments into one to three pages. If you are not able to do this, you likely need to reorganize and tighten your arguments. By writing the final version after you have completed your argument, you will also ensure that your summary accurately reflects your argument.

Example: *Review the summary of the argument in the model brief. Review the above-guidelines and note how the brief effectively uses them.*

F. ARGUMENT

The argument is the core or heart of the appellate brief. It is here that you as counsel have the opportunity to weave the facts and legal authorities together into persuasive arguments that further develop your theme and compel the result you seek for your client.

> **ARGUMENT**
>
> - **Develop your theme**
>
> - **Keep it simple**
>
> - **Include road maps/previews**
>
> - **Use specific argument statements**
>
> - **Liberally use subheadings**
>
> - **Move from the more general to the more specific**
>
> - **Identify the legal test/rule before discussing the facts**
>
> - **Flush out your arguments before rebutting your opponent's arguments**

While the argument often constitutes the bulk of an appellate brief, there are typically few rules governing this part of the brief. Following is a discussion of some principles applicable to the argument section in general and some additional principles pertaining to individual arguments within this section of the brief.

1.   Argument Statements/ Headings

The argument statement or argument heading is the short summary which precedes specific individual arguments. It usually is prominently set forth in a single declarative statement at the start of the argument. In some instances, it may be appropriate for an argument statement to consist of more than one sentence. This statement should, not, however, turn into a narrative summary of the argument. It is intended to be a very short articulation of the argument to follow.

A common flaw in appellate briefs is an argument statement that is too general.

Example: *The trial court erred in granting summary judgment for the appellees.*

Just as your issue statements should be sufficiently detailed to identify the issues for the court, your argument statements also should be detailed enough to identify the essence of your arguments. The argument statement in the above example fails in this respect. It is far too general and says nothing about "why" the trial court committed reversible error.

One way to draft a sufficiently detailed argument statement is to include the word "because" in your statement.[23] If you take the argument statement in the above example and add a because clause to it setting forth the reason for the court's error, the statement is much more indicative of what is to follow.

Example: *The trial court erred in granting summary judgment for the appellees because it erroneously concluded*

---

[23] *E.g.,* LINDA HOLDEMAN EDWARDS, LEGAL WRITING: PROCESS, ANALYSIS AND ORGANIZATION 296 (3d ed. 2002).

> *that the republication of a defamatory statement is not actionable as a matter of law.*

You can also vary this simple structure, for emphasis and/or variety, by starting the argument statement with the because clause.

Example: *Because there was a genuine issue of material fact regarding the landlord's knowledge of the hazardous condition prior to the accident, the trial court erred in granting summary judgment for the landlord.*

Conversely, you do not want to have an argument statement that is too long and convoluted just as you do not want an overly long issue statement. An argument statement that is more than five lines of text is probably too long in most cases. Remember that not every subsidiary point in the argument needs to be found in the argument statement. In fact, if your argument is long and complex, you are likely to have multiple subargument headings that articulate the more specific points and propositions within your argument.

If you have multiple sub-argument headings, you should set these out using a Roman numeral-based numbering scheme and different spacing and typefaces to denote the different levels of the sub-arguments. Following is one example of a hierarchy of argument and sub-argument statements using a typical numbering/typeface convention:

I.   *THE DISTRICT COURT CORRECTLY DECIDED THAT THE CITY COUNCIL COULD NOT HOLD A CLOSED MEETING WITH ITS ATTORNEY TO DISCUSS THE CONSTITUTIONALITY OF A PROPOSED ORDINANCE UNDER THE ATTORNEY-CLIENT PRIVILEGE EXCEPTION TO THE STATE OPEN MEETING LAW.*

   A.   *The Open Meeting Law is to be Liberally Construed to Protect the Public's Right to Know the Decision-Making Process of Public Bodies, to Detect Improper Influences and to Express Its Views on Matters of Public Concern.*

   B.   *The Attorney-Client Privilege Exception to the Open Meeting Law for Discussions Between a Public Body and its Attorney is Limited to Matters of Litigation Strategy.*

       1.   *The Attorney-Client Privilege Exception Should be Narrowly Construed In Light of the Strong Policies Favoring Open Meetings.*

       2.   *The Exception is Limited to Discussions Between a Public Body and its Attorney Regarding Litigation Strategy.*

>   *C. The District Court Correctly Concluded that the Advice*
>   *Sought by the City Council of its Attorney Regarding the*
>   *Constitutionality of a Proposed Ordinance is the Kind of*
>   *General Legal Advice or Opinion to Which the Attorney-*
>   *Client Privilege Exception Does Not Apply[24].*

2. Order of the Arguments

The order of your arguments should track the order of the issues you identified. Typically, each issue will warrant a single argument and argument statement. In most instances, this means that you will lead with your strongest argument. In some instances, logic will dictate a different order, given the nature of the issues and arguments, and will cause you to lead with a somewhat weaker argument.

3. Individual Arguments

Unless your appeal deals with only a single issue and argument, you will have multiple individual arguments within the argument section of your brief. Following are a number of principles to consider as you prepare your individual arguments.

a. Objectives

There are several key objectives you should have in mind when you prepare the individual arguments in your appellate brief.

i. Understand Your Audience

As you prepare your arguments, it is imperative that you keep in mind your audience. Appellate courts are not trial courts and they are not juries. Purely emotional appeals will not impress an appellate court. The appellate court did not see the witnesses at trial and does not have the same sympathy or disdain for your client, your opponent or the witnesses that jurors may have formed. However, it is critical to highlight the key facts for that same reason: this is the appellate court's first impression of your client's story. You want to tell a compelling story, but also one anchored in the law. While your argument should not be completely devoid of emotional appeal, you need to bear in mind that the appellate court is likely to take a more dispassionate view of your case than the judge or jury below.

Appellate courts also are not interested in retrying the facts of your case on appeal. As discussed above, they are confined by deferential

---

[24] Note that heading length, style, and format vary among both practitioners and jurisdictions. Most appellate briefs contain section headings in all-caps. However, the 7th Circuit specifically encourages advocates to refrain from using all-caps, among other jurisdiction-specific preferences. Yet another example of the importance of reading and understanding the local rules in your jurisdiction.

standards of review on factual matters. Your argument must take into account the limited role of the court under the applicable standard of review.

ii. Develop Your Theme

The argument is the place you can establish your theme most directly. While your legal arguments and authorities should persuade the court how to rule in your favor, your theme should give the court a reason to rule in your favor. Whether your theme is that your client was an innocent victim of a fraudulent scheme or a fiscally responsible government body making tough decisions about how to allocate limited resources, your goal is to convince the court that simple fairness and justice compel a ruling for your client. If you can do this, you are well on your way to a successful outcome. Appellate courts will try hard to find the precedent and legal analysis which will support a result they deem just. Your articulation of the public policy reasons supporting your case will help develop your theme.

> **PERSUASIVE ARGUMENT PRINCIPLES**
>
> - Avoid logical fallacies
> - Don't serially digest cases—use them substantively and persuasively
> - Cite to the minimum number of cases necessary
> - Use case parentheticals
> - Deal with opponent's authority/arguments
> - Argue public policy implications
> - Concede losing arguments
> - Don't be too tentative and don't overstate
> - No *ad hominen* attacks
> - Use quotes judiciously

iii. Keep It Simple

Remember that the appellate court comes to your case fresh. It has not lived with the case as you have. It may also be unfamiliar with the law and/or factual subject matter involved in the case. Your job is to make your arguments simple to follow even if the case involves complex facts and complex legal principles. If the judges do not understand you, you cannot possibly persuade them. You cannot assume that the court will have the desire or the patience to sort through an extremely intricate argument. Break complicated arguments into smaller, more digestible parts that build upon one another. Eliminate extraneous details that are only likely to confuse the reader. If you cannot articulate your argument in a relatively simple fashion in your brief, you will almost certainly be unable to do so in your oral argument. Your efforts to show the complexity of the case are likely only to be counterproductive. You should instead try to show that the case is really quite simple and that the reasons why your client should win are equally simple. By and large, judges prefer simple solutions.

iv. Provide a Logical Affirmative Analysis for the Court to Rule in Your Favor

As an appellate advocate, your argument not only needs to provide the court with a reason to rule in your favor through the development of your theme, but it also needs to provide the court with a logical, affirmative legal analysis to get to that result. In cases with multiple legal avenues, be prepared to convince the court why your version is preferable. You should present your own affirmative analysis of your case and not simply rely on a point-by-point attack of your opponent's argument. Your argument should also articulate a rule of law with reasonable limits that will work in other cases. An appellate court will be concerned about whether the result in your case is grounded in principles that would also achieve just results in similar circumstances.

v. Be Fair and Maximize Your Credibility

There are ways you can maximize, and ways you can lose, credibility in the argument section of your brief. You maximize your credibility by accurately and fairly reciting the facts and the applicable law, by conceding losing arguments, by avoiding **ad hominem** attacks, by avoiding hyperbole, and by carefully proofreading and cite-checking your brief.

b. Organization of Individual Arguments

The importance of a well-organized argument cannot be overstated. This may, in fact, be the single most important requirement of a winning argument. Think of an argument's organization as the foundation of a house; a strong foundation is required to build a decent structure. An appellate attorney who is not an especially gifted writer is likely to do well in an appeal if the attorney has laid out a persuasive argument in a very organized, if not eloquent, fashion. Conversely, a highly gifted writer is likely to go down in defeat if the appellate court cannot follow the writer's argument, however eloquent it may be, because the argument is poorly organized. Poor organization results in confusion and unnecessary repetition. Following are several principles to consider regarding the organization of individual arguments in a brief as well as a few comments regarding the organization of the appellee's brief.

i. Provide Road Maps to Preview Points to Follow

One useful organizational tool in a brief is the road map. This is simply a preview of what is to follow—telling the court where you are going. Your overall road maps should be found near the beginning of your individual arguments. For example, a road map at the beginning of an argument might be included in an introductory paragraph as follows:

Example: *The decision of the trial court is erroneous and should be reversed for two reasons. First, the trial court incorrectly held that there is no actionable claim in this state for invasion of privacy. Second, the court incorrectly held that any such claim would be subject to a two-year statute of limitations.*

Review the summary of argument in the model brief. Notice how it roadmaps the three main arguments before expanding on each one in the argument section.

Think of a roadmap as a funnel. By stating your main points "at the top," everything that follows will naturally flow to your conclusion. Similarly, it is helpful to preview subarguments. If, for example, you have two major subarguments labeled "A" and "B," tell the court as much in an introductory road map before subargument A.

The downside to road maps is that they can result in some repetition in the brief. If the road maps are kept short and not overdone, however, this should not be a problem. Remember that your argument summary also helps serve this road map function, thereby eliminating the need for lengthy road maps in your arguments. Certainly, the value of these road maps to the organization of your arguments outweighs the minimal repetition they usually entail.

ii.   Make Liberal Use of Argument Subheadings

Appellate judges generally appreciate the use of argument subheadings. These subheadings, like subheadings in the statement of the facts, not only help break up long passages of text, but they also serve as organizational devices to transition to a new subpoint. Subheadings also allow you to keep your overall argument statement less detailed.

It is not uncommon to have such subheadings every one or two pages in an argument. If you have many pages of text in an argument without such subheadings, go back and see if you can insert some headings. You can do this by asking whether multiple paragraphs or pages seem to be related to the same general topic or proposition. Although the model brief is somewhat artificially concise, notice there is a heading or subheading on almost every page.

iii. State the Law and Apply It to the Facts

Thorough and thoughtful analysis is a hallmark of a strong brief. Whether you have compelling facts, or persuasive and authoritative caselaw, clear and direct application of the law to facts is required.

It is not sufficient simply to state the law and then summarily conclude that you should win. Judges need more than case law. In many appeals, there may be relatively little dispute regarding the applicable law. As an appellate attorney, you need to show how the law applies to the facts in your case. Explain to the court why the relevant cases are similar, or distinct, from the matter at hand. In doing so, you should also make sure to provide citations to the sources in the record where these facts appear. You should do this in the argument even if you have already provided the sources to these facts in your statement of the facts. You do not want to force the judges to have to go back and hunt for these sources in your earlier statement of the facts.

It also is not sufficient simply to laundry list the relevant facts after your discussion of the law. Do not be conclusory. Analyze and discuss the significance of the facts as they relate to the law you just recited. If there is an issue regarding the appellee's control of certain events in the case, and you have cited the pertinent authorities addressing this element, discuss why the facts in your case are similar to those in the cases you cited and how they establish the requisite control even more forcefully than in these cases. If there are facts in your case not found in the cases you cited, be prepared to discuss why these facts may be additionally helpful, or alternatively irrelevant or insignificant.

Another common organizational flaw in the argument section of appellate briefs is the premature discussion of the case facts before the brief has detailed the applicable law. Before the court can appreciate the significance of the case-specific facts in an argument, it needs to know what the applicable legal standard is—what is the legal test for liability against which the facts can be assessed, how has it been applied in similar contexts and how have the courts construed the limits of the available defenses. The skilled appellate advocate will first outline the applicable law and then demonstrate how and why the facts of the case compel a certain result. Keep in mind that the specific facts of your particular case should influence how you articulate the law, including your selection of the cases you will cite, and the facts and analysis you will emphasize from these cases.

There are different ways to organize your discussion of the law and facts in any given case. If, for example, your appeal involves the application of a three-part legal test, you can first discuss the law with respect to all three parts of the test and then discuss the case-specific facts pertaining to each part. Alternatively, you can first discuss the law relating to the first part of the test and then apply that first part of the test to the case-specific facts. Next you would discuss the law relating to the second part of the test followed by an analysis of the facts relating to that part of the test and so forth. The latter organizational structure is preferable if you have a relatively lengthy legal analysis to apply. This structure places the analysis of the facts in close proximity to the relevant legal discussion.

Example: *Review subsection B(3) of the model brief. The first two paragraphs state the law and describe the most apposite case in detail. The next two paragraphs apply the law to the facts at hand and then compare the most apposite to the matter at hand.*

iv. *Organize Your Arguments from the General to the More Specific*

In organizing an individual argument, you usually should move from the more general to the more specific. That is, start with the broadest legal proposition and move to the narrowest. Your goal is to persuade the court to accept an ever-narrowing set of propositions until the court reaches the facts of your case and is led to the inescapable conclusion you seek. This organizational principle can help you organize fairly complicated arguments. For example, here is a set of argument subheadings in a product liability case involving a prescription drug that progressively move from the more general to the more specific:

I. *This State has Adopted Section 402A of the Restatement (Second) of Torts.*

II. *Comment K to Section 402A Provides an Exception to the Strict Liability Rule in the Case of an "Unavoidably Unsafe" Product.*

III. *Prescription Drugs are as a Matter of Law Unavoidably Unsafe Products.*

IV. *A Prescription Drug Manufacturer is Not Liable for Injuries Resulting from its Drugs if the Manufacturer Adequately Warned of the Risks of its Drug.*

V. *A Prescription Drug Manufacturer Fulfills its Obligation to Warn if it Warns the Prescribing Physician.*

VI. *In this Case, ABC Pharmaceuticals Adequately Warned the Prescribing Physician of the Risks of its Drug.*

In cases involving statutory provisions, this usually means that you will want to start with a discussion of the basic language of the statute and progressively move through its purpose, its legislative history, agency interpretations of the statute, and court interpretations.

v. Provide Your Own Affirmative Analysis Before Refuting Your Opponent's Arguments

You may want to refute arguments of your opponent in your brief. Assuming that you do address your opponent's contentions in your argument, it is advisable to do so after you have first laid out your own affirmative analysis. If you challenge your opponent's arguments after you have set forth your own analysis, the court will see your refutations after having the benefit of seeing the case from your perspective. If you attack your opponent's case before you have set forth your own principal arguments, you lose the ability to draw comparisons and to demonstrate the relative weakness of your opponent's position. A premature critique of your opponent's arguments may also be confusing if the court is not able to appreciate the alleged flaws in your opponent's case having not read your arguments and affirmative analysis.

One effective method for incorporating counterarguments is to use the "sandwich" technique. Make your argument and explain why your position is reasonable. Then briefly address your opponent's argument. Finish the "sandwich" by explaining why your argument is superior to your opponent's. In other words, you do not always want to write two entirely separate parts to your brief consisting of your arguments and your response to your opponent's arguments. The weakness of your opponent's arguments often may be best conveyed in conjunction with the recitation of your own affirmative arguments. Also, do not forget to respond to the lower court's analysis. If you are the appellant, the lower court may be your true opponent on appeal.

> **Example:** *Subsection B (5) of the Model Brief is a "separate" section that directly refutes part of the Appellant's argument. It is included in that manner to highlight an effective method for refuting an opponent's argument. From a style perspective, it could easily be reworked into the previous section and therefore embody the "sandwich" technique.*

vi. Use Alternative "Even if" Arguments if Appropriate

Some arguments lend themselves to an "even if" organizational format. In such arguments, you first articulate the main or strongest reasons why you should prevail. After that, you include an "even if" argument—an explanation of why you should still prevail even if the court finds against you as to your first arguments. This is your fallback argument. Looking at the arguments in the prescription drug case in the previous example, an even if/fallback argument might be as follows:

> **Example:** *VII. Because Dr. Smith was Fully Aware of the Risks of ABC Pharmaceutical's Drug at the Time He*

Prescribed it to the Plaintiff ABC Pharmaceutical's Alleged Failure to Warn was Not the Proximate Cause of Plaintiff's Injuries.

Review the first sentence of Section B(4) of the Model Brief. Notice that this argument is placed after the strongest argument.

It is helpful to preview such an alternative argument at the start of the discussion of your principal argument so the reader knows right up front that you have multiple, alternative reasons why you should prevail.

vii. Organization of Appellee's Arguments

The appellee has the advantage in an appeal of seeing what points the appellant has made and thereby knowing what points to attack. The appellee should provide their own affirmative analysis of why the trial court correctly decided the case. This may be particularly important where the appellant has ignored an important ground for affirmance. The appellee should not, however, merely reply to each of the points in the appellant's brief.

The appellee also should try to avoid reinforcing the appellant's arguments by unnecessarily and excessively repeating them. This is the same basic concern a trial attorney has about repeating too much of the direct-examination testimony during cross-examination. While a certain amount of repetition is inevitable in setting up the appellee's refutation of the appellant's arguments, the appellee should avoid spending too much of its brief restating the appellant's contentions.

In some appeals, the appellee may argue that the trial court reached the correct result, but that alternative grounds for the decision are more appropriate. Appellate courts are empowered to affirm lower court decisions for reasons other than those set forth by the lower courts. While this approach places the appellee in the somewhat unusual position of asking the appellate court both to affirm the trial court's ultimate ruling, and to ignore the basis for the ruling, the appellee may need to take this approach if the appellee is concerned that the appellate court may not adopt the trial court's analysis and believes that there are other, stronger reasons for an affirmance.

c. Employing Logical Principles/Avoiding Logical Fallacies

Effective legal arguments are based upon well-established principles of logic. Your arguments should be grounded in inductive or deductive reasoning. With inductive reasoning, one draws a generalized conclusion based upon some number of particular experiences or examples. The strength of the conclusion is related in part to the similarity between the various experiences or examples. This is a form of reasoning by analogy.

> **Example:**   *A misrepresentation regarding the legal effect of a statute is not actionable.*
>
>   *A misrepresentation regarding the legal effect of a state agency rule is not actionable.*
>
>   *A misrepresentation regarding the legal effect of a contract is not actionable.*
>
>   *Therefore, not all misrepresentations of law are actionable.*

A classic form of deductive reasoning is the syllogism involving a major premise, a minor premise and a conclusion.

> **Example:**   Major premise: *Misrepresentations of law are not actionable in this state because everyone is presumed to know the law.*
>
>   Minor premise: *Plaintiff's fraud claim is based on alleged misrepresentations of law.*
>
>   Conclusion: *Plaintiff's fraud claim is not actionable.*

You also should make sure that your argument is free of logical fallacies, such as *post hoc ergo propter hoc* (assuming that one thing caused another because one occurred after the other) and *non sequiturs* (conclusions that do not follow from the underlying premises).[25]

You need to scrutinize the logic of your own arguments and eliminate logical fallacies. You should also scrutinize the logic of your opponent's arguments so you can effectively demonstrate any fallacies in your opponent's reasoning.

d.   Using Favorable Precedent

There are a number of principles to keep in mind in using favorable precedent in support of your arguments. First, focus your argument on the most relevant and persuasive cases. Do not simply digest cases in a serial fashion in your arguments. This is a very common flaw in briefs. Such a brief typically reads something like the following:

In case A, which had these facts, the court held . . .

---

[25]   See RUGGERO J. ALDISERT, WINNING ON APPEAL, *supra* note 14, at 281–87, for a discussion of logical fallacies in appellate advocacy.

In case B, which had these facts, the court held . . .

In case C, which had these facts, the court held . . .

Therefore, the court should rule in favor of Appellant.

This type of brief provides no real analysis and merely serves as a catalogue of relevant authorities. Your job is to direct the court to the most apposite authorities in support of your argument, not all of the authorities. It is not sufficient to digest a string of cases and then say nothing about how the cases support your analysis. Similarly, be cautious of writing an overly long history lesson of how the law has evolved. While that can be helpful if you are requesting a natural extension of the law, it can be unnecessary in other contexts. The court wants to know more than what your supporting cases say. It wants to know how it is that these cases advance your argument.

Second, do not organize your argument around the cases you plan to discuss. You are not asking the appellate court to adopt some group of prior cases. Rather, you are using the cases, and the rules of law from the cases, to argue for a certain result in your case. Determine and organize the legal propositions and conclusions you intend to make and determine where in that outline your cases and other supporting authorities fit.

Third, if you cite to a case which you believe is directly on point with your case, discuss the facts of the cited case in detail. Explain how the facts in that case are similar to your case. It also is helpful to tell the court why you are discussing the facts of this other case in such detail. You can do this simply by telling the court up-front, before you discuss the other case, that the case is nearly identical, or strikingly similar, with your case. It is also persuasive to walk through the reasoning of a similar case, which will give the court a clear legal roadmap to rule in your client's favor.

Fourth, cite to the minimal number of cases and other authorities necessary to make your points. You do not get extra points because you cited twice as many cases as your opponent. In an appeal from a grant of summary judgment, you do not need to cite five cases for the propositions that the appellate court reviews such decisions *de novo* and that summary judgment is improper if there are genuine issues of material fact. Remember that appellate courts appreciate brevity and would much rather that you cite and analyze five cases in your brief than cite without analysis twenty-five largely duplicative cases.

You generally need not, and ought not, cite multiple cases for the same proposition. If you have multiple citations for a particular proposition, you should cite the most recent case from the highest court in your jurisdiction. These are the cases that will have the most precedential value. Alternatively, you may want to cite a case from the highest court within your jurisdiction that is not necessarily the most recent, but is the most factually similar to your case.

There are some circumstances in which you may want to include multiple citations for the same point, however. For example, if a proposition is not clearly established by the highest court in your jurisdiction, it may be appropriate to show that courts in other jurisdictions are in accord with a position you are advocating. Likewise, you may want to show that there has been an unbroken line of authority over time supporting a particular proposition. If, on the other hand, you simply want to cite a case within your jurisdiction that sets forth the elements of a common law defamation claim, a single cite should suffice.

Fifth, make strategic use of parenthetical citations to briefly note information concerning a case and to avoid the need for a more detailed discussion of the opinion.[26] It is not necessary to discuss in detail the facts and reasoning of every case you cite. You can often provide sufficient information about a case by including a parenthetical with the cite. However, remember that parenthetical citations are no substitute for a reasoned discussion of the most apposite authorities. This citation form is particularly well suited for citations to additional cases that support a proposition you have discussed.

> **Example:** *Numerous courts agree that the standard for liability under strict liability and negligence theories is the same in "failure to warn" cases involving prescription drugs. See, e.g., Swayze v. McNeil Lab., Inc., 807 F.2d 464, 467 (5th Cir. 1987) ("these principles merge into one inquiry: the adequacy of the defendant's warnings") DeLuryea v. Winthrop Lab., 697 F.2d 222, 229 (8th Cir. 1983) ("the standards for liability under strict liability and negligence are essentially the same"); Werner v. Upjohn Co., Inc., 628 F.2d 848, 858 (4th Cir. 1980) ("Though phrased differently the issue under either theory is essentially the same: was the warning adequate?"); Basko v. Sterling Drug, 416 F.2d 417, 426 (2d Cir. 1969) ("comment k simply adopts the ordinary negligence concept of duty to warn")*

A parenthetical may be used to briefly describe the type or nature of a case, the basis of the court's ruling and/or the specific legal rule from the case if this is not apparent from your discussion in the argument.

---

[26] *See* Leonard I. Garth, *How to Appeal to an Appellate Judge, in* THE LITIGATION MANUAL, *supra* note 6, at 187, 196 ("The single, easiest way to make a good brief better is by the judicious use of parentheticals following case citations.").

Sixth, look for supportive secondary authorities such as authoritative treatises, annotations, law review articles, uniform laws and restatements. While you do not want to cite to these sources simply to pad your brief and impress the court with the depth of your research, citations to a few such sources can significantly buttress your argument if they are directly on point to a specific argument.

Seventh, be cautious of citing a case for a particular proposition when other parts of the case are harmful to your position on appeal unless the case is a binding authority in your jurisdiction. Occasionally, you may find cases that strongly support one aspect of your case but harm another.[27] Generally speaking, the damage that such a case inflicts outweighs its benefit to your position. If there is other supportive case authority available, you are best off not to cite the case at all, subject, of course, to your ethical obligation to cite controlling adverse authority in your jurisdiction. If the case is the only authority you have for a proposition, you may want to include it and deal as best you can with the negative aspects of the case.

Finally, if you cite a case in your argument, include an internal page cite indicating exactly where in the opinion the statements exist that you are referencing. Electronic legal research programs are extremely accurate. However, you should still personally confirm that your pinpoint citations match the opinion. Judges and lawyers find it extremely frustrating to come across a cite to a lengthy opinion that contains no indication of where in the opinion one might find the proposition for which the case is cited. Almost every case cite you include in your brief should include such internal page cites. These cites will aid the court and only help your credibility. They signal to the court that you know precisely what part of an opinion supports your argument and are willing to stand behind the cite.

e. Dealing with Unfavorable Precedent and Opposing Arguments

As an appellate advocate, you need to be able to deal effectively with unfavorable precedent and opposing arguments. There are various ways you can respond to unfavorable precedent. Ignoring the precedent is not one of these ways.[28] While you do not need to respond to every single case cited in your opponent's brief, you should address your opponent's major cases on the important issues in the appeal. If you do not cite and discuss your opponent's authorities, you may lose your opportunity to try to

---

[27] Obviously, do not stop reading an opinion after you have found a favorable headnote. Many cases present this good case/bad case dilemma.

[28] You must, of course, disclose authority in your jurisdiction directly adverse to your position even if your opponent does not cite it. Failure to do so is likely a violation of your state rules of professional conduct.

convince the court why the authorities are not persuasive or dispositive. Following is a list of twelve possible responses you might make to an unfavorable case cited by your opponent:

1. *Your opponent has misstated the holding of the case. This includes both overextending and narrowing the holding.*

2. *The proposition cited by your opponent is not the holding of the case, but is only dictum.*

3. *Your opponent's case is not well reasoned or contains relatively sparse reasoning.*

4. *Your opponent's case misapplied the law.*

5. *Your opponent's case involved a significantly different procedural posture.*

6. *The material facts in your opponent's case are distinguishable.*

7. *Your opponent's case is from another jurisdiction and, therefore, is not controlling.*

8. *Your opponent's case is against the weight of the authority and/or the modern trend of authority.*

9. *Your opponent's case is old and outdated.*

10. *Your opponent's case has been reversed, overruled or modified.*

11. *Your opponent's case is a split decision and the dissent is more persuasive.*

12. *Your opponent's case was wrongly decided and created bad law.*[29]

As noted above, it is preferable to deal with your opponent's authorities and arguments after you have presented your affirmative analysis and authorities or as part of your affirmative presentation. That way, you can contrast your opponent's cases with the more well-reasoned cases you have already discussed and show how your opponent's cases are distinguishable from the material facts you have already analyzed.

There are some tactical decisions you need to make in dealing with your opponent's arguments. In representing an appellant, you need to decide whether to address arguments that you believe the appellee may make or wait to address them, if at all, in your reply brief. There is some risk in dealing with the appellee's arguments in appellant's principal brief. For one thing, the appellee may not have been planning to make an argument you address. By raising the argument, you will have given the appellee an argument it otherwise might never have made. Moreover, you

---

[29] *See* Clary, Part One, *supra* note 1, at 40–41.

may articulate appellee's argument more effectively than appellee ever would have.

Notwithstanding these risks, it generally is advisable to address the expected arguments of your opponent. The key is to address those arguments quickly and efficiently. Similar to a rebuttal mindset, try to distinguish/dismiss these arguments in two or three points. If you dedicate more space, it will have the countereffect. Think of it this way: if you repeatedly tell someone "don't look at that, don't look at that," the natural reaction is to look at whatever "that" is. On the other hand, if you simply say "there's nothing important over there," it will not generate the same reaction.

In most cases, you will likely already know what these arguments are from the briefs and proceedings below. You also can gain some advantage by stealing your opponent's thunder. By addressing your opponent's expected arguments, you can try to diffuse the force of these arguments before the appellee has had a chance to unveil them. You also may be able to get the court to adopt your characterization of appellee's arguments, and to view appellee's brief through a lens you create. The bottom line is this: If you are sure that the appellee is going to make an argument going to the heart of the appeal, it is best to address the argument up front and not stick your head in the sand and hope that it never appears.

The appellee has a slightly different dilemma with regard to this issue. The appellee already will have seen the arguments the appellant has made in its principal brief. The appellee may, however, anticipate that the appellant will make some new or somewhat different arguments in its reply brief in response to appellee's arguments. The appellee could omit any reference to these anticipated reply arguments and hope that the appellant never makes them. If, however, the appellant makes the arguments in its reply brief, the appellee will have lost an opportunity to brief its position as to the arguments. Consequently, the appellee should address these anticipated arguments if they are significant enough.

Finally, in representing the appellant, you also have to consider whether to address an argument that you believe the appellee will overlook or ignore but that the court likely will recognize. If you are concerned enough about the possible significance of the argument and believe that you have a solid counter-argument, you should probably address the argument in your principal brief lest you lose your chance to address it at all. If the appellee never addresses the argument, you will not be able to address it in your reply brief and may never have a chance to allay the court's concerns about the argument.[30]

---

[30] *See* STERN, *supra* note 10, at 292.

f. Argue the Public Policy Implications

In most appeals, it is not enough to rely on case law and other legal authorities to carry the day. Appellate courts also want to hear about the public policy implications of the rule of law and result you are advocating. In discussing these public policy implications, you let the court know "why" it should rule in your favor and why a decision in your favor will make sense in other cases involving different facts.

While it is important to address these public policy implications, you must support your argument with sound analysis of the relevant case law and other authorities. Do not rely on naked public policy arguments devoid of any legal analysis and precedent. Such an approach will fail in all but the rarest of cases.

Appellate cases implicate many different kinds of public policy considerations. Following are a handful of examples of the kinds of policy interests the appellate court may concern itself with in a given appeal:

- *Preserving the attorney-client privilege*
- *Encouraging freedom of the press and the public's right to know*
- *Preventing further litigation*
- *Protecting public safety*
- *Maintaining the separation of powers between coordinate government branches*
- *Upholding the sanctity of contracts*
- *Avoiding stale claims*

Your job is to articulate how interests such as these will be implicated by a favorable or adverse decision in your appeal. This is also the part of the argument where you usually are best able to argue the equities of the case. You are less constrained by precedent here and can articulate a persuasive case as to why a decision in your client's favor would advance the overall interests of fairness and justice.

Do not be conclusory in discussing the public policy implications of your case. Where possible, back up your analysis of these interests with statistics or examples of the scenarios you predict. Such "policy fact" backup can make the difference between merely a good brief and a great one. For example, point to the adverse consequences that have followed from another state's adoption of a rule your opponent is advocating. Also, consider citing to respected commentators who share your view of the public policy implications of the case.

In terms of the organization of your argument, a discussion of these public policy considerations may fit after you have laid out your legal analysis and may warrant one or several separate argument subheadings.

Examples: *There are Strong Public Policy Reasons Why the Court Should Not Recognize a Cause of Action for Invasion of Privacy.*

The Public Interest in Protecting the Governor's Ability to Have Candid Discussions with His Staff Outweighs the Plaintiff's Purely Personal Interest in Access to the Recordings of the Governor's Staff Meetings.

Keep in mind that these public policy implications are likely to be of even greater concern to the appellate court than the trial court in light of the appellate court's particular concern about the ramifications of its decisions on subsequent cases.

g. Eliminate/Concede Weak Arguments and Avoid Nit-Picking

It is best to jettison your weak arguments entirely or expressly concede the point to your opponent. Doing this will only increase your credibility with the court. Courts realize that counsel are sometimes dealt a bad hand on an issue and appreciate attorneys who have the candor to acknowledge that they cannot prevail on every point in the case. They are more likely to trust attorneys who are honest enough to admit that some parts of the case favor their opponents. Also remember that your case need not be perfect for you to prevail. You likely do not have to win every single point in the appeal to walk away the victor.

You also should avoid making arguments and points, that while perhaps accurate, are inconsequential. Such nit-picking, however personally gratifying, is not going to win you any points with the appellate court and is likely only to distract from the truly important arguments you make.

h. Do Not Be Tentative and Do Not Exaggerate

Watch your word choices in your argument so that you do not come across as tentative. Following are some phrases that connote tentativeness:

Plaintiff submits that. . . .

It can be argued that. . . .

Arguably, ...

It is our contention that. . . .

Eliminate these "wind-up" words from your argument. They only tend to weaken the points you are making. The court understands that your arguments represent your positions. Present them with confidence. Simply make the assertion without these prefatory words.

Conversely, also do not engage in hyperbole in your argument (e.g., "Civilization as we now know it will come to an end if the court rules against my client."). Overused exaggeration is the litigation "floodgates" argument—that the courts will be overwhelmed with new cases if it rules for an opponent. While it may be appropriate in a given case to highlight the likelihood of increased litigation from a certain outcome, be careful not to paint an exaggerated Pandora's Box. The appellate court has heard this argument many, many times before.

You also should avoid efforts to "beef up" your argument by resorting to boldface, underlined, italicized and/or super-sized typeface. Appellate judges get irritated with such artificial attempts to embellish arguments. In a similar, although less egregious vein, avoid over reliance on words such as "clearly," "patently," and "obviously." These conclusory terms are no substitute for a well-developed argument and often signal to the court that the point is anything but clear or obvious.

i. *Eliminate Ad Hominem Attacks and Sarcasm*

You should scrupulously avoid *ad hominem* attacks on your opponent, your opposing counsel or the trial judge in your brief. There is no place for such personal attacks in a brief. Such incivility is sure to anger the appellate court and damage your credibility. It may even make the court sympathetic to your opponent. Remember that your reputation both precedes you and also follows you.

If you are the recipient of such *ad hominem* attacks, avoid the urge to retaliate in kind. Often your best response to such rhetoric is to take the high road and simply ignore it. It also can be effective in some instances to use humor and self-deprecation to defuse such attacks.[31]

Likewise, while it is appropriate to challenge your opponent's arguments, avoid using inflammatory rhetoric and sarcasm in doing so. Refrain from describing your opponent's arguments as "outrageous," "ridiculous," or "specious." You can use alternative language to express the flaws in your opponent's arguments that is not so hostile.[32] It is better to show the court how flawed your opponent's argument is through a

---

[31] If it is necessary to respond to an ad hominem attack, footnotes are an excellent method for clarifying opposing counsel's alleged grievance.

[32] *See* Girvan Peck, *Strategy of the Brief in* THE LITIGATION MANUAL, *supra* note 6, at 264, 272 (The author provides some good examples of less inflammatory words and phrases you might use in challenging the trial court's decision or an opponent's arguments.).

straightforward and sound analysis of the law and facts than to give the argument some conclusory and inflammatory label.

j. Use of Quotations

Quotations can be effective in your argument, but only if used judiciously. You should save your quotes for those instances in which a court or other author has articulated a point in an especially powerful way that you cannot replicate by paraphrasing. If you overuse quotations, you will dilute the effect of them. Generally speaking, there is no need to quote from a case or secondary authority if you can adequately paraphrase the substance. You also may want to quote a court with regard to a very precise definition of a standard or test you are applying in your argument or to articulate a particularly important public policy consideration. By reserving your quotes for these few circumstances, you will enhance their punch and effectiveness.

Even if you determine some quotation is appropriate, avoid lengthy quotations. Appellate judges frown upon long blocks of single-spaced quoted text. In fact, some commentators say that if you decide to include such lengthy quotes, you should assume that the judges will not read them.

It is critical that the quotes you use are accurate and not misleading. If you quote something out of context, you can be assured your opponent, and likely the court, will jump on this and your credibility will be damaged. Similarly, be precise in your use of an ellipsis to designate an omission from the quote. Certainly, you never want to use an ellipsis to omit language that would materially alter the meaning of the quote. Moreover, you should follow the citation rules regarding the use of an ellipsis so that it is clear whether the omission is in the middle of a sentence you are quoting, at the end of a sentence you are quoting or in-between sentences you are quoting. Following are the correct uses of an ellipsis in these circumstances:

- *If you omit text from the middle of a sentence, the ellipsis denotes the omitted text (e.g., TEXT . . . TEXT.).*

- *If you omit text from the end of a sentence, the ellipsis denotes the omitted text and is followed by a period (e.g., TEXT. . . .).*

- *If you omit text between sentences, the ellipsis denotes the omitted text and comes after the period from the preceding sentence (e.g., TEXT. . . . TEXT.).*

You should not use an ellipsis to denote text omitted from the beginning of a sentence.[33]

---

[33] *See* THE BLUEBOOK: A UNIFORM SYSTEM OF CITATION, R.5.1(b), at 46 (Columbia Law Review Ass'n et al. eds., 17th ed. 2000).

k. Use of Footnotes

Appellate advocacy commentators have differing views regarding the appropriateness of footnotes in appellate briefs. Some contend that they should not be used at all primarily because they interrupt the flow of the argument.[34] These commentators believe that if the point to be made in the footnote is important enough, it belongs in the text, and that if the point is relatively unimportant, it should not be made at all. Other commentators believe that footnotes are appropriate in some circumstances to make certain ancillary points that would tend to interrupt the flow of the argument text and/or to locate citations to legal propositions in the text.[35] Even these commentators agree that footnotes should be used sparingly and that counsel should avoid lengthy footnotes.

The authors believe that footnotes can be useful but agree that they should be used sparingly, if at all. You should not use footnotes to make major or elaborate arguments in support of your case or to set up and knock down straw men in order to try to impress the court with the depth of your research. Given the strong views that some judges have regarding the use of footnotes in a brief, and the chance that some judges will simply ignore them, it is wise to ask yourself if it is critical that the court read the material in your footnote. If it is, you should elevate the material to the text of your argument. Never use footnotes to cram additional verbiage in the brief to get around the court's page limits.

If you include a footnote in the text of your argument, consider trying to locate the footnote at a natural break in the text—such as the end of a paragraph or argument section—so that you minimize the disruption to the flow of your argument.

l. Use of String Citations

Generally speaking, you should avoid using string citations in your brief. In most instances, one or just a few citations will suffice. Any more than this are likely only to unnecessarily break up the text and flow of your argument and annoy the reader.

One of the very few situations in which you may want to use a string citation is to show the overwhelming weight of authority supporting a particular proposition. One of the authors was involved in an appeal involving an issue of first impression in Minnesota and was advocating that the Minnesota Supreme Court adopt the position of four other states that had addressed the issue. The other side did a good job of using a long string citation to show that the other twenty-seven states that had considered the issue all went the other way. If you use a string citation for this purpose,

---

[34] *See, e.g.,* GARNER, *supra* note 8, at 22 (suggests a ban on all substantive footnotes).

[35] *See, e.g.,* Daniel M. Friedman, *Winning on Appeal, in* THE LITIGATION MANUAL, *supra* note 6, at 152, 157.

you might consider putting it in a footnote to reduce the interruption of your argument text.

m. Use of Lists, Charts, Diagrams, Etc.

Do not overlook the power of a list, chart, or diagram to illustrate an important point in certain cases. In fact, it is generally recognized that visual aids can significantly improve retention. For example, side-by-side lists are useful for drawing comparisons in a readily understandable fashion. You can use such side-by-side comparisons to quickly show in a shorthand fashion how the facts of your case match the applicable legal test or the facts of another case upon which you are relying. You also can use this device to compare the language of different documents, such as pleadings, discovery responses or contracts, to show how similar or dissimilar they are. Likewise, a timeline chart showing the sequence of particular events can be useful especially if you want the appellate court to focus on the timing of some event, such as the time when your opponent had notice of some facts. Similarly, a diagram or drawing can help illustrate a scene, such as the scene of an accident, or an object, such as an allegedly defective product. Such illustrative devices often are preferable to lengthy narrative descriptions.

G. CONCLUSION

The conclusion of your brief should contain a short, plain statement of the relief you are requesting. You usually can accomplish this in a single sentence.

Examples: *For the above-stated reasons, Viking Enterprises respectfully requests that the Court affirm the decision of the court of appeals in its entirety.*

For the foregoing reasons, Smith respectfully requests that the Court reverse the decision of the trial court and remand the case for a trial on the merits of Smith's claims.

The model brief in Appendix C contains an example of the alternative—a longer narrative that embodies the overall theme of the brief.

You also can ask for alternative relief if that is what you are seeking.

There is some disagreement among appellate practitioners and commentators over whether you should include a narrative summary of your arguments in the conclusion. Some favor such a summary believing that after you have told the judges what you were going to tell them, and having then told them, you should tell them once again what you just told them. The authors do not favor such summaries in most cases, although a short summary may be helpful in a particularly complex matter or a case that implicates personal rights or liberty interests. If you decide to include a narrative summary in your conclusion, do not simply restate your argument headings, which the court will already have read numerous times. Instead, consider using this opportunity to make a final powerful statement about the public policy implications of the case. And keep your summary short. The court will be anxious to finish your brief, no matter how eloquent you are, by the time it gets to the conclusion section.

H. APPENDIX

The first thing you should do in preparing the appendix to your brief is to read the court's rules regarding the required contents of the appendix. These rules spell out the items that must be included in the appendix, such as pleadings, lower court orders and notices of appeal. Some appellate court rules direct the parties to prepare a joint appendix to avoid unnecessary repetition of the same materials in each appendix.

In addition to including the items required by the rules in your appendix, you should consider including any other critical parts of the record that you want the court to access easily. For example, if you are relying upon some testimony from a deposition or trial, you should consider reproducing the relevant testimony in your appendix so the judges will not have to pull the whole case record if they want to examine the testimony. This also applies to critical documents such as contracts, warranties, etc. The appellate judges and law clerks who read your briefs may take them home where they do not have immediate access to the full appellate record. Consequently, if the testimony, admission or stipulation is important enough, you should include it in your appendix so they will have everything they need when reading your brief.[36]

Likewise, you may want to reproduce the language of statutes or regulations in your appendix so the court will have the precise language easily at hand. While you may already have quoted and discussed part of a statute in your argument, you may want to include the remainder of the statute or regulation in your appendix in case the court wants to read it.

You also should consider including in your appendix non-standard or very recent authority cited in your brief if you think the court might not have ready access to it. For example, if you are relying in part upon an older state attorney general opinion that the court is not likely to have, you should consider including this in your appendix.

---

[36] If you have a separately bound appendix, you may be able to include some of these critical excerpts from the record in a short addendum attached to the back of your brief. *See, e.g.,* 8th CIR. R. APP. P. 28A(b) (addendum may include short excerpts from the record that would be helpful in reading the brief without immediate reference to the appendix).

Once you have assembled the contents of your appendix, you should paginate it and prepare an index. Some appellate rules require such an index and require that the appendix be separately paginated.

III. WRITING STYLE PRINCIPLES

WRITING STYLE CONSIDERATIONS

- **Think and organize before you write**
- **Be clear**
- **Be concise**
- **Be precise**
- **Use the active voice**
- **Vary length of sentences/paragraphs**
- **Use clear topic sentences**
- **Avoid legalese**
- **Critically edit**
- **Proofread!**

You will enhance the effectiveness of your brief by employing general principles of good writing. To improve your own writing style, you may want to refer to well-respected and timeless books about writing, such as *The Elements of Style* by William Strunk, Jr. and E.B. White. You also should review stylistic preferences from your jurisdiction.[37] Following are a number of basic writing style principles to keep in mind as you draft your brief.

A. OUTLINE FIRST— THEN WRITE

A comprehensive outline will lay the groundwork for a successful brief. Resist the temptation to start drafting your brief right after you have found a few useful authorities. At this early point, you may not have found all of the relevant law, and may not have reviewed enough to appreciate various nuances or to have found cases that are the most persuasive either in terms of presenting analogous facts or articulating the most powerful reasoning. Your brief will be much better if you spend far more time preparing to write than you spend actually writing.[38] During the preparation stage, do your legal research. At the appellate level, it is common to encounter diverging legal paths. Take your time to understand the legal paths and thoughtfully choose which path you intend to follow. Then start to outline your

---

[37] The Seventh Circuit Court of Appeals has a concise and informative style guide that focuses on the importance of readability from a formatting perspective: http://www.ca7.uscourts. gov/forms/type.pdf. A number of states release state-specific style guides. For example, California (http://www.sdap.org/downloads/Style-Manual.pdf); Illinois (https://courts.illinois.gov/Style Manual/SupCrt_StyleManual.pdf); and New York (http://www.courts.state.ny.us/reporter/new_ styman.htm).

[38] As the late Professor Irving Younger noted, rewriting does not always cure the defects of a rushed draft in that words, once written, take on a permanence and resistance to revision. Professor Younger remarked: "Let those first words be less than your best words and your final version will suffer." Irving Younger, *Ready, Set. . .Wait!*, A.B.A. J., Jan. 1, 1988, at 122.

arguments, case law, supporting facts, public policy arguments and criticism of your opponent's arguments.

There are different outlining techniques you can use. One is the more traditional linear outline using points set off by Roman numerals. Other commentators advocate different outlining techniques.[39] Regardless of what outlining technique you prefer, take the time to collect and map out your thoughts before you start to draft. If nothing else, your brief will be more organized and easier to follow if you take the time to do this.

B. BE CLEAR, CONCISE AND PRECISE

Your writing should be clear to the reader. Keep it simple. Shorter sentences and paragraphs will help the clarity of your brief. Avoid fancy rhetoric. An appellate brief is not a forum for you to display your eloquence or impressive vocabulary. Simple, clear writing should be your goal. If the appellate judges have to reread parts of your brief several times to understand what you are trying to say, you are facing a steep uphill battle in the appeal.

Strive for brevity. Prefer shorter words and sentences for the sake of clarity. Eliminate unnecessary words, sentences, paragraphs and arguments. It is important to write thorough and thoughtful legal analysis. It is just as important to focus on the critical issue(s). For example, if you are applying a legal test with five prongs, and three of them are undisputed, focus on the two contested elements. Judges, like lawyers, have too much to do and not enough time. The court will not only appreciate a shorter analysis, it will recognize that you understand the key part(s) of the argument.

Also get rid of the nit-picking in your text. If the text does not help advance a significant argument, take it out. Put another way: if a sentence does not add a new idea, it needs to be rewritten or removed. If you are uncertain about omitting something, take it out, read the passage again and ask yourself whether the omission of the text is likely to have any appreciable effect on the outcome of the appeal.

Your writing should not only be clear and succinct, it should also be precise. Make sure that you have selected the right words to convey the points you want to make. Sometimes you need to add additional detail to make a point more precise.

---

[39] *See, e.g.,* GARNER, *supra* note 8, at 26 (describing a nonlinear "whirlybird" outlining technique).

C. USE ACTIVE VOICE

Use active voice in your brief. Change passive voice to the active.

Examples: *Change:*   *The contract was breached by the defendant.*

              to: *The defendant breached the contract.*

The word "by" in a sentence is often an indication that your sentence is in the passive voice. While there are situations in which you will want to use the passive voice in your brief for tactical reasons (e.g., you want to de-emphasize the actor and focus the sentence on the object acted upon), your brief should primarily be in the active voice. Active voice is more forceful and concise.

D. AVOID LEGALESE

Eliminate legalese from your briefs. Words and phrases like *a fortiori,* heretofore, said contract and comes now the plaintiff do not impress appellate courts. This is not to say that you must ban all legal terminology from your brief. Some legal words and phrases have well-recognized meanings and are commonly used by courts and attorneys even though not used in everyday parlance, like dicta, *res ipsa loquitur,* consideration and proximate cause.

Other legal words and terms can obscure clarity and disrupt flow. As noted above in subsection B, clarity is key. Use legal terms when needed, while remaining mindful of the effectiveness of writing clearly and concisely.

E. BE APPROPRIATELY RESPECTFUL OF THE COURT

Be respectful of the court in your brief. Avoid snide or sarcastic comments or attacks on the wisdom or integrity of the court. On a subtler note, you should also avoid telling the appellate court that it "must" do something or "cannot" do something. Instead, tell the court what it "should" or "should not" do. Likewise, you should show respect to the trial court no matter how erroneous you think the court's decision. By the same token, you should also avoid gratuitous pandering to the court.

F. REFER TO THE PARTIES BY NAME

Your brief should refer to the parties by their actual names (e.g., John Smith) or some abbreviation of their names (e.g., IBM). Rule 28(d) of the Federal Rules of Appellate Procedure expressly directs parties to keep references to appellant and appellee to a minimum. Using a party's real name also can help personalize the individual and reduce the likelihood of confusion.

It generally is recommended that you do not use titles such as "Mr." or "Ms." after the first time you refer to an individual. This can get rather wordy if you refer to the person frequently. Just use the person's last name (e.g., Jones). While some attorneys like to refer to their clients by their first names at trial to further personalize them with the jury, such informality is generally inappropriate in an appellate brief.

You can group several parties together and give them a collective reference. For example, in a suit against a state, its governor and its legislature, the defendants might be collectively identified as "the State."

Finally, be sure to be consistent in your references to the parties throughout your brief. It can get confusing if you interchangeably refer to the same entity and litigant as the "school district," "District No. 577," the "school board" and the "defendant."

G. INCLUDE TOPIC SENTENCES IN YOUR PARAGRAPHS

Make sure you include topic sentences in the paragraphs in your brief. Each topic sentence should clearly and succinctly convey the subject matter of the paragraph to follow.

Example: *The existence of an agency relationship is primarily a question of fact for the jury. It is only when the evidence is such that reasonable minds could draw but one conclusion that such questions are for the trial court. Leonard v. North Dakota Co-op. Wool Marketing Ass'n, 6 N.W.2d 576, 578 (N.D. 1942). The question in this hospital malpractice case is whether the nurse was an agent of the attending physician. The trial court erred in refusing to instruct the jury regarding the captain of the ship or borrowed servant doctrine. As discussed below, there was ample evidence for the jury to find the existence of an agency relationship in this case. Accordingly, the case should have gone to the jury.*

Your topic sentences should also help to tie your paragraphs together. There are different ways to do this including, for example, using transition words in your topic sentence such as "accordingly" and "moreover." A brief reference in your topic sentence to some topic or language in the previous paragraph is another way to link your paragraphs together. Ideally, you want each paragraph to flow into the next to create a sense of continuity in your text.

H. VARY THE LENGTH OF YOUR SENTENCES/PARAGRAPHS

Make sure you get some variety in the length of the sentences and paragraphs in your brief. In general, you should try to keep your sentences short. Some commentators contend that sentences in a brief should average no more than twenty words.[40] That is not, of course, to say that every sentence should be approximately twenty words. Varying cadence is an effective way to engage your audience. Strive for variety. You can effectively emphasize a point by making it in a short sentence following several longer sentences. Dramatic change in sentence length can create a distinctive punch.

Example: *After learning that one of his teachers was sexually abusing a student, the school principal failed to take reasonable steps to protect the student from additional abuse. The principal could have confronted the teacher regarding the alleged abuse and conducted an investigation of the allegations. He could have notified the district superintendent and the school board and requested that the teacher be suspended pending an investigation. He also could and should have reported the alleged abuse to the police as required by state statute. He did nothing.*

The same advice applies to paragraphs. Keep them relatively short on average but try to achieve some variety in the length. If one of your paragraphs is an entire page long, or close to it, break it up. Remember that a paragraph should concern a single discrete topic. Long paragraphs often contain multiple topics that can be broken out into separate paragraphs. Alternatively, a very long paragraph may be a signal that you need to convey your point more precisely.

I. USE GENDER NEUTRAL AND GENDER INCLUSIVE LANGUAGE

There are different techniques you can employ to avoid using gender specific references in your brief. The pronoun "they" is recognized as a singular, non-binary pronoun.[41] Another technique is to change the antecedent reference to the plural form and then use a plural pronoun.

---

[40] *See* GARNER, *supra* note 8, at 108–09.

[41] "They." *Merriam-Webster.com Dictionary*, Merriam-Webster, https://www.merriam-webster.com/dictionary/they. Accessed 05 Jan. 2021.

Example: *Original:* *Appellate courts do not like it when an attorney fails to follow the courts' rules in preparing his brief.*

                  Revised: *Appellate courts do not like it when attorneys fail to follow the courts' rules in preparing their briefs.*

Another alternative technique is to repeat the gender-neutral antecedent and eliminate the pronoun.

Example: *Original:* *When an attorney drafts the statement of facts in an appellate brief she should include citations to the sources of the facts.*

                  Revised: *When an attorney drafts the statement of facts in an appellate brief the attorney should include citations to the sources of the facts.*

Yet another technique is to select titles that are gender neutral—e.g., "chair" instead of "chairman," "firefighter" instead of "fireman," etc. These are just a few of the different techniques available to ensure you are using gender-inclusive language and avoiding unnecessary "he/she" references in your briefs.

J. CRITICALLY EDIT YOUR BRIEF—MAKE EVERY SENTENCE COUNT

After you have drafted your brief, you must take the time to edit it. As the old adage goes, there are no good writers, only good re-writers. Doing a critical edit of your brief does not mean simply proofreading it for typographical errors. That is another, later level of review. A critical edit means that you examine every paragraph and sentence and every word within every sentence. As you review your draft, you should ask yourself:

- Is this sentence/paragraph clear?
- Does it convey the precise point you wanted to make?
- Does it significantly advance your arguments?
- Is it necessary?
- Can you shorten it and still convey the same point?

A common mistake is writing sentences with "one and a half points." Common elements of an overly complex sentence are: an opening transition (or restating part of the previous point), multiple commas, using more than twenty to twenty-five words. Each sentence should make one point.

This is a difficult part of the process of preparing a brief. Once you have a draft, you may feel that you said everything you wanted to say in the way you wanted to say it. At this point, you must put yourself in the place of the reader and try to look at your brief from the vantage of someone who knows nothing about your case, who has no emotional attachment to any side, and who wants to know what your best arguments are in as few pages as possible.[42]

K. CITE-CHECK AND BLUEBOOK

You must, of course, make sure that you check the validity of your citations before filing your appellate brief. There is nothing more embarrassing than having your opponent, or the court, point out that the authorities you are relying upon have been overruled, vacated or modified. All of the major legal research companies offer cite-checking. With that in mind, cite-checking is not a difficult or especially time-consuming task. You should not wait until your brief is nearly ready to file with the court before first checking your key citations. It can be very frustrating to prepare your brief and find, right before you are ready to file it, that there are serious problems with one or more of the key cases you relied upon. Make sure to check the validity of at least your key authorities early on in the drafting process. Furthermore, always re-check the validity of your citations shortly before your oral argument. It is quite possible that the passage of time from when you filed your brief until your oral argument has resulted in a change in the status of your citations or that important new cases have been decided in the interim.

Also make sure that you conform your citations to the latest edition of the Bluebook, the ALWD Citation Manual or any other citation style manual the court uses.[43] Get your cites in the right form. A relatively small number of Bluebook or Citation Manual rules govern the vast majority of cites in appellate briefs. Accurate citations are another aspect of maximizing your credibility. Appellate judges and their law clerks get rightfully irritated if they cannot locate your authorities because of incorrect citations.

L. PROOFREAD, PROOFREAD, PROOFREAD

Take the time to proofread carefully your brief before filing it with the court. If you have spent many hours researching and writing a strong brief,

---

[42] An additional incentive to critically edit your brief, is to avoid the kind of order the Kentucky Supreme Court issued against a lawyer who wrote a brief the Kentucky Court of Appeals deemed "virtually incomprehensible." Notwithstanding the lawyer's argument that a brief should be valued for its substance over its form, the Kentucky Supreme Court suspended the lawyer for 60 days for bad writing. Ky. Bar Ass'n v. Brown, 14 S.W.3d 916 (Ky. 2000).

[43] THE BLUEBOOK, *supra* note 33; DARBY DICKERSON & ASS'N OF LEGAL WRITING DIRECTORS, ALWD CITATION MANUAL: A PROFESSIONAL SYSTEM OF CITATION (2d ed. 2000).

you do not want to undermine your credibility by filing a brief that has typographical or grammatical errors. If you are converting file formats, the format of your brief may change. For example, converting a Microsoft Word document, or Google Doc, to PDF can wreak havoc on your typography and formatting. Ensure that you review your final version before uploading and filing with the court.

Appellate judges tend to equate sloppy proofreading with sloppy analysis and sloppy research. They are not as likely to trust attorneys who do not take the time and effort to proofread their briefs, just as they are not as likely to trust attorneys who ignore the court's rules.

After you have spent many hours deeply engrossed in a brief, it is often difficult to notice typographical and grammatical mistakes. Your eyes start to glaze over the text you have written, read and rewritten many times and you start to read what you thought you wrote instead of the words on the page. One option is decidedly old-school: print a copy of your brief and read it by hand. The change in format will help you review your brief with "fresh" eyes and is guaranteed to help you spot previously undiscovered typos, along with potentially larger issues.

Another option is to have another person read through the brief to try to detect these kinds of mistakes. Your proofreader need not even be an attorney. In fact, sometimes it is helpful to have someone who is not an attorney read your brief to see if the organization is easy to follow and if it seems to make sense. While it is advisable to enlist some help with the proofreading task, remember that you alone bear the ultimate responsibility for your brief. Do not simply delegate this task to someone else.

Moreover, do not rely on a spellcheck function to catch misspellings in your brief. Spellcheck may miss some of your misspellings because the incorrect words you typed are, in fact, correctly spelled. In other words, the problem is the misuse of similar-sounding words, not just their spelling.

It is not only important that you carefully proofread your brief for the court, but it is also important that you do this for your client. Your credibility with your own client is partly dependent on the quality of your written work. Clients who pay you to prepare their briefs rightfully expect that their briefs will not be riddled with errors that could and should have been corrected with minimal effort.

M. GIVE YOURSELF TIME

Completing an appellate brief takes a great deal of time. You need to create a workplan that includes the necessary time to research, write, revise, and finalize your brief. Much of this time comes after the body of the brief has been drafted. First, you may want others in your office and your client to review the brief and provide comments. You also need to allow enough production time. For example, it can be quite time-consuming to assemble and copy a large appendix. If you need to get your brief printed or bound by an outside entity, this can take days or longer. Once you have copied your brief, you should spot check the copies to make sure the pages were collated properly and that none are missing. Even if briefs are filed online, most jurisdictions still require delivery of paper copies, which can be time consuming.

Needless to say, things can go wrong with any or all of these steps. As a result, you should plan a timetable for the completion of these various tasks that gives you some leeway if things go awry. It is risky to expect to get everything done in the last several hours of the day the brief is due. You do not want to have to ask the appellate court for more time to file your brief because of something you should have anticipated.

IV. REPLY BRIEFS

Appellate courts usually allow appellants to file a reply brief in response to the appellee's brief. The first decision the appellant has to make is whether to file such a reply brief. The decision is similar to the decision whether to conduct redirect examination at trial or whether to do a rebuttal during oral argument. There are different schools of thought regarding reply briefs. Some believe that you should not file a reply brief as an appellant unless absolutely necessary to correct some serious misstatement by the appellee, lest it appear that you have been injured by the appellee's brief. Those who advocate this view believe that it is psychologically advantageous to waive a reply brief insofar as this suggests that there is nothing in the appellee's brief that even warrants a response. Another school of thought is that you should always or nearly always file a reply brief, without much regard to the strength of the appellee's brief, in order to make sure to get in the last word. For the same reason, these attorneys invariably decline to waive rebuttal during an oral argument. There is no universally correct position on this issue. The authors generally file replies, but they always should be brief and focused.

If you decide to file a reply brief, there are several principles to keep in mind. First, make sure your brief is a true reply. In other words, most appellate rules require that a reply brief be limited to the scope of the arguments made by the appellee. It is inappropriate to include new points or arguments in a reply brief that do not constitute a legitimate reply to the appellee's brief. Similarly, do not sandbag the appellee by deliberately withholding significant new arguments from your principal brief and including them in your reply brief so that the appellee has no opportunity to respond to these arguments. Some appropriate purposes of a reply brief include: to correct a misstatement of the facts or law by the appellee; to respond to some significant cases in appellee's brief that were not cited or discussed in appellant's brief; and to address a cross-appeal by the appellee.

Second, keep your reply brief short and address only the most significant points in the appellee's brief. Your reply brief should not be a lengthy refutation of every single point of disagreement with the appellee's brief. Similarly, your reply brief need not critique every case the appellee cites. Even if your criticisms of the appellee's brief are valid, it will look to the court as if you are nit-picking and wasting the court's time. Moreover, the longer your reply brief the less its impact and the more it starts to look to the court like the appellee's brief did some significant damage to your case.

Third, your reply brief should not simply repeat the same arguments made in your principal brief. Tell the court why the appellee's arguments are flawed, why the cases the appellee cites are inapposite, and/or how the appellee misrepresented the facts. In doing this, you will no doubt weave in some of the basic affirmative points and themes set forth in your principal brief. This is not problematic. In fact, ideally, your reply brief should convey the same underlying affirmative analysis and theme as your principal brief and not simply consist of a disjointed response to individual points made by the appellee. What you should not do is merely regurgitate the arguments in your principal brief and all but ignore any real analysis of the appellee's arguments.

Finally, your reply brief should not include all of the same sections in your principal brief (e.g., statement of the issues, statement of the case, etc.). The reply can be limited to an argument and conclusion, and perhaps a summary of the argument, depending on how long the reply is. You are, however, permitted to use your reply brief to address alleged misstatements of facts in the appellee's statement of the facts, misstatements of the issues, and misstatements of the procedural posture. Your arguments in your reply brief can track the same organization as the arguments in your principal brief or you can include somewhat different arguments specifically targeted at the arguments in the appellee's brief.

EXERCISES

For the following exercises on outlining, brief writing, and revising your brief, you can use either case record, *Lane v. Moot State University Law School*, or *Smith, et al. v. Willis, et al.*

1. Outlining and Preparing to Write Your Brief

Review your research and determine the 3–5 most apposite authorities for each issue.

Create a detailed outline of your argument. Determine your strongest and weakest arguments and restructure your outline accordingly.

Ensure that your outline has a sufficient number of headings and subheadings. Determine if your brief would benefit from additional (or fewer) headings.

2. Writing Your Brief

a. Statement of Issues

Draft a Statement of the Issues for the appellant(s)/appellee(s) in either case record.

Consider reordering the issues, based on strongest/weakest argument(s).

Consider incorporating the burden of proof/standard of review in your issue statement.

Review the test of a good issue statement (as discussed above) and revise your issues accordingly.

b. Statement of the Case

Draft a Statement of the Case for the appellant(s)/appellee(s) in either case record.

Consider whether you have you included the necessary procedural aspects of the case.

Consider whether to include particularly well-reasoned (or poorly reasoned) portions of the lower court's reasoning.

c. Statement of the Facts

Draft a Statement of the Facts for the appellant(s)/appellee(s) in either case record.

Be mindful of your overall theme and purposefully reflect that theme in your statement of the facts.

Consider the most effective way to tell your client's story—chronological, reverse-chronological, or perhaps a combination of both.

Consider the 4–6 key facts for your client. Now determine how you will effectively showcase those facts—headings, subtle repetition, or through the use of effective adjectives/adverbs.

d. Summary of Argument

Draft a Summary of Argument for the appellant(s)/appellee(s) in either case record.

Consider whether your summary effectively conveys your theme.

Consider whether your summary tells the court what you want, why you want it, and provides a legal route to reach that conclusion.

Consider whether your summary tracks the overall organization of your argument.

e. Argument

Draft the argument (or the argument for one issue) for the appellant(s)/appellee(s) in either case record.

Determine whether you have incorporated the procedural standard and how that may impact your argument.

Determine how to order your arguments: strongest to weakest, matching the order granting appeal, or a combination.

Use headings and subheadings to both emphasize key arguments and to ensure your compartmentalize each section.

Ensure that you provide a complete statement of the applicable law and methodically apply the law to the applicable facts.

Ensure that you write a complete affirmative argument, as opposed to a piecemeal argument that refutes your opponent's arguments.

Include targeted policy arguments, ensuring they are incorporated into your argument, as opposed to a "naked" policy argument.

Consider the 4–6 most important points for each issue. Review your argument and determine if those points are emphasized.

f. Appendix

Identify what you would put in an Appendix to your brief for the appellant(s)/appellee(s) in either case record.

3. Revising Your Brief

Consider the standard of review. Review your brief and confirm that you properly incorporated it.

Consider the procedural status. Review your argument and determine if your argument sufficiently reflects the impact of the procedural status. For example, if you are the appellants in *Smith*, have you effectively incorporated the favorable standard on a motion to dismiss?

Pick a section of your argument. Review the header and then write down what you think are the 4–6 most important points for that issues. Now review your argument and determine if those points are emphasized.

Pick an issue in your argument. Think about the 2–3 most important authorities for that issue. Now review that issue in your brief and determine if those authorities are emphasized. Consider whether you can eliminate any additional authorities.

Pick an issue in your argument. Think about the 2–3 authorities that the opposing side will rely on. Determine if you want to proactively address any of those cases in your argument.

Print your brief and read it by hand, or read your brief out loud. Focus on being concise. Consider whether each sentence makes one new point.

Print your brief and read it by hand, or read your brief out loud. Focus on clarity and readability. Rework and revise any section that is unclear, hard to understand, or perhaps too long.

PART THREE

ORAL ARGUMENT

■ ■ ■

I. THE PURPOSE OF ORAL ARGUMENT

The most fundamental thing to remember about oral argument is that it is a conversation with the court. Oral argument is not an oral recitation of your brief or a simple synopsis of the brief. Rather, your oral argument should complement your brief, much like a glass of fine wine may complement a nice dinner.

It is helpful to compare an oral argument to a typical law school class. In one sense, you, as the advocate, are the professor. Your appellate brief is the reading assignment you give the students so they can prepare for the class. The reading assignment provides the meat of what the students need to know, while the subsequent class time provides an opportunity for a dialogue between the professor and the class in which they flesh out the meaning of the reading assignment. The difference is that in oral argument your role is to answer questions rather than pose them.

> **WHAT IS ORAL ARGUMENT**
> - **Argument as conversation**
> - **Argument as rebuttal**
> - **Argument as caricature**

Although your brief is the primary vehicle you will use to persuade the court, oral argument is critical in closely contested cases. Judge Paul Michel of the United States Court of Appeals for the Federal Circuit has underscored the importance of oral argument: "In perhaps half the cases, it is clear from the briefs that the lower court must be affirmed. The other half are closer cases where oral argument could influence my vote, and it does so far more than 20 percent of the time."[1] Put another way, in the words of Judge Kermit Lipez of the United States Court of Appeals for the First Circuit ". . . assume that oral argument will make a difference because 'often enough, it does.' "[2]

---

[1] Paul R. Michel, *Effective Appellate Advocacy,* 24 LITIG. 19, 21 (Summer 1998).

[2] McGaughey M. D., (2020) *"May It Please the Court—Or Not: Appellate Judges' Preferences and Pet Peeves About Oral Argument",* 20 Journal of Appellate Practice and Process 141 (Fall 2019).

As you prepare for your oral argument, always reflect on the purpose of this particular form of advocacy. There are three primary goals:

A. ANTICIPATE, DISCOVER, AND ANSWER THE COURT'S CONCERNS

Briefs are like lectures; oral argument is a Socratic dialogue. It is your one opportunity to learn about concerns the court may have and respond to them directly.

ORAL ARGUMENT GOALS

- Discover and address concerns of the court
- Persuade and personalize/focus on theme
- Answer opponent's arguments

A well-prepared advocate will anticipate and prepare for the most difficult possible questions. Listen carefully and hit questions head on. Do not try to evade difficult issues. Oral argument is most valuable when it reveals what the court sees as weaknesses in your position and when you are able to address those weaknesses. It also is a time when you can capitalize on concerns the court articulates through questions addressed to your opponent.

B. PERSUADE AND PERSONALIZE

Oral arguments are short. Use your time wisely. When you are not addressing questions raised by the court, use the time to persuade the court and personalize your case. Rely on your brief to provide permissible routes to allow the court to reach the result you seek; in oral argument, you should focus your precious minutes on convincing the court why it should *want* to reach your proposed result. Personalize your client and speak in terms of fundamental fairness. Make the court want to find a way to rule for your client. Briefs, when well crafted, are highly persuasive documents. At the same time, they generally must follow a given structure. In oral argument, you have more freedom. Find your persuasive theme, articulate it up front, and refer to it throughout your argument.

Be persuasive but remember your audience. This is an appellate argument, not a closing argument to a jury. Appellate courts do not respond well to closing arguments. Rather, they want a reasoned analysis, perhaps accented with a bit of passion, but not overwhelmed by it.

C. RESPOND TO YOUR OPPONENT

Oral argument provides you with your final opportunity to address your opponent's arguments. Take advantage of this opportunity when appropriate, but do not squander the minutes available to you by responding to every point your opponent attempts to make. Keep the big picture in mind and try to read the court. If the court seems to be responding positively to one of your opponent's major points, then by all means address it. On the other hand, if your opponent raises issues that fail to rouse the judges and have little chance of carrying the day, then resist the temptation to score debating points by responding to each argument at the expense of losing the court's interest. Instead, stick to your own theme and ignore those parts of your opponent's presentation.

II. PREPARING FOR ORAL ARGUMENT

The key to presenting an effective oral argument is meticulous preparation. You may know your case backward and forward, but unless you specifically prepare for the oral argument, you may lose an opportunity to seal your success or, worse, you may convert a winning case into a losing one.

A. KNOW YOUR COURT

Try to observe a court before appearing before it. If you are in a jurisdiction that announces in advance the particular panel before whom you will be arguing, then arrange to see those judges in action before your oral argument. You will want to know whether the court is one that interrupts with frequent questions. Do the questions tend to be about the record, the law, or potential future ramifications of the court's ruling? Is the court one that typically is familiar with the facts and the briefs? Do the judges ask questions in a predetermined order? If you are arguing via videoconference, the court may have different protocols (more on that later). Answers to these questions will help you know what to expect and will affect the way you prepare for your argument.

Familiarize yourself with the court's system for timing arguments. At what point will you get signals regarding the time you have remaining? What are the signals? Do you have to ask to reserve some amount of time for rebuttal or is a prescribed amount automatically allocated? Will the clerk keep track of your rebuttal time or will you need to keep track of that time yourself? If you exceed your allotted time during your opening argument, is that time subtracted from your rebuttal time?

You also want to know how strict the court is about time limits. For example, will you need to stop mid-sentence when the red "stop" light comes on, will you be able to complete your sentence, or will the court allow you quickly to conclude your entire thought? Similarly, what is the court's general demeanor? Some courts are friendly, some are impatient, and some relish the opportunity to engage in a Socratic sport. Answers to these questions will help you feel more comfortable on the day of your argument and will help prevent you from becoming discombobulated by unexpected responses from the judges.

A number of courts offer audio and/or video recordings of recent arguments on the court's public website. While observing the court in person is preferable, listening to and analyzing recorded arguments is an excellent way to learn about the court's procedures and the proclivities of different members of the court.

B. REVIEW THE APPELLATE BRIEFS AND THE RECORD

Regardless of who wrote the briefs and regardless of who tried the case below, you, as the oral advocate, need to be intimately familiar with the briefs, with the authorities cited in those briefs, and with the district court record. Know what is in the record and what is not. Be prepared to cite pages of the record for salient facts you may need. It never is effective to say in response to a question about the record that you are unsure of the answer because other counsel tried the case below. Similarly, it never is effective to say that you are not familiar with a particular case cited in the brief because someone else wrote the brief or did the research. Demonstrating a lack of familiarity with either a particular component of the record or a particular case will not just undercut that point, it can undercut your overall credibility with the court.

You also need to be familiar with the record to guard against making arguments on appeal that appear inconsistent with positions you or other counsel for your client took at trial. If you need to take a different position on appeal, be prepared to explain the apparent inconsistency to the court.

Example: *Question: Counsel, you defend the exclusion of the testimony on hearsay grounds, but that's not the objection you made at trial, is it?*

Answer: Your Honor, my initial objection was to leading, but after counsel re-phrased, I objected again. The district judge sustained that second objection before I stated my grounds for the record. So, I don't think there is any inconsistency between our position at trial and our position on appeal. However, even if there were an inconsistency, and even if this court were to find that the grounds stated below were insufficient, the appellate court may properly uphold the district court's ruling so long as legally sufficient grounds exist.

C. UPDATE YOUR RESEARCH

Always cite-check your cases and check to see whether there are any important developments since you filed your brief. This type of updating is especially critical in cases involving areas of law in which different courts have taken differing positions and in areas in which the law is fairly volatile.

D. OUTLINE YOUR ARGUMENT

As you prepare to outline your argument, keep a few pointers in mind. First, remember the forest. Nowhere is this more important than in the limited time you have for oral argument. If your argument is no more than a thicket of individual trees, you do not understand your case in a way that will persuade an appellate court. Just as the trees in a forest rise up to form a seamless canopy of intertwining branches, your goal is to show the court how your individual arguments likewise weave together, supporting each other and proving your overarching theme.

Second, do not simply outline your brief. Rather, put the brief aside for a while and think about how to articulate a unifying theme, the major force behind your argument. Put another way: determine *what the case is about* (protecting individual rights and liberties, allowing a state to constitutionally exercise its police powers, etc.) as opposed to *what happened in the case*. Think about what will persuade the court that it *wants* to rule for you. Personalize your client and your client's situation or the broader policy ramifications of the court's ruling in your case. Remember the purposes of oral argument: persuading the court and personalizing your case, having a dialogue with the court about its concerns, and addressing potentially persuasive arguments of your opponent. If your oral argument is nothing more than a synopsis of your brief, the court will view your argument as a waste of time and tune you out.

Third, remember that arguments speak differently than they write. Oral argument is the time for persuasive conversation regarding the principal reasons you should prevail. It is not the time for the type of details and intricacies more appropriate to a written brief.

One helpful exercise as you prepare your argument outline is to have a conversation with a spouse, a parent, or a friend in which you try to convince that person, in just a few minutes, why it is important for the court to rule in your client's favor. This should help you articulate the theme you want to carry through your real argument to the court. This method is particularly helpful for determining the impact of your theme. If your theme does not resonate with your practice audience, you need to change it. If your practice audience overreacts to your theme, you need to tone it down. If your practice audience engages with your theme, that is a strong sign that you understand the key elements of your argument.

Following is a discussion of the main components of an oral argument that you will want to include in your outline.

1. The Introduction

After telling the court who you are and whom you represent,[3] you should immediately launch into a one-sentence articulation of your theme. Make that first sentence count. Write it out and memorize it. It should set the stage and tone for the rest of your argument. Remember, if you have more than one sentence, you may be interrupted by questions before you finish stating the one most important thing you want the court to think about and remember as it deliberates later.

As you craft your one-sentence theme statement, you may want to pretend that you have just left the courthouse following your argument and are confronted by a reporter. The reporter points a microphone at you and asks for a soundbite describing what your case is about. To make it on the nightly news and to do well by your client, you need to give a one-sentence articulation of the essence of your case that reflects in simple terms what is at stake on appeal. Generalities or legalistic gobbledygook will not make the airwaves.

> **Examples:** *Compare the following examples, each of which accurately states the themes on appeal, but only some of which personalize and persuade:*
>
> #1 *Compare: This case is about whether enforcement of Granite City Zoning Ordinance 241 as applied to my client violates the first amendment.*
>
> *To: This case is about whether Granite City should be permitted to suppress free speech at a private club based on unfounded fears of prostitution and gambling.*
>
> #2 *Compare: This case is about whether enforcement of Granite City Zoning Ordinance 241 constitutes a reasonable time, place, and manner restriction as applied to appellant.*
>
> *To: This case is about whether Granite City has the right to enforce zoning rules that restrict nude dancing at a nightclub and bar located next to a shopping mall and family movie theater.*

---

[3] *See* Part III. A, *infra.* If the court already knows who you are, you may skip this formality and begin with your one-sentence articulation of your theme.

#3   *Compare: This case is about whether the evidence was sufficient to convict my client of murder, given that some witnesses testified pursuant to plea agreements and the remainder of the evidence was primarily circumstantial.*

To: This case is about whether a 21-year-old man should spend the rest of his life in prison based solely on circumstantial evidence with no eyewitnesses where the government purchased the testimony of convicted criminals by offering them substantially reduced sentences.

In each pair of examples, the first formulation offers little more than a prosaic recitation of the applicable legal standard, draped in uninspiring legalisms and depersonalizing references ("my client", "appellant"). The second formulation, in contrast, brings the issue to life by personalizing the party involved, weaving in emotion-laden facts that highlight the stakes involved, and using active phrasing ("suppress free speech", "purchased testimony") instead of sterile legalisms.

The following additional example is a bit lengthy, but even if the court were to interrupt before hearing the entire introduction, the opening phrase identifies the theme.

Example: *The issue in this case is whether Miranda means anything, or whether a 21-year-old should spend the rest of his life in prison in a case where community pressure to assign blame for a crime was so great that police selected a young graffiti artist, tricked him in violation of Miranda into agreeing that he was in the vicinity where the crime took place, and then sealed his conviction through testimony the government bought from convicted criminals who did not witness the crime but who received substantial sentence reductions in exchange for their testimony.*

The remainder of your introduction should briefly identify the specific legal issues you intend to address. This issue road map provides a structure that helps the court follow your argument. Even more importantly, the road map lets the court know which issues you intend to focus on, and gives the court an opportunity to direct you to the particular issue that may be troubling it the most.

Example: *I will begin by addressing the violation of Mr. Smith's Miranda rights and the risk posed to society as a whole if these rights are not held inviolate. Second, I will discuss the district court's error in*

> *refusing to exclude the fruits of the Miranda violation. Finally, I will explain how the district court's error was not harmless. The evidence was insufficient to convict even with the fruits of the Miranda violation; without those fruits, an acquittal is constitutionally mandated.*

In some cases, it is effective to tell the court what the case is *not* about. Such an approach, especially for the appellee, not only helps refine the issues, but also counteracts a particularly effective theme articulated by your opponent.

Example: *The issue in this case is not the continued efficacy of Miranda; the issue in this case is whether a convicted murderer should go free because of a good faith error by a rookie police officer—an error that in no way affected the defendant's constitutional rights in a case where the evidence amassed during a two-week trial was so overwhelming that the defendant would have been convicted even if defendant's admissions to the police officer had been excluded.*

2. The Facts

A common mistake made by less experienced oral advocates is to waste argument time by including a separate recitation of the facts. You should outline the salient facts while you are preparing for oral argument—a timeline is especially useful—but summarizing the factual background during the argument itself usually is unnecessary unless your argument revolves around some critical fact dispute. If you are the appellant (and therefore the first to speak), and are unsure whether the court is familiar with the facts of your case, you may ask the court whether it cares to hear a brief recitation of the facts. Generally, the answer will be "no." If the court says at the start that it has read the briefs, or if you know from observation or experience that the court generally prepares in advance, do not even ask—just assume the judges are familiar with the facts.

We do not mean to minimize the importance of using facts in an appellate argument. Facts are at the heart of legal problems and facts drive solutions to those problems. The argument itself should revolve around your facts; you just usually do not need to present them separately, as you do in an appellate brief. Rather, the best approach is to identify and outline your key facts as you prepare for your oral argument, and then incorporate those facts into your legal analysis rather than in an initial narrative fact summary. An exception to this general rule lies when you represent the appellee. There are times as appellee when you may want to separately and immediately point out material facts the appellant omitted or misrepresented.

Example: *I'd like to start by pointing out that counsel for appellant is mistaken about a critical fact. Counsel said there was no direct evidence that appellant committed the murder. However, the jury heard from three separate people at trial, each of whom testified that defendant not only confessed to shooting Steve Smith, he bragged about it. That's direct evidence.*

3.   The Standard of Review

In all cases, the standard of review is discussed in your brief, and in nearly all cases, the appropriate standard is undisputed and obvious to the court. As with the facts, do not waste your time by articulating the standard again during your oral argument. Instead, during the course of your substantive argument or in response to a question, reference the standard when it bolsters the persuasiveness of your position. Do not take time to separately state an undisputed standard of review prior to diving into the substance of your argument. Always be prepared, however, to state the applicable standard of review if asked.

The following example references the deference typically accorded the district court in a fact-laden case as a means of bolstering the answer to a difficult question. The example further demonstrates the persuasive punch you can obtain by weaving pertinent facts into your substantive argument. The answer concludes with reference to the ramifications of an adverse ruling, and then it transitions back to the advocate's own theme.

Example: *Question: Counsel, appellant argues that by prohibiting his counsel from contacting midlevel employees of ABC Corporation directly, the district court denied appellant the opportunity to solicit testimony that would have verified his fraud allegations and defeated the summary judgment motion. Is that true?*

Answer: Those employees were not unavailable, it's just that they and the corporation were entitled to refuse interviews without corporate counsel present. Furthermore, it is important to keep in mind that a voluminous factual record had been developed prior to the summary judgment motion, and the district court judge was intimately familiar with the case. Her findings should be treated with deference and with regard for the preference to resolve matters through summary judgment motions when possible. The parties appeared before the judge no less than eight times on various matters; the judge permitted extensive discovery; ABC Corporation produced over a million pages of documents; a dozen depositions were taken, eight by appellant; ABC's president was deposed for 12 hours over two days; each party had experts examine the record and submit reports. In the face of all this, the district court found insufficient evidence of fraud to warrant the additional time and expense of undergoing a lengthy trial. If summary judgment can be defeated by speculation in the face of all this evidence that additional time and an expensive trial might reveal a yet unseen smoking gun, district court judges will be reluctant to review and potentially dispose of complicated cases prior to empaneling a jury. And then cases like this one, which is not a fraud case at all, but a case of a disgruntled former employee trying to "get even," will clog the courts' dockets and impose enormous expenses on innocent parties to resolve otherwise frivolous matters.

4. The Argument

Before preparing the substance of your oral presentation, you first must select the arguments you will highlight. Remember, you cannot and should not try to pack all of the arguments from your brief into your oral argument. Think about your theme and about what most likely will persuade the court to rule in your favor. Use this as a guidepost for selecting the arguments you plan to present orally. You should identify two to three main points per issue that are critical to your argument and ensure that you make them. Choose arguments: (a) that are strong and persuasive for you; (b) that speak well and are not too complicated and multi-layered; and (c) about which you want to have a dialogue with the court.

Once selected, you need to craft your arguments with care. Argue on your own terms in the affirmative, centering around your theme. Begin each issue with a statement that weaves in your theme and suggests the appropriate outcome. Explain how application of the legal rule leads to a result in favor of your client. Never waste oral argument time discussing abstract principles of law. Rather, oral argument is the time to persuade the court using the specific facts of your case as applied to the law. Understand, refer, and direct the court to the most apposite cases that support your arguments. Discuss the favorable future implications of a ruling in your favor or the negative implications of a ruling in favor of your opponent. Remember the three-part formula: what result do you want; why should the court *want* to take you there; and where is the permissible route for the court. Try to think of analogies and examples to illustrate your arguments and particularly to illustrate the consequences of a decision for or against your client.[4]

Consider carefully the sequence of your arguments. Generally, you should lead with your strongest argument. You have one opportunity to focus the court's attention on the most critical issue—make the most of it. Taking the opposite approach, and leading with an argument of lower importance, can undercut your entire argument.

> **Example:**   *The Seventh Circuit chided counsel in a written opinion about not only arguing an issue that was frivolous, but about highlighting it by presenting it first; "The first [issue], which actually is frivolous though urged by appellants as their first ground of appeal, is whether the district judge had jurisdiction, after the appeal was filed, to replace 'Chicago Police Department' with 'Chicago Fire Department' in one sentence of the opinion. As this was the correction of a clerical error, it could be made by the district judge 'at any time,' Fed. R. Civ. P. 60(a), even after jurisdiction over the case shifted to this court by virtue of the filing of the notice of appeal. [Citation omitted.] Even if this were wrong, and the error could not be corrected while the case was on appeal, the existence of a trivial error, obviously merely typographical, in the district court's opinion would not be a ground for reversing the judgment." McNamara v. City of Chicago, 138 F. 3d 1219, 1221 (7th Cir. 1998).*

If you are the appellant, focus on creating your narrative of the case, the key authorities that support your position, and why the court should rule in favor of your client. While it may be important to proactively address key aspects of the appellee's arguments, an appellant needs to make an affirmative argument, not simply attack the appellee's arguments. The appellant must show the court that the initial decision was incorrect and give the court sufficient justification to take a different approach.

If you are the appellee, the focus of appellant's argument and the court's questions may make it appropriate to alter your argument order. In that case, deal up front with the argument that seems to be grabbing the court's attention, and then transition to the argument that puts you in your best position.

---

[4] If you craft a good analogy, it can be quite helpful. Be cautious, however. If the analogy is not a perfect one—and few are—it can backfire, giving opposing counsel a golden opportunity to turn the analogy against you.

Always be prepared to alter the organization of your arguments and to jump around your prepared outline in response to the court's questions and interest. You may be required, for example, to jump from argument one to argument three. Alternatively, you may be required to leave argument one before you are done in order to answer a question on a different issue. If that happens, you need to make a judgment call about whether to return again to argument one or to move on. Move on if argument one is a clear winner and the court is on your side; move on if the court clearly is against you and argument one is not an appeal-breaking issue; return to the argument if only one panel member has moved you to a different issue, and you are unclear what the other two think about the issue you had to leave.

The bottom line is be flexible, read the court, and be prepared to depart from the argument sequence you prepared.

5. Conclusion

As with your introduction, write out and memorize your conclusion. We recommend preparing two versions. One should be a brief, one-sentence concluding articulation of your theme. Through this articulation of your theme, you should indicate how the court should rule and why. You often will have no time to recite more than a single sentence, which is why you should prepare the sentence in advance, and make every word count. Your alternative conclusion should be a slightly more comprehensive, 60-second concluding thought. If you are disciplined with your time and not thrown off by questions from the court, you may have the luxury of delivering a few sentences that truly tie everything together and allow you to end on a high note.

Example: *When you prepare your concluding words in advance, you can edit them for maximum impact with minimum verbiage. For example, William Seward suggested that Abraham Lincoln close his first inaugural address with the following words, as civil war threatened the nation:*

"I close. We are not, we must not be, aliens or enemies, but fellow countrymen and brethren."

President Lincoln edited as follows:

"I am loathe to close. We are not enemies, but friends."[5]

---

[5]   *See* William Safire, *Parsing Gore's Speech,* N.Y. TIMES, Aug. 21, 2000, at A25.

E. ANTICIPATE QUESTIONS AND OPPOSING ARGUMENTS

Your outlining efforts do not end once you complete your primary presentation. In fact, anticipating and outlining responses to possible questions and probable opposing arguments may be the most important part of your pre-argument preparation. Attorneys who win or lose cases during oral argument generally do so through responses to questions from the court.

Think about and catalogue the possible weaknesses in your argument and then outline responses to each. Review your balancing chart, as described in Part One. Prepare answers to likely questions and to the hardest questions you can anticipate. Think of Murphy's Law as you consider potential questions; if there are three questions that can potentially sink your case, you should expect to get asked all three of them.

> **"Rhetoric is overrated. Success seldom depends on eloquence. It turns instead on anticipating the inevitable, skeptical questions, and preparing effective answers."**
>
> The Honorable Paul R. Michel, U.S. Court of Appeals for the Federal Circuit, *Effective Appellate Advocacy*, 24 Litigation 19, 22 (Summer 1998).

Preparing for questions is important for both substantive and stylistic reasons. It is much more organized and persuasive to say, for example, "I have three responses to that question," than it is simply to continue talking your way through a question until you find and provide each of your responses. Providing such an organized response is quite difficult unless you anticipate the court's questions and outline responses in advance. Think about how much easier it is to outline a lecture when professors provide internal road maps and guideposts, and actually number their points for you. You want to make it just as easy for the judges to outline your responses to their questions. After all, it is the answers to their questions that interest them the most during oral argument.

F. PREPARE AN ARGUMENT NOTEBOOK

You should never approach the podium in an appellate argument with loose papers or various piles of materials. Rather, you should have everything you need organized behind tabs in a single three-ring binder.[6]

---

[6]   The argument notebook described in this section is not the only organized way to approach a podium. Each of the authors, in fact, has developed a variety of ways to organize a presentation. The point is to be neat, non-distracting, and organized. Do not use index cards: shuffling them in response to questions from the court is distracting and may get them out of order. Do not take briefs to the podium with post-it notes protruding from the margins: this looks messy and unfocussed. Do not use a yellow pad bound at the top: having sheets draped over the top of the

In some cases, all you will need is your argument outline, tabbed for easy reference, and outlined answers to difficult or probable questions. The outline should be in a larger than normal font, so you can find what you need in a quick glance. You also may want to annotate your outline with cites to the record, brief, or appendix. That way, if questions arise, the cites will be at your fingertips. Similar to preparing a law school outline, the *process* of preparing your outline (and notebook) for oral argument can be just as important as the finished outline and notebook.

It is helpful to include a digest of key cases in your notebook so you can quickly recall the facts of the case, the precise holding, the court, and the decision date. On occasion, you also may want to include in your notebook copies of *major* cases with key parts highlighted, your brief, or a few pivotal documents. In no case, however, should you take more than a single binder to the podium.

THE ARGUMENT NOTEBOOK

- **Tab 1: Argument outline**
  - **Tab A: Introduction**
  - **Tab B: First issue**
  - **Tab C: Second issue**
  - **Tab D: Conclusion**
- **Tab 2: Outlined responses to questions**
- **Tab 3: Digest of cases**
- **Tab 4: Highlighted *major* cases (optional)**
- **Tab 5: Key document or transcript excerpts (optional)**
- **Tab 6: Your brief (optional)**

If you do limit yourself, as you should, to a single binder, you will need a place in that binder to take notes on the arguments of your opponent and questions asked of your opponent that you wish to reference and follow through on. Depending on your own personal preference, either include a section of blank sheets or leave space on your own outline for such notes. If you are comfortable doing the latter, that may provide you with the best vehicle for integrating last-minute responses seamlessly into your own prepared presentation.

There is one important exception to the one-binder rule. If your opponent mis-cites a transcript or other critical document, or omits a truly material fact, then take the original source up to the podium, hold it up for the court to see, and read from it directly. This simple visual act is dramatic and persuasive.

Example: *Appellant says there was no evidence linking him to the scene of the crime. Let me read from the trial transcript, volume 2, page 219. " 'I saw a bald man with a bushy beard running from the house moments*

---

podium looks unprofessional, and flipping the pages frequently makes distracting sounds that the microphone amplifies.

after I heard the shots.' Question: 'Do you see that man in the courtroom?' Answer: 'He's sitting over there.' Question: 'Let the record reflect that Mrs. Smith just identified the defendant.'" [In this example, you would hold the transcript and read from it directly, even if the relevant testimony is quoted in your brief, and even if you have committed it to memory.]

G. PRACTICE

All attorneys, regardless of experience level, benefit from practicing—out loud—the arguments they outline.

It is helpful to think of your practice as a three-stage process. First, master the substance of your argument. What is the best description of your theme? What are the key issues and points that you need to focus on? How will you allocate your limited amount of time? Second, polish your presentation. How will you deliver your theme to capture the court's attention? When will you increase, or decrease, your cadence? Are you comfortable transitioning from questions to your argument? Third, perfect your argument. Can you confidently answer the challenging questions? Do you effectively emphasize your points? Are you able to move from issue to issue with clarity?

Practice may begin by standing and speaking at a desk or in front of a mirror. As you start to gain a strong understanding of your argument, record one of your practices. Reviewing your recording is an excellent way to self-assess both the substance and style of your argument. You should also consider practicing your argument without your outline or notebook for two reasons. One, it will help you understand and highlight the most important portions of your argument. Two, it will help you become more comfortable with moving from issue to issue, perhaps in an unplanned order (which is likely to happen during the argument).

Practice may continue in front of a spouse or friend. Many times, receiving feedback from a non-lawyer at this stage is invaluable. If your theme does not resonate with them, you need to rework it. If they cannot follow your argument, you need to restructure it. If they think you are talking too fast, or lack emotion, members of the court will feel the same way.

Practice should conclude with a formal moot court—a dress rehearsal for the real thing. Moot courts are a must for new attorneys, and for all United States Supreme Court arguments. Experienced appellate attorneys preparing to argue important or complex cases also benefit tremendously from participating in at least one moot court.

To make the most of your practice sessions, prepare your outlines and your notebook in advance. Time your formal presentation before your moot court to make sure you have allowed time for questions. Then, treat the moot court as if it were your final argument. When you are finished, ask your colleagues for a detailed critique, and revise or add to your argument outline and your outline of potential questions and responses. In some cases there may be whole arguments or sections of arguments you will need to rework. Be open to that possibility, even if you thought you had everything ready to go. Remember, if one or more of the people assisting with your moot court fails to understand part of your presentation or fails to appreciate the subtleties of a point you attempt to make, it is likely that at least one member of your final argument panel will be similarly confused or unconvinced.

The complexity and import of your case will determine the number of moot courts you should have and the experience level and expertise your moot court panel should reflect. Schedule your moot court well enough in advance of the actual argument that you will comfortably be able to make adjustments in your presentation. In a complex antitrust case, for example, you may want to have one moot court a full week in advance of the argument and another the day before.

III. PRESENTATION POINTERS

Although the substance of your oral argument is of primary importance, your oral presentation skills can enhance or detract from your effectiveness as an advocate. You need not be flamboyant or particularly glib in an appellate argument, but a bit of practice and attention to a few performance basics can pay big dividends. Following are a few basic rules. They are here because, as basic as they are, lawyers violate them with surprising frequency. Train yourself and your ear now. The practice will pay off later.

A. MAKE A STRONG OPENING IMPRESSION

When it is your turn to speak, walk to the podium without hesitation, carrying no more than your argument binder. Adjust the microphone and begin *immediately* (unless the court is not ready). Introduce yourself with the traditional opening line: "May it please the Court, my name is Sarah Smith and I represent John Edwards, the appellant."[7] Then give your one

---

[7] If you will be sharing your allotted argument time with someone else, you should introduce counsel with whom you are sharing the podium and note for the court how you are dividing the argument. Generally, it is far preferable for a single attorney to argue. There are several reasons for this. First, arguments generally are more cohesive and persuasive when presented by a single attorney; splitting issues makes the whole presentation more disjointed. Most important, however, having a single attorney responsible for the entire argument better enables the court to control the direction of the argument. The greatest gift you can receive during argument is to have the court identify the issues in which it is most interested or with which it is having the greatest

sentence substantive introduction that contains your theme and launch directly into your argument.

B. CONNECT WITH THE JUDGES

Generally, the judges will have name plates in front of them on the bench. Familiarize yourself with the pronunciation of their names ahead of time and occasionally refer to them by name, but do not be obsequious or too familiar. Refer to questions a specific judge asked your opponent. Refer to things a specific judge said during the argument. Be cautious, however. Do not try to ascribe a particular point of view to any judge due to a question the judge asks. Remember, a question is just a question, and the judge will tell her colleagues what she thinks when they confer after the argument.

Use similar caution when referring to a prior opinion authored by a judge on your panel. Unless the opinion is a concurrence or dissent, it is an opinion of the *court,* not of the individual authoring judge. Refer to it as the *court's* opinion, not the particular judge's opinion. If you do not use such care, even if you impress the author, you risk alienating the rest of the panel.

C. USE QUESTIONS TO YOUR ADVANTAGE

Questions are the most important part of oral argument because they provide you with an opportunity to discover and address concerns the court has about your case—concerns that if not known or addressed could cause you to lose. Following are guidelines on how to handle this most critical aspect of your oral argument.

1. Prepare for and Welcome Difficult Questions

Do not shy away from questions. Welcome even the most difficult questions and take advantage of the opportunity to persuade the judges on a point that troubles them. In preparing how you might respond to difficult questions, think about how you can turn them around and transition back into the affirmative points you want to make. There are typically three to

---

difficulty. If those issues happen to be the ones your co-counsel plans to address, there may not be sufficient time left when your co-counsel gets to the podium to address the issues to the court's satisfaction. Alternatively, the court may not wait for your co-counsel and instead ask you to address issues for which you are insufficiently prepared.

There are two exceptions to the single attorney rule. First, and most obviously, the law school moot court context may demand sharing argument time. Second, when there are multiple parties, some of whom have issues that are not common to all, it may be necessary to apportion argument time among co-counsel. In that case, it is best to be flexible about the time division, to accommodate the interests of the court. Making multiple precise divisions of the time allocated to one side is tricky, distracting, and frequently wasteful of the court's time. At bottom, in the absence of compelling reasons to share the podium, you generally should try to negotiate for a single presentation.

five challenging questions per issue—how you respond to those questions may determine the outcome of the case.

If you can identify difficult questions in advance and practice your responses, you will put yourself in an excellent position to prevail at oral argument.

2.   Be Direct

Try to answer each question with a direct "yes" or "no" followed by a brief explanation. If you do not understand a question, ask the judge to repeat it or try to restate it yourself and then answer. Do not, however, use this technique of restating the question as a means of skirting a particularly difficult question. The court will know what you are doing and either press you to answer the question at hand or will assume you do not have an answer.

Example: *Question: As I understand it, some guardians are lawyers but many are not, and, in fact, they come from a wide range of backgrounds and educational levels, some with no more than a high school education. Yet these guardians make recommendations the district court relies on—in this case regarding serious financial and medical matters.*

Answer: If I understand the court's question, you would like to know the qualifications of the guardian in this case. Unfortunately, the record does not reflect those qualifications. I wish it did. But the point is, the district court is familiar with the guardian and her qualifications, and is familiar with what is required of a guardian. The court would not have made the appointment if it were not confident that the guardian was qualified to fulfill the responsibilities of the position. Appellant has provided no reason to believe the guardian was unfit or irresponsible in any way.

If you ever get a question to which you do not know the answer, provide a direct and honest response. Do not try to mask the problem by being evasive. That technique will irritate the court more than a direct and truthful response.

Example: *Question: How does Smith v. Jones relate to your case?*

Answer: I'm afraid I'm not familiar with that case, Your Honor, but I would be happy to review it and submit a written response to your question later this afternoon. [Pause for direction from the court on your offer.] In the meantime, I would direct the court to James v. Stewart, which is on all fours with our case. [Then explain.]

If you ever get a question about the record to which you do not know the answer, provide a similarly direct and honest response. Misrepresenting the record will not only undercut your credibility in regard to the record, but your entire argument.

3. Use Questions Directed at Your Opponent

Pay close attention to questions asked of your opponent. These questions are clues to what the court may perceive as weaknesses in your opponent's position. Exploit them. Use them as indications of issues you should emphasize. If you are representing the appellee, be flexible enough to shift the order or emphasis of your argument as a result of the information you receive from the court's questions of your opponent. If you represent the appellant, do the same during your rebuttal. Refer specifically to particular questions asked of your opponent and then give *your* responses to the questions. Exploiting questions in such a way will distinguish you as an oral advocate, and may well help your client prevail in an otherwise close case.

4. Read the Judges

Listen to questions very carefully to try to understand the express question, but also to discern why the question is being asked. What is the judge really concerned about? The judge may not ask the question very artfully because the judge does not know the case as well as you do. If you can glean the real concern behind each question and address that concern, you will greatly advance your cause.

Remember also that judges ask questions at times to educate each other. This tactic can manifest itself in different ways. First, a judge may simply be looking for a strong response that will persuade a colleague who is troubled by a particular issue. Second, a judge may be signaling a response that the judge finds persuasive and that he wants you to elaborate on for the benefit of the other panel members. Learn to read these signals and to take advantage of opportunities a judge may give you to persuade the judge's colleagues. Not all questions are hostile; they are opportunities to persuade. Even if you encounter a judge who truly is hostile, always take the high road and be respectful. If you are confrontational, flip, or sarcastic, you will hurt yourself in the case at hand as well as those you may have in the future.

> **ANSWERING THE COURT'S QUESTIONS**
>
> - **Prepare for and welcome questions**
> - **Stop and answer immediately**
> - **Be direct—not evasive**
> - **Seek clarification when necessary**
> - **Use "Yes/No" with short explanation format**
> - **Use questions directed at your opponent**
> - **Do not become confrontational**
> - **Do not assume all questions are hostile**
> - **Anticipate difficult questions**
> - **Read the court; know when to back down/when to stand your ground**
> - **Transition from the question back to your argument or theme**

Example: *Judges may use questions to persuade each other. This example concerns whether a county followed all procedural requirements before permanently terminating parental rights:*

Question: Did the county make reasonable efforts to assist the mother before or after the child was placed in foster care?

Answer: Both.

Question: But doesn't the statute say that to permanently terminate parental rights, the county must make reasonable efforts to help the mother after the child is placed in foster care?

Answer: Yes, that is the statutory requirement.

> *Question: So is our inquiry limited to looking only at the efforts the county made to help the mother after the child was placed in foster care?*

> *Answer: The efforts made after the child was placed in foster care certainly should be considered, as the statute directs, but the efforts the county made even before the child was removed to foster care show just how seriously the county undertook its responsibilities. Let me briefly review those efforts for you. . . .*

As you learn to use questions to read the court, an important skill to develop is knowing when to back down off a losing argument. If you receive multiple questions about the same point, that may be an indication the court expects you to concede that point. Doing so helps you maintain credibility on other critical issues. At the same time, know when to stand your ground. You should not retreat, for example, when: (1) the issue will make or break your appeal; (2) you may have lost one judge but not necessarily the others; or (3) the issue is an important one you need to preserve for the next level of appeal.

> **Example:** *Even if the court remains troubled by the grant of summary judgment against the appellant individually, the district court's refusal to certify a nationwide class action was justified and in fact required by proper application of the Rule 23(c) standards. [Then proceed to review application of the standards to the case at hand.]*

5. Use Caution with Hypotheticals

Be on guard for questions that pose hypotheticals. Answer the question directly, but try to point out any salient differences between the facts in the hypothetical and your case. Sometimes judges will use hypotheticals to take you down a slippery slope, or to try to demonstrate a pernicious effect that a ruling in your favor may have on some future case. Try to anticipate these slippery slope or line-drawing problems; this will help prepare you for potentially difficult hypotheticals posed by the court.

> **Example:** *The opinion in Wittmer v. Peters, 87 F.3d 916, 919 (7th Cir. 1996), demonstrates the perils posed by well-crafted hypotheticals, and the need to respond not only to the hypothetical as framed by the court, but to the ultimate point the court may be attempting to make through the hypothetical. Wittmer was a case challenging the promotion of a black correctional officer by a warden of a boot camp over two white*

officers who received higher scores on a test given to applicants for the position. The following found its way into the court's opinion: "At argument the plaintiffs' counsel conceded, in response to a question from the bench, that separation of the races in a prison that was undergoing a race riot would not violate the Constitution. That is a clearer case for discrimination than this, but our point is only that the rectification of past discrimination is not the only setting in which government officials can lawfully take race into account in making decisions."

6. Answer Questions Immediately; Do Not Talk over the Court

When a judge begins to ask a question, stop immediately—even if you are in mid-sentence. Never respond by saying, "I'll get to that." It does not matter how disruptive you think the interruption. If the court asked the question now, it is interested in an answer *now*. After you fully respond, you can transition back to your original issue or, based on information you get from the question about the court's concerns, you may decide to continue on in a different direction. The flexibility to read the court and alter the course of your argument is the mark of a truly effective oral advocate.

> **Example:** *When interrupted mid-sentence by a question, it is very tempting to try to finish your thought, even at the expense of talking over the judge, much as you might naturally talk over a sibling or spouse who interrupts you mid-sentence. One author witnessed the following fiasco: A high-ranking but inexperienced government attorney arguing before a federal circuit court thought it best to complete whatever he had to say regardless of the court's interest in interrupting with questions. After the argument, while the attorney explained to those accompanying him the need to "just shout these judges down," a clerk came out with a note from the panel which read: "The judges of this Court may be old, but we are not deaf." Never speak over a judge, regardless of the eloquence of the sentence the judge may be interrupting. [Additional lesson: always take advantage of the opportunity to engage in a moot court.]*

Not only should you stop immediately when a judge begins a question, you need to wait until the judge finishes the question before you start your answer. There are two points here. First, *listen* to the entire question. Do not anticipate based on just a few words and then tune out the balance of the question while you consider your answer. You may end up answering the wrong question. Second, do not interrupt the judge either to finish the question yourself or to begin your answer before the judge finishes articulating every word. Given the extent of your preparation you may know immediately the point the judge is trying to make and you may be able more quickly to articulate it, but doing so is rude and will gain you no points. As painful as it may be on occasion, let the judge get every word of the question out before you presume to be able to answer it.

If you need a moment to compose your response, pause, and formulate your response. Talking your way into your response is ineffective. Taking a moment to pause, reflect, and then provide a thoughtful response is much more persuasive than empty filler; do not fear a few beats of silence.

TWELVE TYPICAL QUESTION TOPICS AT A GLANCE

1. Record Questions: Where is that in the record? How do the unfavorable facts impact your position? Are you asking us to assume a fact not in the record? Can we take judicial notice of that fact?

2. Procedural Posture Questions: How did we get here? Did the district court have jurisdiction? Do we have jurisdiction? Do you have standing? Were the issues now on appeal all preserved for review?

3. Burden of Proof/Standard of Review Questions: Who had the burden on a particular issue in the district court? Is that a factual or legal issue? What is the standard for our appellate review of the district court's decision on the issue—de novo; clear error; abuse of discretion? Do we have to apply different standards of review to different issues? Do we have to assume facts or well-pled allegations in favor of your client/in favor of the opposing party?

4. Requested Remedy Questions: What exactly do you want us to do? Affirm? Reverse? Remand?

5. Legal Test Questions: What legal test do you want us to use? Why is that test a good one? Why is the opposing party's alternative proposed test a bad one? What authority supports your test? If you rely on multiple authorities, what is your best authority? Is that authority binding or merely persuasive?

6. Test Application Questions: How does the correct legal test apply in the present case? Why do you win under that test? Why does the opposing party lose?

7. Hypothetical Questions: Suppose we added/subtracted/ changed fact[s] X [and Y]. Would your test still apply? Who would win? Is that consistent or inconsistent with the result you want in your case?

8. Caselaw Questions: How is case X factually similar/distinct from the present matter? Did the court in case X apply the standard you want applied here? Why should this court adopt the reasoning in case X?

9. Policy Questions: If we adopt your test, will that be a slippery slope for future cases? Is your test consistent with the development of the law in this subject area? Is your test a broad one or a narrow one? Is the problem you want us to resolve better left to a different decision-maker, e.g., the Congress; the legislature; an administrative agency; the executive branch?

10. Concession-seeking questions: Would you lose if we applied the test proposed by the opposing party? Would you lose if we cannot distinguish binding authority X? Would you lose if we do not overrule binding authority Y? Would you lose if the fact-finder made an error in determining fact Z?

11. Responding to opposing arguments questions: Opposing counsel argues X. How do you respond specifically to that argument?

12. Writing the opinion questions: Counsel, give us a sentence that states the rule you want us to adopt in this case. Counsel, give us a sentence that states the holding you want us to deliver in this case.

NOTE: Not all questions will necessarily be hostile. Some may be friendly. Do not be afraid to agree with the latter.

D. NO NAME CALLING

No matter how low your opponent stoops, no matter how egregious your opponent's misrepresentation, always take the high road. To stoop to your opponent's level or to characterize your opponent's misstatements with inflammatory words of your own will further offend the court and will damage rather than enhance your own credibility. Being direct but slightly understated often is most persuasive in the appellate context.

Examples: *Appellant's counsel says that parental rights should not have been permanently severed because the mother's problems of neglect are all in the past; that they are from two years ago when the mother herself was a child. It would be nice if that were true. But* *missing eight out of twenty-four visitations during the three months preceding the district court's ruling is not "in the past." One of those missed visitations was even the child's birthday. As the district court ruled, the child does not have time to wait any longer for her mother to grow up. The child needs a mother now, and needs permanency now.*

Counsel for appellant is mistaken. There was no objection whatsoever to the jury instructions at trial. I'd refer the court to volume 5 of the trial transcript, page 340. "The Court: Are there any objections to the jury instructions? Mr. Hill: No, Your Honor."

E. SPEAK AND ARGUE DIRECTLY; AVOID "FILLERBLUSTERING"

The court will understand that your arguments and positions represent your client's arguments and your client's positions. Always avoid words and phrases that distance you from your client or your client's position. Examples, which you may hear even from seasoned advocates, include: "it is my client's position that. . ." or "it is our contention that. . ." or "we believe . . ." Not only are such phrases inartful and wasteful of the precious minutes you are allotted, they have the effect of making it appear as if you may not really be standing behind your client's position—that you merely are paying lip-service to arguments your client has instructed you to make.

On the other hand, do not become so personally involved in the advocacy on behalf of your client that you begin to blur the distinction between you and your client. You are counsel for your client, arguing on your client's behalf, not on your own behalf. Your client has a personal stake in the outcome, you do not. It may occasionally be difficult to keep a separate perspective, but just as distancing yourself too far from your client has the effect of reducing your credibility, so too does blurring the distinction and becoming too personally involved.

GOOD ORAL ADVOCATES NEVER SAY:

- "Okay"
- "Um" or "Uh'
- "It is our contention"
- "We believe"
- "Like"

You also should practice overcoming speech tics and avoiding filler words. Take the following words out of your vocabulary: "um," "uh," "like," "okay." Attorneys frequently, and without noticing it, will respond to a judge's question first with the word "okay," or bluster a moment or two with an "um" and "uh," and then follow with the substantive answer. To catch yourself, you may need to practice in front of someone or record yourself and then listen for bad speech habits. As noted above, it is far better to pause for a moment to collect your thoughts than to begin with meaningless filler words. Do not overdo it, but become comfortable with pauses. Experienced advocates occasionally will pause on purpose as a technique for adding emphasis.

F. NO QUOTES OR SPECIFIC CASE CITES

It rarely is appropriate or effective to use direct quotes from cases during oral argument. Think about the etiquette of a normal conversation. Conversations involve your own words; not the words of others. Similarly, while you may refer to a book by name in a conversation, you never would cite the publisher, edition, year and page number. If you refer to a case cited in your brief, refer to it by name, but do not waste your time and detract from your thought by following the name with citation details. The only exception to this is if you refer to a newly-decided case that is not in your brief.

G. NO VISUAL AIDS

During jury trials and even during district court arguments, visual aids may not only be helpful, they may be critical. During appellate argument, by contrast, visual aids generally are too distracting and wasteful of the limited time you have. Again it bears repeating that appellate argument is not a speech, it is a conversation. You are not lecturing with the assistance of an overhead projector, PowerPoint® presentation, or posterboard chart or picture; you are engaging the judges in a discussion of critical legal issues and public policy considerations. If your argument is so complicated you need a visual aid, you need to re-think your argument.

H. KNOW WHEN TO STOP

Be aware of the time and know when to stop—either immediately when your time has expired or when you sense that you are on the winning end of things and the court has heard enough. Try to end on a high note. Being able to read the court and stop before time has expired takes practice and tremendous discipline, but it shows confidence, experience, and respect of the court and its time. In return, you will gain additional respect from the court.

Although you may occasionally be able to end your argument before your time has expired, you often will use all of your time and wish you had more. To help ensure your ability to end on a high note, do not start a new issue when time is close to running out. It is far better to give a strong conclusion than to begin an argument you cannot complete. When you have about a minute left, it is time to move to your conclusion so you are not left in the awkward position of being in mid-sentence when the red "stop" light goes on. If you move to your conclusion with a minute to go, it also gives the court the opportunity to ask any final questions that it otherwise may simply skip in order to stay on schedule and to give equal time to both sides.

If you end up in mid-thought, you should pause, acknowledge that you see your time has expired, ask if you may briefly conclude, and then deliver a single, *very* brief concluding sentence. (You should prepare such a sentence in advance so you do not ramble or use 15 words where 10 will do.) If you are in the middle of answering a question, seek permission to finish your answer, then do so expeditiously. If you are in mid-sentence but at a logical stopping point when the red light comes on, conclude the sentence without taking time to ask permission. Then, pick up your notebook and step down as quickly as you rose. If your case is over, leave the counsel table promptly so the next case can begin without delay.

Example: *Counsel: I notice my red light. May I briefly conclude?*

Court: Briefly.

Counsel: In the end, this is a case not about fraud, but about responsibility—about the responsibility appellant should himself bear for the injury he incurred as a result of using a properly manufactured product for an unintended use. Thank you.

I.   REMEMBER ELEMENTARY SPEECH TECHNIQUES

Just as fundamental principles of good writing enhance the effectiveness of your brief, so do fundamental principles of speaking enhance the effectiveness of your oral argument. Following are a few basics to keep in mind as you practice.

1.   Volume, Speed, and Pitch

Speak with sufficient volume to be heard easily; speak with a slow enough cadence to be understood easily; and speak with a low enough pitch to make your voice pleasant and credible. Once you have mastered these basics, you should practice varying your volume, your speed, and your pitch. Use these variations both for emphasis and to make your argument less monotonous to the ear. Although perhaps counterintuitive, it is enormously effective to pause and slightly **lower** your volume and slow your speed when you want the court to pay particular attention. Remember that oral argument, to a degree, is a performance. Mastering these techniques will add another layer of persuasion to your argument.

2.   Eye Contact

The importance of maintaining eye contact with each individual judge cannot be overstated. This is one reason why you should have an outline rather than a narrative in front of you. Practice enough that you are comfortable using the outline only for guideposts. An oral argument is a conversation with the court. When you converse with someone, you look that person in the eye. A common mistake is to "argue to the courtroom ceiling." Practice looking straight ahead and maintaining regular eye contact.

3.   Posture and Appearance

Many attorneys are so focused on the substance of their oral argument that they fail to notice their posture at the podium. Even the most seasoned advocates have extra adrenaline flowing when it is their turn to speak. Frequently the touch of nervousness manifests itself in bad habits that the attorneys themselves fail to notice, but that can be quite distracting to the court and that can detract from the effectiveness of an otherwise eloquent presentation.

Plant your feet squarely on the floor and stand in one position; do not move around and do not rock or shift your weight from one leg to the other. Do not stray from the microphone. Do not lean on the podium. Stand straight and keep your hands free for relaxed, natural gestures. Resist the temptation to take a pen or pencil to the podium. Not only does taking notes or checking things off detract from the formality of your presentation, but more often than not pens and pencils end up being waved around and even pointed at the judges while the attorney is trying to make a point. You may not notice what you are doing, but the judges will. Think back to elementary school when your teacher pointed a pencil at you and then leave yours back at your table and out of reach.

4.   Distracting Habits

Identify and eliminate distracting movements and habits. For most people, nervousness manifests itself in ways they are completely unaware of, but ways the court will find distracting. You may need to have a friend tell you whether you have adopted any nervous habits, then work to overcome them. Here are some common distracting habits: fiddling with hair; waving glasses around; clicking a pen; sucking on the bow of one's glasses; rubbing the back of one's neck or one's chin; jingling change or keys in one's pocket. If you are at all prone to do this, try to keep your hands at your side or place them lightly on the podium. Just in case, however, empty your pockets before you enter a courtroom.

Recordings are ruthlessly honest. Try recording a practice argument to see whether you have posture problems at the podium or other distracting mannerisms to which you otherwise may be oblivious.

J. OBSERVE PROPER COURTROOM DECORUM

Despite the formality of the courtroom setting, some lawyers forget that they are always "on" in a courtroom, regardless of whether it is their turn at the podium. Keep the following simple but important rules in mind:

1. *Never* visibly or audibly react to your opponent's presentation, no matter how egregious your adversary's error or accusation.

2. *Always* stand when addressing, or being addressed by, the court regardless of where you are in the courtroom and regardless of how brief your response (e.g., "Is appellee ready?" [stand] "Yes, Your Honor.").

3. *Never* bring a beverage or food into the courtroom.

4. *Always* sit at attention. Do not, for example, read the newspaper during the argument of another case, even if you are sitting in the gallery. When at counsel table, do not lean back in your chair, as you may at the desk in your office.

5. *Never* whisper. If more than one attorney is at counsel table, keep a small pad handy and communicate by passing notes. Whispering is distracting to the court, and could cause you and your co-counsel to miss an important point.

6. *Always* turn off electronic devices. Remind your client to do the same.

Proper appellate court decorum also means that, unlike at trial, your client should remain in the gallery at all times. Do not have your client sit at counsel table and do not introduce your client to the court during your argument. Formality reigns in an appellate court. Never attempt to be folksy, cute, funny, or familiar. Be respectful and reserved.

K. APPELLEES NEED TO BE FLEXIBLE

Each of the above preparation pointers applies both to appellants and to appellees. An additional charge to appellees, however, is that flexibility is key. As appellee, you should have a presentation outline ready, but be prepared to depart from it or reorganize it depending both upon the appellant's argument and questions asked of the appellant. If those questions reveal a weakness the court has identified, exploit that weakness, and consider opening your argument with it. If the appellant has failed adequately to answer a question, reference the question and provide your own response to it. If the appellant through her presentation or through an answer to a question from the court has exposed a weakness in your position, address the argument directly and show the court a route around the weakness that will allow the court to rule in your favor.

Although you should be flexible and responsive, do not structure your presentation around the other side's argument. Always prepare and present an affirmative argument on your own terms, weaving in specific responses to the appellant's major theme and argument. Fight on your own high ground. An appellee's argument should never follow simply the format of "appellant's counsel said X; my response is Y." In short, do not lose sight of your own theme and the need to argue your case from your own point of view, but be responsive to the appellant's presentation when necessary or helpful to your case.

L. REBUTTAL: KEEP IT SHORT

Rebuttal is the most difficult argument to do effectively, yet it is an argument with potentially great payoff. The key to good rebuttal is to be brief. Limit yourself to true *rebuttal*. Never attempt to answer every argument made by your opponent. Pick no more than two-three points (fewer is even better) that truly warrant a response, and then answer each in bullet format. Rebuttals need no introduction; brevity and directness are key. Walk to the podium, tell the court you have two (or three) points to make, then make them and sit down. A brief rebuttal focused on truly critical issues has much more impact than a shotgun, point-by-point response to as many arguments as time permits.

Example: *Two quick points.*

> *First, the Appellee has failed to provide any valid justification for firing for Mr. Smith. Each of the alleged reasons given by XYZ's counsel for the firing of Mr. Smith is a Johnny-come-lately attempt to justify the company's desire to get rid of an effective union organizer. First, contrary to the impression XYZ's argument attempts to create, not a single one of these justifications was provided to Mr. Smith, despite his request, at the time he was fired. In fact, no reason for his discharge was articulated at all until after this lawsuit was filed. Second, other, non-activist employees suffered no consequence whatsoever for committing the same alleged offenses. This is retaliation and union-busting, pure and simple. And no effort to sugar coat it makes it any more palatable under the law.*
>
> *Second . . . .*

Generally, you should reserve no more than two minutes for rebuttal. There are three reasons for this. First, brief rebuttals have far more impact. Second, if you reserve more time, you may lack sufficient time during your initial presentation to reach one of your critical issues. And if you miss an issue during your main argument, you may be foreclosed from presenting it during rebuttal. Third, judges frequently are done with a case by the time of rebuttal. Only if you are brief and speaking to something critical will you capture the court's attention.

When deciding whether and how to use your rebuttal time, consider whether: (1) your opponent made a critical misstatement of law or fact that cannot go uncorrected; (2) there is an obviously weak or mishandled part of your opponent's presentation that you can exploit to your advantage; or (3) you need an opportunity to correct or supplement a weak answer you gave during your opening presentation. Although counsel for appellant should always reserve a brief time for rebuttal (assuming you are not in a jurisdiction where time is given automatically), waive your time if nothing truly critical remains. The act of waiving rebuttal itself tells the court your opponent said nothing deserving of response and that you are confident in your argument and brief.

Example: *"Unless there are any questions the court would like me to address, I have nothing further."*

M. ORAL ARGUMENT VIA VIDEOCONFERENCE

In response to the COVID-19 pandemic, many appellate and supreme courts modified both the mode and method of oral arguments. Many courts switched to remote arguments held via videoconferencing platform. Although the argument procedure and format generally remained the same, there were some notable changes. The virtual setting also required advocates to adjust their presentation. While virtual arguments are unlikely to fully replace in-person arguments, we've provided guidance on virtual arguments, should you find yourself in that setting.

1.   **Changes to procedure and format.**

   a.   **Dedicated time for an introduction/roadmap.** Many courts provided advocates with a set amount of uninterrupted time at the beginning of their argument (typically two or three minutes). Video arguments are a somewhat unnatural setting, which makes it harder to duplicate the conversational aspect of courtroom arguments.

   b.   **Set order of questions.** Many courts advised advocates that judges would ask questions in order, based on seniority. At the beginning of an argument, the court would announce that order to assist advocates in understanding the order of questions. This method was used so that each judge would have an opportunity to ask at least one question, and also helps advocates anticipate where the next question would come from.

 c. **Altered visual layout.** In a courtroom, advocates typically see the judges in front of them, a timer below them, and opposing counsel in their peripheral vision. In a virtual setting, the judges, opposing counsel, and timer, are on the same screen and in the advocate's line of sight at all times. Practicing will ensure advocates are comfortable with the visualization.

2. **Preparing for a virtual argument.**

 a. **Proper technology.** The microphone and webcam on your laptop may not be sufficient for a virtual argument. Many built-in microphones produce distorted audio in a virtual argument. Wired headsets generally produce the best sound. Wired (and wireless) headsets will also reduce background noise and help advocates focus on the judge's questions.

 b. **Audio/visual preferences.** Some courts require that advocates use a designated virtual background to ensure that every advocate appears the same. Other courts prefer that advocates use a virtual background if their background may not appear professional. For example, if an advocate is arguing from a bedroom or basement, choosing a neutral virtual background is a must.

 c. **No distractions.** Not only should you strive to control the framing of your setting/background, limit any potential distractions—both inanimate and animate. For example, you would not bring clever pop art or political symbols into the courtroom—don't bring them into the virtual courtroom. The same goes for your spouse, significant other, children, or even pets. While law students may find it funny to meet your cat, the court is unlikely to share that same sense of amusement.

 d. **Silence is golden.** Turn off all visual and audio notifications on your computer and phone. You may also need to sever any link between your phone and computer, as some devices will send notifications to both devices simultaneously.

 e. **Camera placement.** Place your camera at eye level to make it easier to maintain eye contact with the court. If possible, use a standing desk. Other options are a laptop stand, or using legal textbooks to elevate your computer and camera.

f. **Eye contact.** Practice looking at your camera, as opposed to your computer screen. While the difference may appear minor, the impact is significant. Looking at the camera is the equivalent of making direct eye contact. Looking at your computer screen is the equivalent of looking at the judge's feet.

g. **Dress the part.** Advocates are still expected to maintain a professional appearance. The video image may only reveal an advocate's head and shoulders. However, you should not assume that the image will remain static. For example, if you need to stand at any portion of the proceeding, revealing that you're wearing shorts with a suit is not ideal.

h. **Substantive changes.** Capturing and maintaining the court's attention is more challenging. Starting with an emotive theme is an excellent way to engage the court. Focusing on your four to six critical arguments will allow you to maintain a strong connection with the court.

i. **Personal style.** The virtual setting impacts advocates appearance, volume, and style. For the most part, it suppresses most elements of personal style. Practicing, recording, and reviewing your argument will help you maintain those important elements of personal style that add to your effectiveness as an advocate.

j. **Immediately stop for questions.** Video arguments, even with the proper technology, are subject to technical challenges, including video lag. Because of that, you may not hear a judge's question immediately. Which makes it more important than ever to stop talking when you hear the start of a question. If needed, ask a judge to repeat the question.

k. **Mute as needed.** Just like an actual courtroom, you should not speak unless it is your portion of the argument. Be sure to mute your audio during your opponent's argument. Muting your video should only happen if absolutely needed, and for as short of a duration as possible.

l. **Tech support.** Have the court's contact information on hand in the event of a technology issue. A best practice is to program the court's number into your phone, so you can quickly call, if needed.

m. **Print your outline.** Your screen should be dedicated to your video conference. You want to maintain eye contact and watch for visual clues that a judge is about to ask a question, losing focus, or engaged in your current argument. If your outline is on your screen, you will not pay as much attention to the video window. In addition, viewing your outline on screen requires you to scroll, which may cause an accidental technical issue. Print your outline and keep it in front of you, just as you would in the courtroom.

The next chart provides a quick guide to presentation rules. Explanations for the rules, along with a few caveats, are contained in the text of Part Three.

PRESENTATION GUIDELINES AT A GLANCE

<u>DO</u>

Begin without delay.

Tell the court what you want it to do.

Stop mid-sentence if a judge interrupts.

Immediately answer questions.

Directly answer questions. (Yes, because . . ./No, because . . .).

Try to ascertain the underlying purpose of a question.

Refer to questions asked of your opponent.

Remember your theme.

Use analogies and examples.

Use short sentences.

Speak slowly and conversationally.

Speak loudly.

Maintain eye contact.

Stop immediately when time expires.

<u>DON'T</u>

Bring a pen or loose papers to the podium.

Talk over a judge.

Be evasive.

Read a prepared speech or simply summarize your brief.

Read quotes or provide case citations.

Give a narration of the facts.

Discuss an undisputed standard of review.

Use filler words (um, uh, okay).

Use words that distance (It's my client's position *that*. . .).

React visibly or audibly to opponent.

Engage in personal attacks.

Be folksy, funny, or too familiar.

Continue speaking when time has expired.

EXERCISES

Note: *Each exercise can be done from the perspective of the appellant(s) or the appellee(s). It may be helpful for students to do the exercises—or at least some of them—twice, once for appellant(s) and once for appellee(s).*

1. Review the record in *Lane v. Moot State University Law School* or *Smith, et al. v. Willis, et al.,* and index facts or other information for which you may want cites readily available during your oral argument.

2. Update your research for the cases from your brief in *Lane* or in *Smith* to see whether there have been any recent developments in the law that you will want to highlight during your oral argument.

3. Think about and articulate the theme around which you want your oral argument to revolve. Consider the effect of a ruling for or against your client. Are there broader policy and societal ramifications of a ruling for or against your client? What societal interests would be served by a ruling in your favor or harmed by a ruling in favor of the opposing party? Talk about your case with a non-lawyer/non-law student friend or family member. If this were a real case, why should it be important to them that you prevail in the appeal?

4. Draft an introduction to the equal protection argument relating to the law school's admissions process in *Lane.*

5. Draft an introduction to the protective order issue in *Lane.*

6. Draft an introduction you would use if both of the issues in *Lane* were on appeal.

7. Draft an introduction to the racial discrimination issue in *Smith.*

8. Draft an introduction to the wealth discrimination issue in *Smith.*

9. Draft an introduction to the poll tax issue in *Smith.*

10. Outline the salient facts pertaining to your appeal in *Lane* or in *Smith.* Do you believe it will be helpful to present any of these facts in a separate narrative statement? Why or why not? Are there facts you will want to incorporate into your main argument presentation?

11. What is the standard of review applicable to each issue you are arguing in *Lane* or in *Smith*? Will you want to reference any of the applicable standards during your argument? Why? How?

12. Select the arguments you will want to present orally. What is an appropriate sequence? Outline each argument. Remember that arguments speak differently than they write.

13. Write a one-sentence conclusion for your oral argument presentation.

14. Write a one-minute conclusion for your oral argument presentation.

15. Outline three to five questions you may be asked for each issue and practice responses to those questions.

16. Outline the primary arguments your opponent may present. What are your opponent's strongest arguments? What are your responses?

17. Prepare an argument notebook.

18. Practice your argument by yourself, stopping only to make notes/changes to the substance of your argument.

19. Practice your argument by yourself and record your argument. Review the recording and note stylistic changes and areas of improvement.

20. Practice your argument without notes and record your argument. Review the recording to see how you naturally address the key points.

21. Practice your argument with a spouse/significant other/family member/friend. Provide them a list of simple questions to ask during your argument.

22. Moot your argument with one or more colleagues. Provide them your list of the three to five most challenging questions per issue.

APPENDIX A

CASE RECORD #1

■ ■ ■

LOIS LANE V. MOOT STATE UNIVERSITY LAW SCHOOL, ALICE ANDERSON, LISA PACKER, AND BARRY BADGER

Note: The events and persons in this case record are fictional. No reference to persons living or dead, or to real events, is intended. Depending on instructor preference, the included dates may require modification.

STATE OF MOOT   DISTRICT COURT

COUNTY OF PROSPER   SECOND JUDICIAL DISTRICT

Lois Lane,   Court File No.: CIV 56789

      Plaintiff,

                                  COMPLAINT

v.

Moot State University Law School,
Alice Anderson, Lisa Packer, and
Barry Badger,

      Defendants.

     Plaintiff Lois Lane, for her Complaint against Defendants, states and alleges that:

PARTIES

    1.   Plaintiff is, and was at all relevant times, a resident of Prosper County in the State of Moot.

    2.   Defendant Moot State University Law School ("Moot State") is the only state-sponsored law school in Moot and is located in the city of Metropolis in Prosper County. Moot State is chartered by state statute and receives public funding. Moot State and its officials, including Defendants Anderson, Packer and Badger, are state actors subject to the Fourteenth Amendment of the United States Constitution and were at all relevant times acting in their official capacities.

    3.   Defendant Alice Anderson is the dean of Moot State and has overall supervisory authority over all aspects of the law school's admissions program.

    4.   Defendant Barry Badger is the chair of the Admissions Committee of Moot State.

    5.   Defendant Lisa Packer is the Associate Dean of Admissions at Moot State and supervises new student admissions.

FACTS

    6.   In February 2020, plaintiff applied for admission into the fall 2020 entering class at Moot State.

    7.   Plaintiff scored a 157 on the Law School Admissions Test ("LSAT") in December 2019 and had a grade point average of 3.20 on a four point scale at Prosper Community College, from which she graduated in May

2017, shortly after the death of her spouse from cancer. She is a single mother, and a reporter for KRYP-TV.

8. Moot State automatically admits and automatically denies admission to some of its applicants based on their Applicant Scores. An Applicant Score is calculated by adding the applicant's LSAT score to the product of ten times the applicant's grade point average (LSAT + (10) GPA = Applicant Score). In addition to considering Applicant Scores, Moot State considers the residency status and race of the applicants in determining which students are automatically admitted and automatically denied admission.

9. Plaintiff is white, and is and was at all relevant times a resident of Moot. Her Applicant Score when she applied to Moot State was 189.0. Upon information and belief, Moot State automatically admitted to the fall 2020 class resident and non-resident applicants who were Black or Latinx who had scores of 189.0 or higher. Plaintiff included a diversity statement with her application. Even though plaintiff's score was only one point lower than the 190.0 automatic admission cut-off score applied to her, plaintiff was placed on a waiting list.

10. On or about July 1, 2020, Moot State notified plaintiff that her application had been denied.

11. Upon information and belief, Moot State admitted to the fall 2020 class resident and non-resident Black and Latinx applicants who had lower Applicant Scores than plaintiff. Moot State purportedly created this race-based admissions program in an effort to increase minority admissions and achieve targeted racial quotas in the school's entering classes.

12. After learning that she had been denied admission to Moot State, plaintiff enrolled in a small private law school outside of Metropolis. The tuition at this other school is more than three times as much as the tuition at Moot State. Moreover, the average earnings of graduates of this law school are substantially less than the average earnings of graduates of Moot State.

EQUAL PROTECTION CLAIM

13. Through the actions of Defendants Anderson, Packer and Badger, as alleged above, Moot State created and administered a racially discriminatory admissions program in violation of plaintiff's rights under the Fourteenth Amendment of the United States Constitution.

14. Moot State's unconstitutional race-based admissions program caused Moot State to deny plaintiff's application for admission to the fall 2020 entering class.

15. As a result of Moot State's unconstitutional actions in denying plaintiff's application for admission, plaintiff has had to pay higher tuition

costs to attend another law school and has suffered a permanent loss of future earning capacity as an attorney.

WHEREFORE, plaintiff prays that the Court enter judgment in her favor and requests the following relief:

1.   A judicial declaration that Moot State created and administered an unlawful race-based admissions program in violation of plaintiff's rights under the Fourteenth Amendment of the United States Constitution;

2.   A temporary and permanent injunction precluding Moot State from continuing to administer its unconstitutional race-based admissions program;

3.   An order that Moot State admit plaintiff to its law school at the start of the fall 2021 semester;

4.   An award of compensatory damages to compensate plaintiff for the higher tuition expenses that she has had to pay to attend her current law school and will have to pay her school if she is not admitted to Moot State;

5.   An award of compensatory damages to compensate plaintiff for her permanent loss of future earning capacity if she is not admitted to and allowed to graduate with a degree from Moot State;

6.   An award of punitive damages for the defendants' willful violation of plaintiff's constitutional rights;

7.   An award of plaintiff's costs and attorney fees incurred in bringing this action;

8.   An award of prejudgment interest as allowed by law; and

9.   Such other further relief that the Court deems just and equitable.

Dated: July 15, 2020   Respectfully submitted,

                                 _____

                                 Jennifer Adams, No. 45832
                                 Adams and Tomkins
                                 675 Main Street
                                 Metropolis, Moot X7914

STATE OF MOOT   DISTRICT COURT

COUNTY OF PROSPER   SECOND JUDICIAL DISTRICT

Lois Lane,   Court File No.: CIV 56789

        Plaintiff,

v.   **JOINT ANSWER OF
                                                DEFENDANTS**

Moot State University Law School,
Alice Anderson, Lisa Packer, and
Barry Badger,

        Defendants.

_____

    Defendants Moot State University Law School, Alice Anderson, Lisa Packer, and Barry Badger, for their Joint Answer to Plaintiff's Complaint, state and allege that:

    1.   Defendants are without knowledge or information sufficient to form a belief as to the truth of the allegations in paragraph 1 of Plaintiff's Complaint.

    2.   Defendants admit the allegations in paragraphs 2, 3, 4, 5, and 6 of Plaintiff's Complaint.

    3.   Defendants are without knowledge or information sufficient to form a belief as to the truth of the allegations in paragraph 7 of Plaintiff's Complaint except to admit upon information and belief that plaintiff scored a 157 on the December 2019 LSAT, that she graduated from Prosper Community College in 2017 with a 3.20 GPA on a four-point scale, and that she has served as a reporter for KRYP-TV.

    4.   Defendants admit the allegations in the second sentence of paragraph 8 of Plaintiff's Complaint. Defendants deny the remaining allegations contained in paragraph 8 of Plaintiff's Complaint, except to state that Moot State does consider residency when determining whether an applicant's Applicant Score falls in a presumptive admit range or a presumptive reject range.

    5.   Defendants are without knowledge or information sufficient to form a belief as to the truth of the allegations in the first sentence of paragraph 9 of Plaintiff's Complaint with respect to plaintiff's residency "at all relevant times." Defendants admit the allegations contained in the second sentence of paragraph 9 of Plaintiff's Complaint. Defendants deny the allegations in the remaining sentences in paragraph 9 of Plaintiff's Complaint, except to admit that Defendants did receive and review

Plaintiff's diversity statement and that all Black and Latinx applicants to the fall 2020 class who had Applicant Scores of 189.0 or higher were admitted, and that plaintiff was placed on a waiting list until July 1, 2020, when her application for admission was rejected.

6. Defendants admit the allegations in paragraph 10 of Plaintiff's Complaint.

7. Defendants admit the allegations in the first sentence of paragraph 11 of Plaintiff's Complaint. Defendants deny plaintiff's characterization of Moot State's admissions program as "race-based" as alleged in the second sentence of paragraph 11 of Plaintiff's Complaint. Defendants further allege with respect to this sentence of Plaintiff's Complaint that Moot State considers the race of its applicants in its admissions program to further the school's compelling state interest in achieving a diverse student body. Defendants otherwise deny the allegations in this sentence of paragraph 11.

8. Defendants are without knowledge or information sufficient to form a belief as to the truth of the allegations in paragraph 12 of Plaintiffs Complaint.

9. Defendants deny the allegations in paragraph 13 of Plaintiff's Complaint.

10. Defendants deny the allegations in paragraph 14 of Plaintiff's Complaint and assert that plaintiff was denied admission to Moot State because of her residency status and her relative qualifications as compared to other resident applicants. Plaintiff was not denied admission because of her race.

11. Defendants deny the allegations in paragraph 15 of Plaintiff's Complaint.

12. Plaintiff's Complaint fails to state a claim against defendants upon which relief can be granted.

WHEREFORE, defendants pray that plaintiff take nothing by her complaint, that the Court enter judgment dismissing Plaintiffs Complaint with prejudice and on the merits, and that Defendants be awarded their costs and attorney fees incurred in defending this action.

Dated: July 25, 2020   Respectfully submitted,

_____

Thomas Crane, No. 64123
Schuster and Williams
2122 Second Avenue South
Metropolis, Moot X7913

STATE OF MOOT   DISTRICT COURT

COUNTY OF PROSPER   SECOND JUDICIAL DISTRICT

Lois Lane,   Court File No.: CIV 56789

      Plaintiff,

v.   **STIPULATION AND FIRST
                                        PROTECTIVE ORDER**

Moot State University Law School,
Alice Anderson, Lisa Packer, and
Barry Badger,

      Defendants.

WHEREAS, discovery in this action will involve substantial amounts of confidential information,

IT IS HEREBY ORDERED, UPON CONSENT OF THE PARTIES, THAT:

1.   All information produced by the parties in the litigation shall be subject to the following restrictions:

    a.   The information will be used only for purposes of the litigation;

    b.   The information will not be given or made available to anyone other than the parties and their respective legal representatives, and such other persons who must be shown the information for purposes of the litigation, including the Court;

    c.   There will be no reproduction of the information except as necessary for use in the litigation; and

    d.   Each person who is given or shown the information in the context of the litigation agrees to maintain it as confidential, for use only in the litigation.

2.   Discovery shall be delivered to counsel without being filed unless required by further proceedings.

3.   Any party may designate selected information as especially confidential, and may require that such information, to the extent filed with the Court, be filed under seal, subject to the Court's further determination as to the propriety of the claim of especial confidentiality.

4.   Any party may seek modification of this order from the Court at any time with respect to the treatment of any specific material.

5. Nothing in this order is intended to apply to the trial of the case.

Dated: August 6, 2020   Respectfully submitted,

_____

Jennifer Adams, No. 45832
Adams and Tomkins
675 Main Street
Metropolis, Moot X7914

Dated: August 6, 2020   Respectfully submitted,

_____

Thomas Crane, No. 64123
Schuster and Williams
2122 Second Avenue South
Metropolis, Moot X7913

Dated: August 11, 2020   SO ORDERED:

_____

Wendall W. Washington
Judge of District Court

STATE OF MOOT   DISTRICT COURT

COUNTY OF PROSPER   SECOND JUDICIAL DISTRICT

Lois Lane,   Court File No.: CIV 56789

      Plaintiff,

v.   **AFFIDAVIT OF LISA PACKER**

Moot State University Law School,
Alice Anderson, Lisa Packer, and
Barry Badger,

      Defendants.

Lisa Packer, being first duly sworn, states as follows:

1. I am the Associate Dean of Admissions for Moot State University Law School (the "Law School"). We are the public law school in the State of Moot, chartered by state statute. We are funded by the legislature, tuition monies, and private donations.

2. I graduated from the Law School with a Juris Doctor degree in 2007. I am admitted to practice law in the states of Moot and New York.

3. After graduating from the Law School, I worked for two years as an associate attorney at Evergreen and Cash in New York City. While there, my work was primarily in the areas of employment law and civil rights.

4. In 2009, my spouse took a job in Metropolis. The Law School was looking for an Associate Dean at the time. I applied for the position, was hired, and have been in the position ever since. I supervise all new student admissions for the Law School.

5. I submit this Affidavit in support of the Law School's motion to dismiss Plaintiff's complaint. I submit the Affidavit under the provisions of the Court's existing protective order, and I designate Attachment A and Attachment B as especially confidential, to be filed and maintained under seal pursuant to paragraph 3 of the protective order.

6. The admissions process at the Law School is time-consuming and complex. For the fall 2020 entering class, we received exactly 500 applications (which is about our annual average) for only 100 places. As we receive applications, members of the Admissions Office create a single-page cover sheet for each applicant. This cover sheet includes basic information, such as the applicant's name, contact information, previous employment and education, undergraduate grade point average (GPA), their Law

School Aptitude Test ("LSAT") score, and whether the applicant submitted a diversity statement. If an applicant's diversity statement describes diversity other than, or in addition to, racial diversity, the Admissions Office adds an asterisk to the cover sheet. The purpose of the asterisk is to ensure that the Admissions Committee considers all types of diversity, in addition to racial diversity. The Admissions Office then calculates an "Applicant Score" based on a combination of the applicant's undergraduate GPA and LSAT score and adds that Applicant Score to the applicant's cover sheet. To calculate the Applicant Score, we add the applicant's LSAT score to the product of ten times the applicant's undergraduate GPA, so the mathematical equation looks like this: LSAT + (10) GPA = Applicant Score. An asterisk is not worth any points in the calculation of the applicant score (described below). All GPAs are converted to a standard four-point scale before we plug them into the equation. The LSAT is scored by an outside testing agency. The scores on the LSAT range from a possible low of 120 to a possible high of 180.

7.   If an Applicant Score is above a certain number, the Admissions Office drafts an acceptance letter and sends it, together with the applicant's file, to me for signature. If an Applicant Score is below a certain number, the Admissions Office follows this same procedure, except it drafts a rejection letter for me to sign. I independently review the files, and retain the discretion to refuse to sign an acceptance or rejection letter if I believe further consideration is warranted.

8.   We regularly track the performance records of our enrollees relative to their initial Applicant Scores, and have found that persons with scores above particular levels tend to do well. We have found a correlation between our Applicant Score and an applicant's first-year grade point average, although, as with any numerical performance predictor, there are exceptions.

9.   Each year, we start with the presumption that students with Applicant Scores of 185 or more will be admitted, and students with Applicant Scores lower than 178 will be rejected. We then adjust the scores each year once we have a sense of the overall applicant pool, to take into account the vagaries of different years. For the fall 2020 entering class, the numbers were:

	Presumptive Admission	Presumptive Denial
Residents	190 or more	Less than 183
Nonresidents	187 or more	Less than 178

10. For the fall 2020 entering class, 10.0 percent of the applicants overall (i.e., fifty persons) had Applicant Scores of at least 190, and another 10.0 percent overall (i.e., fifty persons) had Applicant Scores of at least 185.

An additional 20.0 percent of our applicants overall (i.e., one hundred persons) had Applicant Scores of at least 178. The balance (60.0 percent of the applicants overall = three hundred persons) had scores below 178, and ultimately received rejection letters no matter what admissions classification they were placed in.

11. It became apparent fairly early in the process that fully seventy-six percent of our applicants overall were going to fall into the resident classification this year. Twenty-four percent were nonresidents. Additionally, eight percent of the overall applicant pool were Black, and six percent were Latinx. These last three percentages are lower than they have been historically, which is a matter of some concern to us.

12. The faculty and dean have directed the Admissions Office to compose a geographically and racially diverse student body, focusing especially on Black and Latinx students, as these groups tend historically to be underrepresented in the legal profession, at Moot State University, and in Moot State University Law School. In fact, between ninety and ninety-five percent of our Black and Latinx applicants come from out of state. The faculty has further directed that applicants from such underrepresented groups be admitted in numbers great enough to attempt to create a critical mass. We did hire an expert, Barbara McGuire, who worked with the Office of Institutional Research to design a recruiting system to aid in achieving our diversity goals. She looked at the possibility of implementing scholarships for those who have overcome adversity. She also looked at the possibility of advertising and recruiting (a) in economically disadvantaged areas and (b) at colleges who historically have higher percentages of students who are the first in their families to go to college. But it was determined that we did not have sufficient funds to implement these approaches on a sustained basis as a state law school in tight budget times, except for one or two additional scholarships through alumni appeals.

13. I concluded we would likely have no opportunity to achieve an appropriately diverse student body if we presumptively admitted every resident applicant with a score of 185 or more. As a result, I raised both the presumptive admission and the presumptive rejection thresholds in that classification. I also raised the presumptive admission threshold in the nonresident classification. My fear was that, without the adjustment, our entire entering class this year might consist of presumptive admissions, which would not allow us to take into account any applicant life experiences, special achievements, perspectives, and other factors not necessarily reflected in the numerical Applicant Scores. The practice of law will increasingly require our graduates to encounter and work with judges, lawyers and clients of many diverse backgrounds. Our student body needs to reflect that diversity.

14. In the Law School's admissions program, we try to at least match, if not exceed, the previous years' percentages of Black and Latinx students. Historically we found that achieving this goal aides in the creation of a critical mass of diverse students, achieving an increasingly diverse student body. For example, for the five most recent prior entering classes, the percentage of Black students has ranged from 12 percent to 15 percent, and the percentage of Latinx students has ranged from 9 percent to 12 percent. The racial composition of students currently pursuing undergraduate degrees at Moot State, by contrast, is 63 percent white, 15 percent Black, 12 percent Latinx, and 10 percent other. The racial composition of attorneys currently licensed to practice law in Moot is 74 percent white, 9 percent Black, 8 percent Latinx, and 9 percent other.

15. When the Law School received Plaintiff Lois Lane's application, we created her one-page cover sheet. We noted Lane as a resident of Moot and noted her diversity statement. Because Lane's diversity statement described her status as a single mother, in addition to her work experience, we did mark an asterisk on Lane's cover sheet. She resides in Moot. Her Applicant Score was 189.0. This did not qualify her for presumptive admission, and her application was moved forward for further review.

16. When an Applicant Score exceeds the presumptive rejection threshold, but does not qualify for a presumptive admission letter, we send the application to a subcommittee of the Admissions Committee. The Admissions Committee is composed of six faculty members and three students. These nine persons are divided into three subcommittees, each consisting of two faculty members and one student. One subcommittee considers the resident applications. Another subcommittee considers the nonresident applications. A final subcommittee (the "Special Consideration" subcommittee) considers all applications flagged for additional consideration. This would include all applications from the presumptive admission and presumptive rejection categories that I flag for additional consideration following my initial review, and all applications that include a special "diversity statement."

17. An application consists of the application form itself, the single-page cover sheet created by the Admission Office, the LSAT report, transcripts from all post-secondary institutions attended, two letters of recommendation, a personal statement, and an optional diversity essay in which any applicant is invited to write a statement explaining how that applicant would contribute to the diversity of the class. Each applicant may define diversity in his or her own way; "diversity" for purposes of this statement is not limited to racial diversity.

18. The resident and nonresident admissions subcommittees review applications beyond the LSAT and undergraduate GPA, and may, in their discretion add one additional quality point for each of any of the following:

non-residency; economic disadvantage; growing up in a single-parent home; race; upward trend in the undergraduate GPA or especially challenging academic program or achievement; exceptional letters of recommendation; leadership potential; and other exceptional features, such as a special talent for multiple languages, or overcoming some hardship. No more than a total of six additional points may be added to any individual's Applicant Score.

19. The special consideration subcommittee follows the same review system as the resident and nonresident admissions subcommittee. Applications marked with an asterisk occasionally receive one or more extra point(s) added to their applicant score, based on the quality points described above. An asterisk, however, does not automatically result in additional point(s). The special consideration subcommittee also has the authority, if it so chooses, to take an application out of the "point system" and recommend a straight admit or reject decision. The special consideration subcommittee is granted this authority in those cases where the overall strength or weakness of the application is not adequately reflected by the applicant's numerical Applicant Score, even when subject to subcommittee quality points. Any admit or reject decision by the special consideration subcommittee is subject to veto by the committee as a whole. However, I am aware of no such veto in the eleven years I have been Associate Dean.

20. After the presumptive admissions are processed, the Admissions Committee calculates the number of spaces remaining for resident and nonresident applicants. We also assess our racial diversity at this point. Separate resident and nonresident waiting lists are maintained by the resident and nonresident subcommittees.

21. Each member of the admissions committee is instructed to conduct an individualized review of each application, and to consider each application as compared to the quality and diversity of the applicant pool as a whole when making admissions decisions. They are also told that no single factor considered in isolation should be decisive.

22. Competition is keen among law schools for especially outstanding Black and Latinx students, and thus we get a higher rejection rate from Black and Latinx offer recipients, who receive attractive financial aid packages from competing law schools, than we get from our other applicants. We typically have a 20 percent rejection rate from our White applicants, while we typically have a 35 percent rejection rate from our Black and Latinx offer recipients. As we attempt to enroll a critical mass of underrepresented minority students, we need to take these matriculation rates into account.

23. We ultimately enrolled 63 residents and 37 nonresidents for the fall of 2020. Of these, we had 13 Black and 10 Latinx students. Their

respective final Applicant Scores are listed on Attachment A to this Affidavit. Two of the Black students were residents and one Latinx student was a resident.

24. Every Black applicant, every Latinx applicant, and every nonresident applicant with an Applicant Score of 189.0 or more was accepted into the entering class for the fall of 2020.

25. Every Black student, every Latinx student, and every nonresident student currently enrolled at the Law School is in good standing.

26. The Applicant Log lines for Lane and each of the applicants listed on Attachment A are collated on Attachment B. Every applicant folder at Moot State University Law School is identified in a book which we call the Applicant Log. This log is not used in making decisions regarding individual applicants, but merely to keep track of applications. At Plaintiff's request during discovery, I compiled Attachment B containing the lines for the listed students.

Dated: October 15, 2020   _____

                                           Lisa Packer

Signed and sworn to before me
this 15th day of October, 2020

_____

Linda Roberts, Notary Public

ATTACHMENT A TO AFFIDAVIT
OF LISA PACKER

Black Students	A/S	Latinx Students	A/S
William Russell	195	Rosa Garcia	195
Andrea Bell	194	Nick Rodriguez	193
Robert Penn	193	Christina Martinez	193
Natasha Johnson	191	Ben Valdez	189
Ashley Hamilton	190	Alexandra Hernandez	188
Marcus Nelson	189	Victor Baker	187
Todd Smith (resident)	186	Jose Leonardo	184
Brenda Allen	185	Robert Mendoza	184
Cassandra Calder	185	Vince Ramos (resident)	182
Isaiah Mitchell	184	Isabelle Gonzales	178
Jessica Thomas	183		
Byron Wilson (resident)	181		
Parker Evans	179		

ATTACHMENT B
APPLICANT LOG EXCERPTS

Name	A/S	Birthdate	Sex	Background	Resident	Diversity Statement	Race (If Noted)
L Lane	189	9/20/91	F	TV Reporter	Yes	Yes*	W
W Russell	195	4/05/95	M	Engineering student	No	Yes	B
A Bell	194	6/10/96	F	English student	No	Yes	B
R Penn	193	2/05/95	M	History student	No	Yes*	B
N Johnson	191	5/10/94	F	American studies student	No	Yes	B
A Hamilton	190	3/09/89	F	Computer Programmer	No	No	B
M Nelson	189	7/04/93	M	Business student	No	Yes*	B
T Smith	186	10/26/95	M	Economics student	Yes	Yes	B
B Allen	185	9/11/96	F	Math student	No	Yes	B
C Calder	185	8/04/96	F	English student	No	No	B
I Mitchell	184	6/23/96	M	Political science student	No	Yes	B
J Thomas	183	1/01/95	F	History student	No	No	B
B Wilson	181	5/14/96	M	Biology student	Yes	Yes	B
P Evans	179	12/02/88	M	Musician	No	Yes*	B
R Garcia	195	2/12/95	F	Education student	No	Yes	L
N Rodriguez	193	4/30/95	M	Chemistry student	No	Yes*	L
C Martinez	193	1/26/95	F	Economics student	No	No	L
B Valdez	189	8/23/88	M	Accountant	No	Yes	L
A Hernandez	188	10/22/91	F	Teacher	No	No	L
V Baker	187	11/06/95	M	Engineering student	No	Yes	L
J Leonardo	184	12/03/93	M	Mechanic	No	Yes*	L
R Mendoza	184	5/15/94	F	Political science student	No	Yes	L
V Ramos	182	7/10/95	M	Math student	Yes	Yes	L
I Gonzales	178	9/15/96	F	English student	No	Yes	L

* Applicant's diversity statement describes diversity other than, or in addition to, racial diversity.

STATE OF MOOT	DISTRICT COURT
COUNTY OF PROSPER	SECOND JUDICIAL DISTRICT

Lois Lane,

Court File No.: CIV 56789

　　　　Plaintiff,

v.

TRANSCRIPT OF PROCEEDINGS ON MOTION TO DISMISS AND MOTION TO MODIFY PROTECTIVE ORDER

Moot State University Law School, Alice Anderson, Lisa Packer, and Barry Badger,

　　　　Defendants.

This matter came on for hearing before the Honorable Wendall W. Washington, Judge of District Court, on November 12, 2020, upon the Defendants' Motion to Dismiss and the Plaintiffs Motion to Modify Protective Order. Plaintiff Lois Lane appeared through her counsel, Jennifer Adams. Defendants Moot State University Law School, Alice Anderson, Lisa Packer, and Barry Badger appeared through their counsel, Thomas Crane. The Court called the hearing to order at 8:45 a.m.

THE COURT: Good morning counsel. I understand we are here this morning on Defendants' collective motion to dismiss and Plaintiff's Motion to Modify the Protective Order in the matter of Lois Lane v. Moot State University Law School, Alice Anderson, Lisa Packer, and Barry Badger. May I have appearances of counsel for the record please.

ATTORNEY ADAMS: Good morning, Your Honor. I am Jennifer Adams, from Adams and Tomkins, appearing for Plaintiff Lois Lane. Ms. Lane is also in the courtroom today.

THE COURT: Thank you, Ms. Adams. Good morning, Ms. Lane, and welcome.

ATTORNEY CRANE: Good morning, Your Honor. Thomas Crane, from Schuster and Williams, appearing for all of the Defendants. As the Court is aware, Alice Anderson is the Dean of Moot State Law School, Lisa Packer is the Associate Dean, and Barry Badger is the Admission Committee Chair. They are also all present today.

THE COURT: Welcome to you all. Counsel, I regret to say that I have limited time for you this morning. We are about to commence a major criminal trial today, and I have 200 prospective jurors arriving for voir dire in about 30 minutes. However, I can assure you that I have read all of the parties' submissions to date, and have familiarized myself thoroughly with the case and the pending motions. As a result, I prefer to proceed this morning by simply asking you certain questions that are on my mind.

Let me begin with a couple of questions for you, Mr. Crane, about the motions. First, on your Motion to Dismiss, is it your basic position that there is a compelling state interest in having a diverse law school student body, and that Moot State's admissions program survives any equal protection attack because the program is narrowly tailored to achieve the law school's compelling interest in a diverse student body?

ATTORNEY CRANE: Yes, Your Honor, that is essentially correct.

THE COURT: And are you saying that is a legal conclusion for the Court to reach?

ATTORNEY CRANE: Yes, Your Honor.

THE COURT: If I find that the question of whether Defendants' admissions program is narrowly tailored is really a fact question on the present record, do you lose this motion?

ATTORNEY CRANE: No, Your Honor, because in any event, the record indicates the Plaintiff was denied admission by reason of her residency status, and not her race.

THE COURT: Ms. Adams, do you have a comment to add on this point?

ATTORNEY ADAMS: Yes, Your Honor. I respectfully disagree with Mr. Crane regarding the appropriateness of summary judgment for Defendants. For one thing, Defendants cannot at this point establish that the law school's admissions program was narrowly tailored to achieve the school's diversity objectives. In fact, it clearly was not. At best, Moot State appears to be focused on specific kinds of diversity, at the expense of other kinds of diversity. Furthermore, there is at least a genuine issue of material fact regarding the question of whether my client was denied admission because of her race. Among other issues, the asterisk system used by Moot State is suspect at worst, and unclear at best. Finally, even if my client cannot prove that she was denied admission because of her race, she can still prove that Moot State administers a constitutionally impermissible admissions program and request that the Court enjoin the further operation of the program.

ATTORNEY CRANE: I would just further add, Your Honor, that, if Plaintiff cannot prove she was denied admission to Moot State because of her race, then she would have no standing to assert the interests of others who might claim to have been aggrieved by any use of racial classifications in the admissions program. Accordingly, the Court would have no basis for using Plaintiff's Complaint to enjoin the operation of the program.

THE COURT: All right. Now, Mr. Crane, I have a question about Plaintiff's Motion to Modify the Protective Order, which would give

Plaintiff the ability to give the public a copy of Ms. Packer's Affidavit and the Attachments. What do I do about Moot Statute Section 100.03? Isn't there a presumption that the data in Ms. Packer's Affidavit is public?

ATTORNEY CRANE: I don't believe so, your Honor. It is true that data maintained by government entities, and we concede we are such an entity for purposes of the Statute, is ordinarily public. The Statute exists to make sure that government policy making is done in the open, and not behind closed doors. But Moot Statute Section 100.04 really trumps the general presumption in the case of educational data, and Section 100.06 says the normal protective order rules apply to civil litigation anyway. I see no useful purpose served by parading the admission scores and personal data of minority applicants before the public.

THE COURT: What about that, Ms. Adams?

ATTORNEY ADAMS: The Court is quite correct that there is a general presumption of public access to government entity data. The burden should be on Mr. Crane to rebut the presumption, and he has not done so. I am sensitive to the concerns of specific students about having their Applicant Scores released, and Ms. Lane means no disrespect to those students. But the fact of the matter is that Moot State utilizes a racially-based admissions system that has caused Moot State to admit students who scored fully 11 points below Ms. Lane under Moot State's own methodology. The public cannot fully appreciate the reality of the system by mere reference to abstract principles and lofty rhetoric. The public should see that the system impacts real people with real numbers.

THE COURT: Mr. Crane, what if I order release of Attachments A and B to the Packer Affidavit, but redact student names and replace them with number or letter codes? That would at least get the relevant scores out in the public domain, while protecting the identities of individuals.

ATTORNEY CRANE: Unfortunately, Judge, I don't think that solves the problem. Moot State is a small law school, with a small minority student population. There is a substantial risk that, even using codes instead of real names, people will be able to identify specific students, and, in any event, there is a certainty that people will know the scores of each small group of 13 and 10 students, respectively.

ATTORNEY ADAMS: Your suggestion is acceptable to the Plaintiff, Your Honor, although we don't see any problem with making Attachments A and B available to the public as they are. After all, you are going to use them as evidence in your decision, presumably. I just don't see how you can properly seal evidence relied upon in connection with a dispositive motion.

THE COURT: Thank you, Counsel. I appreciate your efforts to answer my questions. My clerk has just given me a note that potential jurors are arriving for my criminal trial, so I will now have to conclude these proceedings. I plan to take everything under advisement for now and will do my best to rule promptly.

WHEREUPON, the hearing concluded at approximately 9:20 a.m.

Rebecca Loughlin, Official Court Reporter, District Court, Second Judicial District.

STATE OF MOOT	DISTRICT COURT
COUNTY OF PROSPER	SECOND JUDICIAL DISTRICT

Lois Lane,

     Plaintiff,

v.

Moot State University Law School,
Alice Anderson, Lisa Packer, and
Barry Badger,

     Defendants.

Court File No.: CIV 56789

**MEMORANDUM OPINION
AND ORDER**

This matter comes before the Court on Defendants' Motion to Dismiss the Complaint and on Plaintiff's Motion to Modify the Protective Order in the case to permit Plaintiff to share with the public certain information filed under seal in connection with the dismissal motion.

ORDER

Based upon the files and evidence, the briefs and arguments of counsel, and the accompanying Memorandum of the Court, the Court hereby orders that:

1.   Defendants are entitled to summary judgment; and

2.   Attachments A and B to the Affidavit of Associate Dean of Admissions Lisa Packer will remain sealed until further order of the Court.

Let judgment be entered accordingly.

Dated: December 10, 2020

Wendall W. Washington
Judge of District Court

MEMORANDUM OPINION

1. FACTS

Plaintiff Lois Lane is a resident of Metropolis, Moot. Lane worked her way through Prosper Community College as a reporter for a local Metropolis television station—KRYP-TV. She ultimately graduated from college in May 2017 with a Bachelor of Arts degree in English and a grade point average of 3.20 on a 4.0 scale. While attending her sophomore year in college, Lane and her spouse had a baby girl. Lane's spouse subsequently died of cancer about six months before Lane's graduation.

Lane continued to work as a KRYP-TV reporter after graduating from college. In the spring of 2020, Lane decided to apply for admission to law school with the hope of becoming an attorney for a television station or other media entity. Lane took the Law School Aptitude Test ("LSAT") in December 2019. Lane learned a short time later that she scored a 157 on the LSAT. Lane applied to Moot State University Law School ("Moot State") for admission into the fall 2020 semester entering class.[1]

As applications are received at Moot State, members of the Admissions Office create one-page cover sheets. The cover sheet contains basic information, such as the applicant's name, employment history, and whether the applicant submitted a diversity statement. The Admissions Office adds an asterisk to the cover sheet if the applicant submitted a diversity statement that describes diversity other than, or in addition to, racial diversity. The asterisk does not automatically award the applicant an additional point(s) at any stage of the application review. The Admissions Office then calculates an "Applicant Score" based on a combination of the applicant's undergraduate grade point average and LSAT score.[2]

If an Applicant Score is above a certain number, the Admissions Office drafts an acceptance letter and sends it, together with the applicant's file, to the Associate Dean for her signature. If an Applicant's Score is below a certain number, the Admissions Office follows this same procedure except they draft a denial letter. For the fall 2020 entering class the numbers were:

	Presumptive Admission	*Presumptive Denial*
Residents	190 or more	Less than 183
Nonresidents	187 or more	Less than 178

All remaining applications are sent to the Admissions Committee for further review. In addition, the Associate Dean independently reviews the applications and can refuse to sign a letter of acceptance or denial if, in her sole discretion, further consideration is warranted.

The Admissions Committee is comprised of six faculty members and three students. The Committee is divided into three subcommittees; each subcommittee is comprised of two faculty members and one student. One

---

[1] Moot State University Law School is the only state-supported law school in Moot and is located in the city of Metropolis.

[2] The Applicant Score is calculated by adding the applicant's LSAT score to the product of ten times the applicant's grade point average (LSAT + (10) GPA = Applicant Score).

subcommittee considers the resident applications. Another subcommittee considers the nonresident applications. The final subcommittee considers all applications flagged for additional consideration, including presumptive admit and presumptive reject files flagged by the Associate Dean, and files that include a "diversity statement." The diversity statement is an optional essay that students may write about how they would contribute to the diversity of the class. Diversity for purposes of this statement may be defined in any way the applicant sees fit, and is not limited exclusively to racial diversity.

This third subcommittee, called the "Special Consideration Subcommittee," may take an application out of the point system and recommend a straight admit or reject decision, due to strengths or weaknesses that are not adequately reflected in an Applicant Score, even when the score is adjusted through the normal point process. Although Special Consideration Subcommittee decisions are subject to review and veto by the Admissions Committee, Moot State reports no such vetoes in recent years.

Moot State's admissions process, for the five most recent classes, has resulted in the percentage of Black students ranging from 12 percent to 15 percent and the percentage of Latinx students ranging from 9 percent to 12 percent.[3] The Moot State University Law School faculty and administration have determined that it is important to the academic goals of their program to attain geographic diversity in their student body and to attain a critical mass of underrepresented minority students, specifically, Black and Latinx students.

When Moot State received Lane's application, it created a one-page cover sheet for her application file. Based on Lane's diversity statement, which described diversity other than racial diversity, Lane's application was marked with an asterisk. Lane's Applicant Score was 189.0. Even though her Applicant Score was only one point below the presumptive admission number, Lane's application was referred for subcommittee review. After the subcommittee reviewed Lane's application, it placed her on the resident waiting list. Because a high number of qualified resident applicants had Applicant Scores in the presumptive admission category, Lane was ultimately denied admission on July 1, 2020. Every nonresident applicant with a score of 189.0 or higher was granted admission. Likewise, every Black and Latinx applicant with a score of 189.0 or higher was granted admission.

I.   PROCEDURAL BACKGROUND

Lane commenced this action against Defendants Moot State University Law School, Alice Anderson, Lisa Packer and Barry Badger

---

[3]   Moot State's typical entering class size is 100 students.

alleging that, through the actions of its officials, Moot State created and administered a racially discriminatory admissions program in violation of the Fourteenth Amendment of the United States Constitution.[4] Lane is seeking a declaration that Moot State's admissions program is unconstitutional, injunctive relief, compensatory damages for increased tuition costs and diminished earning capacity,[5] and recovery of her costs and attorneys fees.

Defendants have collectively moved for dismissal of the Complaint pursuant to Moot R. Civ. P. 12 and 56,[6] contending that Moot State's admissions program does not violate the Fourteenth Amendment as a matter of law because the program is narrowly tailored to serve the State of Moot's compelling interest in achieving a diverse law school student body. Defendants further assert that Lane cannot prove that she would have been admitted to Moot State under an admissions program that did not consider race as a factor.

Plaintiff Lane has in turn moved the Court under Moot R. Civ. P. 26,[7] for an order amending the existing protective order in the case to permit the unsealing of Attachments A and B to the Affidavit of Moot State's Associate Dean of Admissions, Lisa Packer. Moot State replies that these Attachments reveal sensitive data about individual students and groups of students.[8] Plaintiff Lane argues there should be public access to the data, and that the sealing of the Attachments to the Affidavit violates both First Amendment and common law rights of public access.

II. LEGAL ANALYSIS

A. The Standard for Summary Judgment.

Moot R. Civ. P. 56 governs summary judgment in this jurisdiction when the court, in considering a motion to dismiss a Complaint, takes into account matters outside of the pleadings. Rule 56(c) provides in relevant part that:

> The judgment sought shall be rendered forthwith if the pleadings, depositions, answers to interrogatories, and admissions on file,

---

[4]   Defendant Moot State University Law School is a state actor subject to the Fourteenth Amendment of the United States Constitution.

[5]   After Moot State denied her application, Lane decided to accept an offer to attend a small private law school just outside of Metropolis. The tuition at this school is more than three times the tuition at Moot State. Lane is seeking to recover this difference as compensatory damages. The average earnings of graduates from this law school are substantially less than the average earnings of law school graduates from Moot State. Lane also seeks to recover this difference as compensatory damages.

[6]   Moot R. Civ. P. 12 and 56 are identical to Fed. R. Civ. P. 12 and 56.

[7]   Moot R. Civ. P. 26 is identical to Fed. R. Civ. P. 26.

[8]   Plaintiff's counsel deposed Associate Dean Packer, Law School Dean Alice Anderson, and Admissions Committee Chair, Barry Badger during discovery. However, the transcripts do not include the data from the Packer Affidavit because it was not collected in that form yet. The parties have stipulated to the authenticity of the data for purposes of Defendants' dispositive motion.

together with the affidavits, if any, show that there is no genuine issue as to any material fact and that the moving party is entitled to a judgment as a matter of law.

The meaning of this rule is well-established. The Supreme Court of the United States has held that summary judgment should be used to dispose of claims which are factually unsupported or which are based on undisputed facts. *Celotex Corp. v. Catrett,* 477 U.S. 317, 323–324, 106 S. Ct. 2548 (1986). Summary judgment is proper when an examination of the evidence in a light most favorable to the non-moving party reveals no genuine issue of material fact and the moving party is entitled to judgment as a matter of law. *Anderson v. Liberty Lobby, Inc.,* 477 U.S. 242, 106 S. Ct. 2505 (1986).

B. The Equal Protection Issue.

A line of Supreme Court decisions from *Grutter v. Bollinger,* 539 U.S. 306, 123 S. Ct. 2325 (2003) to the more recent *Fisher v. University of Texas* cases (I and II), 570 U.S. 297, 133 S.Ct. 2411 (2013) and 136 S.Ct. 2198 (2016), dictate that the equal protection issue in this case boils down to whether Moot State's admissions procedures are narrowly tailored to achieve the school's diversity objectives. Plaintiff asserts that the *Fisher* decisions have altered the landscape for affirmative action in admissions. The Court disagrees with that overly broad characterization.

The Court finds that this inquiry principally presents a question of law and that there are no disputed issues of material fact precluding summary judgment. For the reasons explained below, the Court agrees with Defendants that Moot State's admissions policy on its face and as applied to Plaintiff does not and did not violate the Fourteenth Amendment as a matter of law, and orders the entry of summary judgment in favor of Defendants. The Court further finds that Plaintiff was denied admission to Moot State for a reason other than her race and that her claim, therefore, necessarily fails even if Moot State impermissibly considered the race of its applicants in its admissions process.

1. The admissions program is narrowly tailored.

Even though student body diversity in a public law school such as Moot State is a compelling interest that may justify consideration of race in the application evaluation process, application procedures that consider race must still be narrowly tailored to serve the state's compelling interest. The Court concludes for the reasons outlined below that Moot State's admissions program is narrowly tailored to serve the school's interest in achieving a diverse law school student body.

The Supreme Court has articulated various factors to consider in determining whether a race-based measure is narrowly tailored. These factors include: the necessity for the relief and the efficacy of alternative remedies; the flexibility and duration of the relief; the relationship of the numerical goals to the relevant market; and the impact of the relief on the rights of third parties. *United States v. Paradise,* 480 U.S. 149, 170, 107 S. Ct. 1053 (1987).

Subsequently, in *Grutter* the Supreme Court emphasized the importance of individualized consideration of each application in a way that does not insulate minority applicants from competition with all other applicants. Then, in *Gratz v. Bollinger,* 539 U.S. 244, 123 S. Ct. 2411 (2003), the Court found that a system which added an automatic and substantial number of points to all applicants who identified as underrepresented minorities was not sufficiently tailored to pass constitutional muster. Building on this precedent the Supreme Court announced in *Fisher* I that strict scrutiny is the necessary standard for assessing whether a school's policy is narrowly tailored. The Court then applied strict scrutiny in *Fisher* II to find that a University's admission policy was constitutional because race was considered a "subfactor" rather than a deciding factor.[9] And most recently, the First Circuit affirmed a District of Massachusetts decision holding that Harvard's race-conscious admission program was constitutional. *Students for Fair Admissions, Inc. v. President & Fellows of Harvard Coll.,* 980 F.3d 157 (1st Cir. 2020).

Applying these factors to the present case, it is clear that Moot State's admissions program, like the programs in *Grutter and Fisher,* and unlike the program in *Gratz,* is narrowly tailored.

First, as discussed above, the program clearly is necessary to achieve a diverse student body at the law school. If race were not considered in the admissions process, there is no doubt that there would be fewer minority law students at Moot State or elsewhere.

Second, Moot State's admissions program is flexible and limited in duration. It is important to note that Moot State's admissions program does not involve a quota system such as the admissions system struck down in *Regents of the University of California v. Bakke,* 438 U.S. 265, 98 S. Ct. 2733 (1978). Moot State maintains "goals" for the percentage of Black and Latinx students in each class. These are not rigid quotas. Rather, they are flexible goals. Although Moot State does consider race in its admissions program, it is simply one of many factors. All applicants may submit a diversity statement describing their diversity in their own words. And in fact, diversity statements that discuss diversity other than racial diversity are designated with an asterisk to ensure they are carefully reviewed.[10]

---

[9] The Court in *Fisher* II specifically noted that its analysis of the University's admissions program is limited in in its instructive capacity.

[10] The Court acknowledges there is uncertainty about the impact of an asterisk. However, the Court believes the asterisk exemplifies Moot State's commitment to individual consideration of each applicant.

Third, Moot State's admissions program bears a reasonable relationship to the relevant applicant pool. In *City of Richmond v. J.A. Croson Co.,* 488 U.S. 469, 109 S. Ct. 706 (1989), the Supreme Court said that it was improper to compare the percentage of all minorities in Richmond to the percentage of minority businesses that received city contracts. Rather, the proper comparison was the percentage of minorities in the relevant geographic area with the percentage of minorities in the area who were qualified to perform the jobs. *Id.* at 509. Likewise, the relevant pool in this case is the students with undergraduate degrees who are qualified to attend law school. The racial composition of students with undergraduate degrees at Moot State is 63 percent white, 12 percent Latinx, and 15 percent Black. *See* Affidavit of Lisa Packer, at ¶ 14. Moot State's admissions goals bear a reasonable relationship to the relevant pool of applicants.

Moot State's admissions program also does not impose an undue burden on the rights of others given that all applicants are compared against each other. In the final analysis, the added diversity in the classroom will actually benefit third parties, including the students who do not receive any preference in the admissions process. Accordingly, Moot State's admissions program is narrowly tailored to serve the school's compelling interest in diversity.

Nothing in the U.S. Supreme Court's Opinion in *Parents Involved in Community Schools v. Seattle School District No. 1,* 127 S. Ct. 2738 (2007) changes the result. The Court has analyzed the *Seattle* decision and has concluded that it does not change the outcome of the present case, most notably because *Seattle* did not involve education at the graduate and professional level (and thus *Seattle* is unlike the case at hand). All the Supreme Court really concluded in the *Seattle* case is that "racial balancing" in grades K–12 is not a compelling interest, *id.* at 2757 (citing *Croson,* 488 U.S. at 498), and that narrow tailoring requires "serious, good faith consideration of workable race-neutral alternatives," *id.* at 2760 (citing *Grutter,* 539 U.S. at 339). However, the *Seattle* case does not fundamentally change the strict scrutiny test. *See Rothe Development Cor. v. U.S. Dept. of Defense,* 499 F. Supp. 2d 775 (W.D. Tex. 2007). Moreover, the decision reaffirms what case law had suggested all along: "government action that 'rest[s] solely upon distinctions drawn according to race' [must] be 'subjected to the 'most rigid scrutiny.'" *Parents,* 127 S. Ct. at 2774 n.10 (2007) (citing *Loving v. Virginia,* 388 U.S. 1, 11 (1967) (quoting *Korematsu v. United States,* 323 U.S. 214, 216 (1944)). As a result, the *Seattle* decision has no effect on the outcome of the case at bar.

2. Plaintiff's residency was controlling, not her race.

Finally, Plaintiff's Complaint fails as a matter of law even if Moot State's admissions procedures are not sufficiently narrowly tailored because Plaintiff was denied admission as a result of her residency status and not because of her race. In other words, Plaintiff cannot prove that she would have been admitted to Moot State had the school not considered race in its admissions process. By contrast, if Plaintiff had applied as a nonresident, she would presumptively have been admitted based on her GPA and LSAT score. Because Plaintiff's residency status, and not her race, ultimately resulted in the denial of her application, her Equal Protection claim cannot stand.

C. The Protective Order Issue.

Defendants have filed Attachments A and B to Associate Dean Lisa Packer's Affidavit under seal pursuant to a protective order. Plaintiff Lane in turn has filed a motion seeking to modify the existing order to make clear that the Packer affidavit involves public data that may be disclosed to anyone. The Court denies Plaintiff's request to modify the protective order.

1. First Amendment analysis.

The first question the Court must decide is whether the protective order is governed by Moot R. Civ. P. 26 and the common law, or instead by the First Amendment of the United States Constitution as applied to the state of Moot through the Fourteenth Amendment.[11]

The United States Supreme Court has made clear that the public and the press have a presumptive right under the Constitution to be present for trials. *See, e.g., Richmond Newspapers, Inc. v. Virginia*, 448 U.S. 555, 576–80, 100 S. Ct. 2814 (1980). The Court noted that "historically both civil and criminal trials have been presumptively open." 448 U.S. at 580, n.17. But the present proceeding is not in trial; indeed, the whole point of a defense summary judgment motion is to avoid a trial.

Moreover, even at a trial, the public and the press do not have First Amendment rights to access all proceedings and all evidence. Consider the decision of the Supreme Court in *Nixon v. Warner Communications,* 435 U.S. 589, 98 S. Ct. 1306 (1978). In that case, the issue was whether a district court has a duty to disclose to the public copies of tape recordings (the famous Nixon "Watergate" tapes), portions of which are played in evidence at an open criminal trial. The Court held in relevant part that the press can report what is in the public domain, but has no First Amendment right to what the public itself has never had physical access to. *Id.* at 609. In the present matter, the public has never had access to Associate Dean Packer's affidavit. It was filed in camera with the undersigned's chambers, and has never been filed in the Clerk of Court's office. (It will, however, most certainly be transmitted, albeit under seal, as part of the record on

---

[11] Plaintiff's employer, KRYP-TV, sought to intervene in this case to obtain access to the entire Packer Affidavit, asserting the First Amendment. This Court denied the intervention request on the basis that Lane, as one of its reporters, is an adequate representative of any rights KRYP-TV may have.

appeal to the Moot Supreme Court, if Plaintiff elects to appeal this Court's decision.)

The Court also notes the Supreme Court's opinion in *Seattle Times Co. v. Rhinehart,* 467 U.S. 20, 104 S. Ct. 2199 (1984). One of the parties there wanted to disseminate in advance of trial information gained through the pretrial discovery process, and claimed a First Amendment right to do so. The Court held that a protective order under Fed. R. Civ. P. 26 does not offend the First Amendment when limited to control of information gained through the court process, because of the substantial governmental interest in orderly court proceedings, which is an important interest unrelated to the suppression of speech. *Id.* at 32, 37. Of course, in the present matter, we have an affidavit which is more than simply a discovery item; it was introduced into evidence in support of the summary judgment motion.

In the end, this Court concludes that the First Amendment is not substantially implicated by an order to seal Attachments A and B to the Packer Affidavit. This conclusion does not end the analysis, however.

2.   Rule 26 analysis.

There is, of course, a common law right of access to judicial records and documents. *Nixon,* 435 U.S. at 597. The right is not absolute. Every court has supervisory power over its own records and files, and access to those can be denied where court files might become a vehicle for improper uses. *Id.* at 598. A court has discretion to weigh all of the facts and circumstances. *Id.* at 599. This Court's supervisory powers are in fact codified in the Moot Rules of Civil Procedure, including in particular Rule 26, for present purposes.

There are many factors the courts can weigh in making the analysis. Moot Rule 26 instructs courts to enter protective orders when "justice requires to protect a party or person from annoyance, embarrassment, oppression, or undue burden or expense." In addition, the court should weigh such factors as (a) the presumption in favor of public access to the business of the courts and (b) the gains in public understanding of the courts' actions, on the one hand, against (c) fairness to the objecting party, (d) avoidance of the courts becoming pawns in efforts by others to create scandal, gratify spite, or harm competitors, and (e) the ability of the public and the press to gain information by other means, on the other hand. *See Nixon,* 435 U.S. at 598–99, 602–03.

When the Court weighs the competing factors in the present matter, it concludes that the sealing of Packer Attachments A and B under the existing protective order is appropriate. The Moot State Entity Data Act, Moot Stat. § 100.04(c) (1994), supports this conclusion, as does the sensitive nature of the data.

Accordingly, the Court denies Plaintiff's motion to modify the protective order to permit the unsealing of the contents of Attachments A and B to Associate Dean Packer's Affidavit. *See* Moot Stat. §§ 100.04(c), 100.06.

State of Moot, State Entity Data Act, Selected Excerpts
Moot Statutes, Chapter 100

100.1.   This Chapter may be cited as the "Moot State Entity Data Act."

100.2.   All state agencies, state political units, state universities, and other statewide systems ("state entities") are subject to this Chapter.

100.3.   There shall be a presumption that all data maintained by state entities is public data, and shall be accessible to members of the public and the press, so that free and open government shall be preserved.

100.4.   Notwithstanding Section 100.03, state entities shall limit disclosure of information under certain circumstances as follows:

(a) . . . .

(b) . . . .

(c) Data relating to specific students or prospective students at Moot state universities shall be considered nonpublic data, accessible only to officials of the universities and the individual students or prospective students themselves, except as broader access may be necessary in the public interest and a court orders disclosure pursuant to section 100.06.

(d) . . . .

(e) . . . .

100.5.   The provisions of Section 100.04 shall not apply to summary data that does not reveal specific nonpublic data.

100.6.   This Chapter shall not govern the discovery or disclosure of information pursuant to discovery in court proceedings, which shall instead be governed by the relevant rules of civil and criminal procedure, and orders made pursuant thereto. However, the courts of Moot shall give due consideration to the provisions of this Chapter in interpreting the relevant court rules.

State of Moot, State Entity Data Act
Selected Legislative History

State of Moot, Hearing on Senate Bill No. 64
Senate Judiciary Committee, March 10, 1994

Present: Senator Jones, Chair, and Senators Smith, Nelson, Vandalia, Brown, Wilson, Tobias, Grant, and Ernest

Senator Jones called the hearing to order at 10:00 a.m.

Senator Jones: Good morning everyone. It appears we have a quorum, which is good in light of the important issues on the agenda today. The first item before us is Senate Bill No. 64, which is the proposed State Entity Data Act, sponsored by Senator Gooden. We are here to listen to testimony from several persons both in support of and expressing concerns about the Bill. I ask each of our witnesses to keep their remarks concise and to the point, and ask that you not simply repeat testimony given by other persons. The first witness will be State Tax Commissioner Melissa Sandstone. Good morning, Commissioner.

Commissioner Sandstone: Thank you Senator Jones. I would like to thank you and the Committee for letting me speak today. I am not here this morning to object in general to Senate Bill No. 64, or the open government principles which the Bill seeks to further. However, the Tax Department of the State has grave concerns over the Bill if it does not except certain kinds of state-maintained data from public scrutiny. We receive and process literally three million tax returns annually from the residents of Moot. For most people, that information is extremely private. We believe it would seriously hamper the State's efforts to ensure that all qualified residents file timely and accurate returns if they thought the data would be accessible to any member of the public or press who happened to want to see it. Therefore, the Tax Department of the State requests that the Committee include appropriate exceptions in the legislation, one of which would be an exception for the tax filings of the State's individual and corporate residents, and all records at the State reflecting those filings.

Senator Jones: Thank you Commissioner. We will take your thoughts seriously. The next witness is Deputy Assistant Commissioner Audra Gillan from the Department of Public Safety. Good morning.

Deputy Assistant Commissioner Gillan: Thank you Senator. I too thank the Committee for its time this morning. We at the Department of Safety have similar concerns to Commissioner Sandstone's. In the Department of Safety, we have many confidential files relating to criminal investigations. We don't want existing or potential criminals to be able to search our data under Senate Bill No. 64, or any version of it. Do you really want criminals to be able to obtain identification data on our undercover police officers? Do you really want criminal x to find out that he is under suspicion in an open investigation? If our data is open to the public and the press, the result will be a disaster for law enforcement in our state.

Senator Jones: Thank you for your comments. We will take these into account in thinking about the legislation. Our final witness this morning is Moot State University President, John Fielder.

President Fielder: Thank you Senator, and thank you Committee. Senate Bill No. 64 presents some unique problems for Moot State University. As the State's public school of higher education, we very much believe that what we do should be out in the open for the public to see. But we have all kinds of sensitive data. We have admissions profiles for prospective students. We have tenure review files for professors. We have grade records. We have honor code investigation files. Public access to these kinds of materials raises serious privacy concerns. Yes, there may be times when data from our files should be available for review by the public or press under carefully controlled parameters. But the rights of the individuals involved need to be weighed. Moreover, no institution can function efficiently if it is constantly looking over its shoulder on access issues. For example, can you imagine the number of requests we would get from prospective employers of the 10,000 students who graduate every year, if they thought they could simply send us an e-mail asking about a student's grades? And what about the functioning of our admissions offices in each of our college units? They compete for top students from around the country and from within Moot. They offer students scholarship money to attract top applicants. We don't want every law school, medical school and business school in the United States, for example, to be able to find out our formulas for offering students places and financial aid. It would be a serious competitive problem. I would ask that you simply exempt records of Moot State University entirely from the legislation.

Senator Jones: Thank you, President Fielder. Do any of our Committee members have any questions for one or more of our witnesses before they are excused?

Senator Nelson: I have a question, and a concern. I understand the difficulties the legislation presents for specific state entities. But how do we craft exceptions that make sense and are sufficient, but do not swallow the basic rule? If we start making a lot of specific exceptions, then we run the risk of forgetting to except something important. At the same time, if we draft a whole bunch of exceptions, there may be no important data left that the public actually has access to.

Commissioner Sandstone: I would like to answer that if I may. You simply must have some exceptions. You cannot have every telemarketing company in the United States downloading our income data on Moot residents from the State's tax files. The better solution frankly would be to decree that public entity data is presumed confidential except insofar as the data directly relates to government policy-making functions, and then make only the latter data easily accessible to the public. But I understand why that could be politically unappealing to the legislature.

Senator Nelson: Well, you are certainly right about the last point. The public already thinks that we are hiding the ball too much on them. So I suppose you are right that, if we are going to presume most things are public, we will have to go ahead and draft some exceptions for nonpublic matters. I fear, however, that we are simply opening up a real can of worms. What happens under present law in the absence of a statute?

Senator Brown: My understanding is that the courts simply deal with any dispute currently on a case-by-case basis. They look at the public's interest in the data, and the historical treatment of the data, and balance all that against the privacy rights of the individuals involved.

Senator Nelson: So what's wrong with that?

Senator Wilson: Nothing, except it's an election year and Senator Gooden is in a tight race. Just kidding. Is that on the record? (Off the record brief discussion.) The problem is that a number of our colleagues think there needs to be a firm statement from this body to guide the courts.

Senator Jones: Any more questions? (Pause) Hearing none, I thank the witnesses for their remarks. We will take them under advisement. We will now take a fifteen-minute break before considering the next item on the agenda.

Whereupon, the Committee went off the record for a break at 10:35 a.m.

State of Moot, State Entity Data Act
Selected Legislative History

State of Moot Legislative Record, April 6, 1994, page 5.
Debate on Senate Bill No. 64, the proposed State Entity Data Act

Remarks of Senator Alice Gooden, chief sponsor:

"With the ever-expanding amount of data maintained by state agencies, I believe it is vital that we enact a law regarding accessibility. Many citizens already think that "big brother" is watching them. Many are suspicious of the amount of information on file, and the need for government to gather it. Still others are afraid that we are compiling mounds of inaccuracies that will never be noticed until some disaster. We need to reassure the public that government in this state is still 'by the people, for the people,' and that they can look at any government records they want."

Questions from Senator Joyce Andersen:

"I understand your logic, Senator Gooden, but I have two questions: First, what are we going to do about specific data that I think really ought to be private? For example, what about income tax files? What about school report cards? What about police investigations? Surely, you don't mean that anyone and everyone can just waltz into the relevant agency and expect to be handed any information they happen to want.

Second, what about court proceedings? When the legislature is not in session, I go back to my travel agency business. We were recently in a nasty court fight with one of my former employees, who left for a competing agency in violation of my non-competition agreement with him. I was very worried that my business plan and client contact names would wind up in a public fight, and my lawyer convinced the court to enter a protective order to keep those things confidential. Would the effect of your bill be that state entities in litigation would not be able to do the same?"

Response of Senator Gooden:

"Your points are well-taken Senator Andersen, and have also been raised on the counterpart House Bill (No. 56). I have tried to anticipate certain exceptions to the full-disclosure presumption in the statute, as well as the special issue of the courts. My suggestion is that this body refer this legislation to a joint conference committee to iron out any differences, and to report back a common bill in both houses for passage."

Whereupon, a vote was taken, and proposed Senate Bill No. 64 was referred to a joint committee of the Senate and the House for resolution of common language.

State of Moot, State Entity Data Act
Selected Legislative History

State of Moot 101st Legislature, Joint Report of Conference Committee on Senate Bill No. 64 and House Bill No. 56, dated April 27, 1994

"We the Joint Committee appointed to resolve differences between Senate Bill No. 64 and House Bill No. 56 now declare that such differences have been resolved. We adopt Senate Bill No. 64, as amended in this Joint Committee, and recommend that both the Senate and the House approve the legislation.

By way of summary, we adopt the broad presumption of public accessibility to data maintained by state agencies. This presumption is found in the third subdivision of the present amended text.

At the same time, we recognize the need for certain limited exceptions to the presumption of access to ensure appropriate privacy for individual citizens so that data is not misused by unauthorized persons or the press to harass or to embarrass individuals, and to ensure efficient government operations in such areas as income tax collection, criminal investigations, and the like. The purpose of the presumption of broad public access to state entity data is to ensure that when state agencies make policy and carry out the business of government, they do so in the open. The purpose is not to make all state entity data available to anyone who may happen to want it. Although the balance between individual privacy and open government can be difficult to maintain, we believe the present legislation achieves an appropriate balance. The exceptions to broad accessibility are found in the fourth subdivision of the present amended text.

Summary data prepared by state entities tends to raise relatively few privacy concerns for specific individuals. By definition, the aggregation of data in summary form makes it hard to identify specific persons with specific information. Accordingly, notwithstanding the exceptions in the fourth subdivision, we declare in the fifth subdivision that summary data is presumptively accessible to the public.

Finally, we recognize that the peculiarities of court processes may require the courts to fashion their own rules to handle access to state entity data in litigation matters. Nothing in this legislation is intended to overrule the Moot rules of civil or criminal procedure insofar as those rules relate to the handling of data obtained in litigation. This principle is found in subdivision six of the present amended text."

Senate Bill No. 64, as amended by the Joint Committee, was passed on May 5, 1994, by the Senate, and on May 6, 1994, by the House. The Governor signed it into law on May 9, 1994. It is codified as Chapter 100 of the Moot Statutes.

APPENDIX B

CASE RECORD #2

■ ■ ■

SMITH, ET AL. V. WILLIS, ET AL.

Note: The events and persons in this case record are fictional. No reference to persons living or dead, or to real events, is intended. Depending on instructor preference, the included dates may require modification.

United States District Court
District of Moot

Drew Smith, on behalf of Plaintiff Group One, and Logan Blake, on behalf of Plaintiff Group Two, Plaintiffs, v. Secretary of State Parker Willis, Governor Taylor Apple, Defendants.	Court File No. 20-CV-00878 Judge: Jordan Packard **Complaint** **JURY TRIAL DEMANDED**

Introduction

1. Plaintiffs are suing the Defendants because Section 6 of the Moot State Constitution disproportionately disenfranchises Black voters, in violation of the Equal Protection Clause of the Fourteenth Amendment. Plaintiffs are also suing Defendants because a recently enacted re-enfranchisement statute discriminates on the basis of wealth in violation of the Equal Protection Clause of the Fourteenth Amendment. The re-enfranchisement statute also operates as an unconstitutional tax under the Twenty-Fourth Amendment.

Jurisdiction

2. Jurisdiction of this Court arises under 28 U.S.C. §§ 1331 and 1343 for Plaintiffs' Constitutional claims.

3. This Court has personal jurisdiction over the Defendants.

4. Venue is proper pursuant to 28 U.S.C. § 1391(b) because the acts and transactions occurred in the State of Moot, Plaintiffs reside in the State of Moot, and the individual Defendants reside in the State of Moot.

5. This Court has authority to issue declaratory and injunctive relief pursuant to 28 U.S.C. §§ 2201 and 2202.

Parties

6. Plaintiff Group One is composed of Plaintiffs 1–4. These four Plaintiffs are similarly situated individuals. Plaintiffs 1–4 are all residents of the state of Moot.

7. Plaintiff One, Drew Smith, is a Black resident of Capital City, state of Moot.

8. Five years ago, Smith was the victim in a car accident. Smith hired an attorney to represent them against the other driver, and ultimately sued the driver that injured them. Smith prevailed in that lawsuit and obtained a monetary judgment.

9. Due to bad legal advice from Smith's attorney, Smith filed an insurance claim seeking to recoup lost wages from their own insurance company. Smith ultimately obtained lost wages from the driver's insurance company. Later, Smith also obtained lost wages from their own insurance company. Smith did not realize that they had received "double" payments for lost wages.

10. After the resolution of Smith's lawsuit against the driver, Smith was charged with insurance fraud—a fifth-degree felony. Only at that point did Smith realize what had happened. Smith repaid the funds and entered a plea of "nolo contendere" in December 2018. Given the underlying facts, the prosecutor agreed to three years' probation, and automatic expungement at the end of the probationary term. However, Smith still has a criminal conviction of "insurance fraud" on their record.

11. When Smith attempted to register to vote in August 2019, Smith was denied on the grounds that their conviction was a crime involving moral turpitude.

12. Plaintiffs Two, Three, and Four are each residents of Moot. Plaintiffs Two, Three, and Four are Black. Like Smith, each of them was denied voter registration on the grounds that their individual conviction(s) constituted a crime involving moral turpitude.

13. Voting is extremely important to each individual in Plaintiff Group One. As members of an underrepresented community that has faced historical discrimination, each of them strongly believes in exercising their civic duty.

14. Plaintiff Group Two is composed of Plaintiffs 5–12. These eight Plaintiffs are similarly situated individuals. Plaintiff Five, Logan Blake, is a resident of Marvelville, state of Moot. Plaintiffs 5–12 are all residents of the state of Moot. Plaintiffs 5–12 have each been convicted of a felony and have each completed their incarceration. Plaintiffs 5–12 are members of a variety of races and ethnicities. Plaintiffs 5–12 are all currently indigent. As a result, each of them is either unable to pay their entire restitution, or a balance remaining despite previous payments. Plaintiffs 5–12 were each denied voter registration on the grounds that by failing to pay their court-ordered fines and/or constitution, they had not completed all terms of their sentence.

Defendants

15. Defendant Parker Willis is the Secretary of State of Moot and, as such, is the chief election official in the state and responsible for providing uniform guidance and promulgating administrative rules for election activities. Defendant Willis is sued in their official capacity only.

16. Defendant Taylor Apple is the Governor of the State of Moot and, as such, is the chief executive officer and is charged with taking care that the laws be faithfully executed. Defendant Apple was also directly responsible for the implementation of the re-enfranchisement statute. Defendant Apple is sued in their official capacity only.

Preliminary Statement Regarding Felony Disenfranchisement

17. The State of Moot has a history of discriminating against its Black citizens. *See generally* Aff. Dr. C. Menendez.

18. At the time of statehood in 1829, the Moot Constitution excluded "from suffrage those convicted of bribery, perjury, forgery, or other high crimes or misdemeanors."

19. In 1894, after an all-white constitutional convention, the list of crimes that barred individuals from the ballot box was dramatically increased. Article VII, Section 6 ("Section 6") of the Moot Constitution provided:

   . . . those who shall be convicted of the following crimes shall be disqualified from registering and from voting: treason against the state, perjury, embezzlement of public funds, malfeasance in office, larceny or receipt of stolen property, assault and spousal battery, adultery, crimes against nature, rape, or any crime involving moral turpitude. Furthermore, any person who shall be convicted of being a vagabond or tramp, or of violating any State election law, shall be similarly disqualified.

20. The intended purpose of Section 6 was to disenfranchise Black citizens. William F. Johnston, who chaired the 1894 convention, told the delegates that the change was needed to thwart the 15th Amendment without actually running afoul of it. We are, he told the delegates, "discriminating not on account of race *per se*." *See* Aff. Dr. C. Menendez, ¶ 9.

21. Additionally, the delegates added a catch-all category, "crime involving moral turpitude" (CIMT). The intentional vagueness of this category, which was never defined by statute, allowed election officials to deny voter registration applications of prospective Black voters while allowing prospective white voters, who were convicted of similar crimes, to register and vote. *See* Aff. Dr. C. Menendez, ¶¶ 10–12.

22. Voters ratified the new constitution in November 1895 and the racially discriminatory impact soon became apparent.

Disproportionate Impact from 1895–1968

23. Between 1895 when Section 6 was ratified, and 1968 when it was amended, hundreds of thousands of individuals were convicted of felonies.

24. During this time period, voting registration was conducted in person by a voting registrar. The voting registrar would check the criminal records and if the individual had been charged with a felony, the registrar compared the charges to those listed in Section 6 of the state constitution. If there was no match, the registrar could still make a discretionary determination that the crime was one involving moral turpitude

25. Upon making the eligibility determination, voting registrars had to indicate why the registration was denied. Although there are multiple reasons why an individual could be denied, only one reason required a discretionary decision by a voting registrar: whether an individual committed a crime involving moral turpitude.

26. As part of the voting eligibility determination, along with the reason for a denial, voting registrars also had to determine, and indicate, the race and/or ethnicity of the applicant.

27. Because "crime involving moral turpitude" is neither defined in the Moot Constitution nor by statute that determination was made solely by voting registrars on an individual evaluation of each registration.

28. During this time period, 1895–1968, twenty-three percent (23%) of voting registration denials—listed the stated reason as "crime involving moral turpitude." *See* Aff. Dr. K. Williams, ¶ 7.

29. Of prospective voters subject to those discretionary denials, forty-seven percent (47%) were Black, forty-four percent (44%) were white, and nine percent (9%) were individuals identifying themselves as a member of another race or ethnicity[1]. *See* Aff. Dr. K. Williams, ¶ 8.

30. During this time period, 1895–1968, the demographics of Moot remained essentially static: 80% white, 14% Black, and the remaining 6% were members of another race or ethnicity. *See* Aff. Dr. K. Williams, ¶ 10.

---

[1] The categories as originally recorded in publicly available documents do not tally with modern census categories, but Plaintiffs' expert Dr. Kelly Williams was able to convert the information to the definitions used in the 2020 census. "Black" corresponds to the category "Black or African American alone"; "white" corresponds to "White alone, not including Hispanic or Latino" whereas "Other race and/or ethnicity" captures all of the remaining categories, including but not limited to Latinx, Native American, Pacific Islander, Asian, and individuals of two or more races. *See* Aff. Dr. K. Williams.

31. In other words, from 1895–1968, based on the population of the state, voting registrars disproportionately determined that prospective Black voters were unable to register to vote on the basis of "crime involving moral turpitude." *See* Aff. Dr. K. Williams, ¶ 11.

Constitutional Reform in 1968 Still Causes Disproportionate Impact

32. In 1968, after coming under sustained pressure from civil rights and civil liberties groups, the Governor of Moot stated "it is long overdue that we rewrite our history, our Constitution, and our criminal code, to ensure that all of our citizens are subject to both the same laws and same penalties."

33. Shortly thereafter, during the 1968 legislative session, Senator T.L. Brixton introduced a bill to amend Section 6 of the Moot Constitution by removing its racial taint.

34. When introducing the bill, Brixton explained that it was "time to clean the slate." He quoted at length from the minutes of the all-white 1894 convention with delegates explaining that the purpose of the changes was to disenfranchise Black citizens without running afoul of the Fifteenth Amendment.

35. As further proof of discriminatory intent, Brixton cited an 1896 summary *per curiam* Moot Supreme Court decision, which upheld the litany of Section 6 crimes as not discriminating against Black citizens despite express legislative intent to do just that. *See State v. Smith*, 100 Moot 26 (1896).

36. Brixton also homed in on the "crime involving moral turpitude," noting its "lengthy, and disturbing, history of being used as a thinly veiled phrase to justify discrimination against Black citizens." *See* Aff. Dr. C. Menendez, ¶ 14; Floor Debate on SB 68–42 (Oct. 10, 1968) (Remarks of Senator Brixton).

37. The version of the bill that Senator Brixton introduced would have removed all the previous disqualifying offenses from Section 6, instead replacing them with murder in the first and second degrees, felony sex offenses, burglary, robbery, and grand larceny.

38. However, an eleventh-hour amendment to the bill revived the 1892 constitution by adding "any felony crime involving moral turpitude." The sponsor, Senator LeBlanc, explained that there was nothing inherently discriminatory about the phrase, which had long been used in immigration law. It was also used by the American Bar Association in its Model Rules of Professional Conduct.

39. Senator LeBlanc is quoted in the legislative history as saying:

> The phrase 'moral turpitude' has no racial taint. Some crimes that in 1895 were thought to involve moral turpitude may not even exist today for all I know. And some might only develop in the future. And some might be committed primarily by white citizens. How do we know? We need flexibility . . . [w]e must have a catchall phrase that allows some flexibility to voting registrars.

40. LeBlanc's amendment allowed both for the state to continue with the case-by-case determination and for the legislature to define by statute the felonies that involve moral turpitude.

41. The bill with LeBlanc's amendment tacked on passed with a slim margin in both houses of the legislature and was put on the citizenry's general election ballot the same year when it passed with fifty-two percent of the votes.

42. As a result, Moot Const., Article VII, Section 6 was amended to its current form:

> . . . those who shall be convicted of the following crimes shall be disqualified from registering to vote and from voting: murder in the first and second degrees, felony sex offenses, burglary, robbery, grand larceny, and any felony crime involving moral turpitude.

43. The civil liberties and civil rights organizations that had pushed for the change supported the constitutional amendment but some of them expressed reservations about LeBlanc's amendment. The Mootville chapter of the NAACP, for example, urged its members to support the ballot initiative but made clear that "better is not good enough."

44. LeBlanc's stated rationale for introducing his amendment was most likely disingenuous. It is true that he frequently expressed concerns about Soviet electoral interference and warned about the dangers of technology and computerization. But it is equally true that he thought the 1968 debate was "political correctness run amok." *See* Aff. Dr. C. Menendez, ¶¶ 20–22.

45. While we may never know the "true" motivation behind LeBlanc's statements, we know for certain that (1) the phrase "crime involving moral turpitude" was directly transplanted from the 1892 constitution; and (2) it was added to that constitution with the express purpose of disenfranchising Black citizens.

46. Even though it had the opportunity to do so, the legislature declined to further define CIMT by statute. Instead, the meaning was determined solely by registrars on a case-by-case basis.

47. In March of 1970, the Governor of Moot expressly delegated to the Secretary of State the authority to interpret and provide guidance as to the meaning of "crime of moral turpitude." At the time, the Governor stated that the Secretary of State is "expressly charged with overseeing the transparency and validity of elections."

48. Shortly thereafter, the Secretary of State sent a two-sentence memo to all current, and future, voting registrars. The memo stated:

    "Each individual registrar shall determine the meaning of 'crime involving moral turpitude' on a case-by-case basis to allow for a comprehensive determination. If unclear, registrars are tasked with reviewing the legislative history for additional guidance."

49. Notably, that memo has not been revised, contradicted, or otherwise modified since it was distributed in 1970.

50. During this time period, 1968–2018, fifteen percent (15%) of voting registration denials listed the stated reason as "crime involving moral turpitude." *See* Aff. Dr. K. Williams, ¶ 15.

51. Of prospective voters subject to those discretionary denials, thirty-two percent (32%) were Black, ten percent (10%) were individuals identifying themselves as a member of another race or ethnicity, and fifty-eight percent (58%) were white[2]. *See* Aff. Dr. K. Williams, ¶ 16.

52. During this time period, 1968–2018, the State of Moot's population remained fairly static, 80% white, 14% Black, and the remaining 6% were members of another race or ethnicity. *See* Aff. Dr. K. Williams, ¶ 18.

53. As a result of the latest disenfranchisement provision, approximately 5% of Moot State's voting-age population has been disenfranchised.

54. That percentage rises sharply when looking at Black citizens of voting-age. 11% of Moot State's Black citizens of voting-age have been disenfranchised.

2018 Reform to Restore Voting Rights Discriminates on Basis of Wealth

55. In response to public pressure and sentiment, Governor Apple implored the legislature to enact a re-enfranchisement statute that would allow individuals convicted of a felony to register to vote.

---

[2] The categories as originally recorded in publicly available documents do not tally with modern census categories, but Plaintiffs' expert Dr. Kelly Williams was able to convert the information to the definitions used in the 2020 census. "Black" corresponds to the category "Black or African American alone"; "white" corresponds to "White alone, not including Hispanic or Latino" whereas "Other race and/or ethnicity" captures all of the remaining categories, including but not limited to Latinx, Native American, Pacific Islander, Asian, and individuals of two or more races. *See* Aff. Dr. K. Williams.

56. Governor Apple stated "[f]ifty years ago we amended our constitution to ensure that our criminal penalties are equally applied. We must continue that progress by allowing our citizens who have repaid their debt to society to exercise their voting rights."

57. In response, the Moot State legislature passed Moot Stat. § 680.95 which was signed into law by Governor Apple on April 30, 2018. Section 680.95 did not change the grounds for disenfranchisement, but it did provide an automatic mechanism for restoring the right to vote once an individual has completed "all terms of their sentence."

58. Crucially, the bill defined "all terms of sentence" as:

"(1) incarceration, probation, and/or parole; and (2) payment of all restitution, (pursuant to Moot State Stat. § 550.611), along with any additional financial obligations or penalties/fines ordered by the court as part of the sentence (collectively referred to as "legal financial obligations" or "LFOs")."

Restitution, as Defined by Moot Stat. § 550.611, Includes an Illegal Poll Tax

59. Moot Stat. § 550.611 defines restitution as:

(a) Compensation in full, which may include uninsured property loss, lost wages, uninsured medical expenses, or other losses as determined by the court, as specified in the criminal sentence;

(b) a surcharge equal to five (5) percent of the total amount determined in (a). The state shall designate a majority of the surcharges to be allocated to non-profit organizations that provide rehabilitation services to persons convicted of a felony in an effort to prevent recidivism.

The sum of these amounts comprises the restitution for each individual case and shall be payable to the clerk of court. Moot Stat. § 550.611 (last revised 2005).

60. The restitution surcharge in subsection § 550.611(b) was added in 2005, after lobbying by a handful of non-profit organizations that worked with individuals recently released from incarceration, and were seeking an additional method of funding. It is noteworthy that some similar organizations did not join the lobbying and in fact, actively lobbied against the implementation of the surcharge.

61. After hearing testimony from both sides, and engaging in a contentious debate, subsection (b) was added to the statute.

62. Since the addition of section (b) of Moot. Stat. § 550.61, the state has collected surcharges totaling $1,561,560.43. *See* Aff. Dr. K. Williams, ¶ 26.

63. Of that total, $978,450.13 has been distributed to non-profit organizations that work with individuals recently released from incarceration. Among other laudable missions, the organizations provide housing, meals, job training, and mentoring to individuals that have recently been released or paroled. *See* Aff. Dr. K. Williams, ¶ 27.

64. Despite claiming that the majority of surcharge funds would be used for rehabilitation programs, the state has fallen short of that goal. Approximately $583,110.30 have been transferred to various state departments and agencies. That amount represents 37.3% of the collected surcharges. *See* Aff. Dr. K. Williams, ¶ 28.

65. The surcharge places an additional, and unpayable, burden on persons convicted of a felony. These individuals are unable to repay the alleged financial harm they caused, per Moot Stat. § 550.611(a), let alone an additional surcharge.

66. By requiring indigent persons to pay an amount—any amount—that they are unable to pay, the state is imposing an illegal tax.

67. In the alternative, when an individual makes a partial payment towards restitution, the state applies the partial payment to the amount(s) due per Moot Stat. § 550.611(a) first. The state only applies a partial payment to the surcharge described in Moot Stat. § 550.611(b) after an individual has fully paid the amount in Moot Stat. § 550.611(a).

68. Some members of Plaintiff Group Two were able to satisfy their obligation under Moot Stat. § 550.611(a), but are currently unable to satisfy their obligation under Moot Stat. § 550.611(b).

69. As a result, the surcharge represents an illegal tax.

Summary

70. The state of Moot has a history of racial discrimination. The State may claim good intentions in amending its disenfranchisement provision, but the impact is clear: Section 6 disproportionately disenfranchises Black voters.

71. The state of Moot's recent attempt to balance these inequities, in the form of a re-enfranchisement statute, falls woefully short of its stated purpose.

72. The re-enfranchisement statute is nothing more than veiled wealth discrimination and a means for the state to collect a tax from indigent persons convicted of a felony. The newly enacted re-enfranchisement statute discriminates on the basis of wealth. It also operates as an unconstitutional poll tax.

73. Plaintiffs have suffered concrete and particularized harm because they are being denied the right to vote, in violation of their constitutional rights.

Trial by Jury

74. Plaintiffs are entitled to and hereby respectfully demand a trial by jury. US Const. Amend. 7; Fed. R. Civ. P. 38.

Causes of Action

Count 1:
Impermissible and Unconstitutional Racial Discrimination

75. Plaintiffs incorporate the foregoing paragraphs as though fully stated herein.

76. The addition of the catch-all provision "crimes involving moral turpitude" was intended to circumvent the Fifteenth Amendment and strip Black citizens of their constitutional right to vote.

77. When the state of Moot amended Section 6, it did so with the stated intention of removing the racial taint from its constitution.

78. However, the amended Section 6 still disqualifies anyone convicted of a crime involving moral turpitude from voting. That phrase is no less racist today than when it was added to the Moot Constitution and to the constitutions of similarly-situated states in the late 19th century.

79. Even since the amended Section 6 went into effect, it continues to disproportionately impact Black citizens of Moot.

80. Section 6 violates the Fourteenth Amendment because it has the effect of denying equal protection of voting rights to Black citizens of Moot on account of their race. *See Hunter v. Underwood*, 471 U.S. 222 (1985);

Arlington Heights v. Metropolitan Housing Development Corp., 429 U.S. 252 (1977).

Count 2:
Unconstitutional and Impermissible Wealth Discrimination, Fourteenth Amendment

81. Plaintiffs incorporate the foregoing paragraphs as though fully stated herein.

82. The Supreme Court has held that voting is a fundamental right. *See Richardson v. Ramirez*, 418 U.S. 24 (1974).

83. The Supreme Court has applied heightened scrutiny in cases involving wealth-based discrimination. *See Harper v. Virginia Bd. of Elections*, 383 U.S. 663 (1966); *see also Griffin v. Illinois*, 351 U.S. 12 (1956); *see also Bearden v. Georgia*, 461 U.S. 660 (1983).

84. The Supreme Court has not expressly ruled on whether heightened scrutiny applies in a situation where wealth-based discrimination implicates the right to vote. *See M.L.B. v. S.L.J.*, 519 U.S. 102, 124 (1996).

85. At least one court has relied on *M.L.B. v. S.L.J.* in applying heightened scrutiny to a claim of wealth discrimination that impacted voter rights.

86. A person convicted of a felony that is not required to pay restitution (or any other monetary amounts as part of a sentence), but has otherwise completed the terms of their sentence is eligible to vote in the state of Moot.

87. A person convicted of a felony that is required to pay restitution (along with other monetary amounts as part of their sentence), is unable to do so through no fault of their own, but has otherwise completed the terms of their sentence, is not eligible to vote in the state of Moot.

88. By requiring that individuals who are otherwise unable to pay, make payments in order to restore their voting rights, the state of Moot is impermissibly discriminating against them on the basis of wealth to deprive them of their fundamental right to vote. *See Bearden v. Georgia*, 461 U.S. 660 (1983).

89. As a result, the state of Moot is intentionally and impermissibly violating the equal protection clause of the Fourteenth Amendment.

Count 3:
Disenfranchisement for Failure to Pay LFOs, Poll Tax, Twenty-Fourth Amendment

90. Plaintiffs incorporate the foregoing paragraphs as though fully stated herein.

91. The Twenty-Fourth Amendment prohibits denying the right to vote based on failing to pay any poll or other tax.

92. The Supreme Court has applied a functional analysis to determine whether a fee is a tax or a penalty. *National Federation of Independent Business v. Sebelius*, 567 U.S. 519, 565–66 (2012).

93. A person convicted of a felony is required to pay a fixed 5% "restitution surcharge" to the State of Moot in order to register to vote.

94. That 5% surcharge is nominal and arbitrary. It is imposed in addition to monetary penalties of a criminal sentence. It bears no relationship to the crime, only the total amount of their LFO.

95. The State of Moot says that the funds are distributed to non-profits that rehabilitate persons recently released from incarceration.

96. Public records indicate that the state, however, retains a significant portion of the funds for its own purposes.

97. Despite being called a restitution surcharge, the restitution surcharge is the functional equivalent of a tax. *National Federation of Independent Business v. Sebelius*, 567 U.S. 519, 565–66 (2012).

98. For those who are otherwise eligible to vote, because they have completed all the terms of their sentence, except for the complete repayment of restitution, Moot Stat. § 680.95 denies the right to vote by implementing and requiring payment of an unconstitutional poll or other tax.

99. For those who are otherwise eligible to vote, because they have completed all the terms of their sentence, including repayment of any court-ordered restitution, but they are unable to pay the restitution surcharge, Moot Stat. § 680.95 denies the right to vote by implementing and requiring payment of an unconstitutional poll or other tax.

100. Moot Stat. § 680.95 directly conflicts with the prohibition of the Twenty-Fourth Amendment.

Request for Relief

Wherefore, Plaintiffs respectfully request that this Court:

- Issue a declaratory judgment that the above-described section of the Moot State Constitution, by its terms and as applied, violates the Fourteenth Amendment of the United States Constitution;

- Issue a declaratory judgment that Moot Stat. § 680.95, by its terms and as applied, violates the Fourteenth Amendment of the United States Constitution;

- Issue a declaratory judgment that Moot Stat. § 680.95, by its terms and as applied, violates the Twenty-Fourth Amendment of the United States Constitution;

- Enjoin Defendants, their agents, employees, and successors, and all those persons acting in concert or participation with them, from enforcing the above-described provisions of the Moot State Constitution and State Statute.

Respectfully submitted,

The Law Firm, LLC

Date: July 12, 2020

s/Austin Kennedy
Austin Kennedy (#5x9845)
509 First Avenue NE, Suite 2
Minneapolis, MN 55413

phone · 612.424.3770
email · email@thelawfirm.com

Attorney for Plaintiffs

Verification of Complaint and Certification

STATE OF MOOT

COUNTY OF CLARK

Pursuant to 28 U.S.C. § 1746, Plaintiffs having first been duly sworn and upon oath, verifies, certifies, and declares as follows:

1.   We are the Plaintiffs in this civil proceeding.

2.   We have read the above-entitled civil Complaint prepared by our attorney(s) and we believe that all of the facts contained in it are true, to the best of our knowledge, information and belief formed after reasonable inquiry.

3.   We believe that this civil Complaint is not interposed for any improper purpose, such as to harass any Defendant(s), cause unnecessary delay to any Defendant(s), or create a needless increase in the cost of litigation to any Defendant(s), named in the Complaint.

4.   We have filed this civil Complaint in good faith and solely for the purposes set forth in it.

We declare under penalty of perjury that the foregoing is true and correct.

Executed on: <u>July 12, 2020</u>   */s/Plaintiffs 1–12*
                                          Plaintiffs 1–12

United States District Court
District of Moot

Drew Smith, on behalf of Plaintiff Group One, and Logan Blake, on behalf of Plaintiff Group Two, Plaintiffs, v. Secretary of State Parker Willis, Governor Taylor Apple, Defendants.	Court File No. 20-CV-00878 Judge: Jordan Packard **Affidavit of Dr. Catherine Menendez, Ph.D.**

1. I, Dr. Catherine Menendez, having been first duly sworn, provide this Affidavit insofar as it relates to the state of Moot's history of disenfranchising voters.

2. I obtained a Ph.D from State University in New Orleans. My thesis was a broad look at the disproportionate impact of voting restrictions on diverse communities in the United States.

3. I am a tenured professor of American History at Moot State University, and I have held that position for the past fifteen years.

4. For the past ten years, the primary focus of my academic research has been on voting and labor rights during the Reconstruction—primarily on the various strategies employed by Southern states to disenfranchise Black voters. I have also published research on labor organizing among sharecroppers in Moot during the Great Depression.

5. In my view, there is little doubt that Article VII, Section 6 of the Moot State Constitution is discriminatory when considering its historical genesis.

6. After the 1870 ratification of the 15th Amendment, which prohibited states from abridging the right to vote on account of "race, color, or previous condition of servitude," at least a dozen states—including Moot—imposed various obstacles as prerequisites for voting or registering to vote. They did so in an attempt to suppress Black voters without violating the letter of the 15th Amendment. These obstacles included near-impossible literacy tests and tests of moral character, property restrictions, and grandfather clauses, which exempted voters whose ancestors could vote before the Civil War from the restrictions and tests. The intent and effect of such mechanisms were to disenfranchise Black voters while ensuring that white voters had access to the ballot box.

7. In addition to these obstacles that *de facto* disenfranchised Black citizens, states also passed laws that allowed them to do so *de jure*— that is, laws that gave them legal sanction to officially disenfranchise them. I am referring to the disenfranchisement of persons convicted of a felony. It is true that disenfranchisement for certain crimes— especially those involving fraud and dishonesty and known as "infamous" crimes—has a long history in English law. It was thought that disenfranchising criminals served both the purposes of retribution and deterrence, and this philosophy informed colony charters and state constitutions. Between 1776 and 1821, for example, eleven state constitutions either expressly prohibited those convicted of certain crimes from voting or empowered the state legislatures to pass laws to the same effect.

8. The state of Moot was no exception. The 1829 constitution gave the "general assembly the power to exclude from offices of trust within the State, and from the right of suffrage, all persons convicted of bribery, perjury, or other infamous crime." After the Civil War and with the passing of the Fifteenth Amendment, Moot legislators decided to radically expand the disenfranchisement provision to expressly bar Black citizens from voting.

9. During the all-white 1894 constitutional convention, chairman William F. Johnston did not mince his words. Johnston told delegates that the change was needed to thwart the 15th Amendment to the U.S. Constitution without running afoul of it. "We are," he told the delegates, "not discriminating on account of race per se . . . we all know what moral turpitude means."

10. The amended disenfranchisement provision included a litany of crimes. Based on my review of the legislative history and my expertise in this area, I believe that some of the originally enumerated crimes were included based on a racist intent to disenfranchise Black voters.

11. As noted in the seminal Supreme Court case *Hunter v. Underwood*, this deplorable and racist tactic was used in at least one other comparable southern state.

12. The amended Section 6 also permitted disenfranchisement for "crime involving moral turpitude" Based on my review of the legislative history, and documents related to the constitutional convention, that phrase was included as a means to discriminate against Black voters by disenfranchising them.

13. When Moot rehauled its disenfranchisement provision in 1968, the sponsor of the original amendment stated the goal was to "clean the slate." The sponsor, Senator T. L. Brixton, was well aware of the discriminatory intent of the original provision.

14. Senator Brixton unequivocally sought to eliminate "crime involving moral turpitude" from Section 6, because he knew that phrase was being applied differently to Black citizens and white citizens that were attempting to register to vote. Senator Brixton also sought to eliminate certain crimes from the provision—on the basis of disproportionate prosecution based on race.

15. At least one other state Senator, F.T.B Me, expressly supported that change. Senator Me's remarks indicate they believed the statute had been improperly applied in the past based on race. Perhaps more importantly, Senator Me clearly believed that some legislators intended to use the statute as a means to punish people based on race.

16. Immediately following that comment, Senator LeBlanc proposed the still-current version of the provision. Senator LeBlanc claimed that "crime involving moral turpitude" was necessary to give voting registrars the ability to make flexible decisions. Senator LeBlanc's comments and justifications were supported by at least one additional senator.

17. Senator Brixton was keenly aware that failing to remove that language—crime involving moral turpitude—would simply revert the state back to 1894.

18. Senator Brixton was correct. Although the updated provision contained fewer enumerated crimes, it still contained "crime involving moral turpitude." As a result, the state legislature failed to make any meaningful change.

19. With that said, there is no clear mention of discriminatory intent in the legislative record from 1968. Senator LeBlanc, for example, remarked that the phrase is used both in immigration law and in the Model Code of Professional Responsibility for lawyers with no racial taint. But this ignores the historical context of the phrase as it was used to disenfranchise Black voters in the state of Moot. It was not transplanted from the Immigration and Nationality Act nor from the American Bar Association's Model Rule. It traces its history directly back to the all-white 1894 constitutional convention and the attempts to subvert the voting rights of Black citizens.

20. However, given Senator Me's comment, I suspect that any legislator that harbored discriminatory intent would have expressed their intent by their voting in favor of the watered down amendment to Section 6 (or voting against the original proposed amendment), as opposed to expressly stating their views. For example, when the amendments were being considered, Senator LeBlanc insisted that there was no racial taint to the term moral turpitude despite clear historical evidence to the contrary. Moreover, Senator LeBlanc repeatedly said in press conferences that political correctness had run amok in this

state and had never been a good reason to alter a perfectly good voting regime. During at least one of those press conferences, Senator Post also said the good news was everyone still knew what moral turpitude meant.

21. Based on my education and specific focus on studying this area of the law, I believe the originally 1968 amendment, proposed by Senator Brixton, was intended to eliminate the racism that is a bedrock of the disenfranchisement provision.

22. However, I do not believe the latter amendment, proposed by Senator LeBlanc, shared that goal.

23. A closer review of the votes on both proposals in the state Senate supports my conclusion. In addition, when the amendment was on the general election ballot, the citizens of Moot barely voted in favor of its passage.

24. Like many other similarly situated states, the 1968 amendment appears to have done little to change the racially discriminatory impact of the provision.

I declare under penalty of perjury that the foregoing is true and correct.

Executed on: <u>July 10, 2020</u>   */s/ Dr. Catherine Menendez*
                                         Dr. Catherine Menendez, Ph.D.

United States District Court
District of Moot

Drew Smith, on behalf of Plaintiff Group One, and Logan Blake, on behalf of Plaintiff Group Two, Plaintiffs, v. Secretary of State Parker Willis, Governor Taylor Apple, Defendants.	Court File No. 20-CV-00878 Judge: Jordan Packard **Affidavit of Dr. Kelly Williams, Ph.D.**

1. I, Dr. Kelly Williams, having been first duly sworn, provide this Affidavit insofar as it relates to the state of Moot's history of disenfranchising voters.

2. I obtained my Ph.D in sociology from State University in Philadelphia. My thesis was a social equity analysis of public transit access in underrepresented and low-income communities from the passage of Title VI to 2005. I developed a novel methodology that combined census demographic data with automatically collected data on passengers' movements.

3. Over the past fifteen years, I have drafted expert affidavits and reports, in over sixty-seven cases. The majority of those cases contained allegations of racial discrimination.

4. My expertise is statistical analysis using heterogeneous datasets, and I have been retained by both plaintiffs and defendants in matters involving alleged racial discrimination.

5. According to my review of publicly available records from the Secretary of State's Office, the state has documented that 175,514 persons with criminal records had their voting applications rejected between 1898 and 1968.

6. At the time of an attempted voting registration, a voting registrar had to write the reason for a voter registration denial, along with the prospective voter's race or ethnicity. Many of the original paper records have been scanned and tallied and are electronically searchable. I reviewed all of the available records when compiling this information.

7. In the 1898 midterm election, the first after the amended Moot Constitution was ratified, twenty-three (23%) percent of the denials

were because of a "crime involving moral turpitude" (CIMT). This number remained remarkably stable from 1898 to 1968.

8. In the aggregate, during the time period of 1898–1968, of would-be voters subject to those discretionary denials, forty-seven percent (47%) were Black, forty-four percent (44%) were white, and nine percent (9%) were individuals identifying themselves as a member of another race or ethnicity[3].

9. However, it is important to evaluate changes over time rather than looking at the aggregate numbers. I decided to focus on three data points: 1898, 1932, and 1966—that is, the first election after the new provision had been in effect, a midpoint year, and the election before the 1968 amendments were ratified. The racial breakdown remained stable:

% Denials Based on Crime Involving Moral Turpitude	1898	1932	1966	% Overall Population
Black	48%	47%	46%	14%
White	44%	43%	44%	80%
Other race and/or ethnicity	8%	10%	10%	6%

10. During this time period, 1895–1966, the racial demographics in the State of Moot remained essentially static: 80% white, 14% Black, and the remaining 6% were members of another race or ethnicity.

11. Comparing the racial breakdown of these discretionary denials with the population distribution during this time period, it is clear that Black voters were disproportionately affected and to a very great extent. The proportion of Black voters who were denied is more than three times larger than would be expected.

12. I also reviewed the data for the period 1968–2018. Please note that 2018 was the most recent year of publicly available data.

13. In 1968 the state of Moot ratified an amended Section 6, purporting to remove the language it found to be inherently discriminatory against Black voters.

14. During this time period, 1968–2018, at the time of the attempted registration, a voting registrar had to either mark a checkbox, or

---

[3] The categories as originally recorded in the documents do not tally with modern census categories, but I was able to convert them. "Black" corresponds to the category "Black or African American alone"; "white" corresponds to "White alone, not including Hispanic or Latino" whereas "Other race and/or ethnicity" captures all of the remaining categories, including but not limited to Latinx, Native American, Pacific Islander, Asian, and individuals of two or more races.

simply write, the reason for the registration denial. The state has maintained these records in both paper and electronic format. I reviewed all of the available records when compiling this information.

15. During this time period, 1968–2018, fifteen percent (15%) of voting registrants were denied on the grounds of "crime involving moral turpitude."

16. In the aggregate during this time period, of prospective voters subject to those discretionary denials, fifty-eight percent (58%) were white, thirty-two percent (32%) were Black, and ten percent (10%) were individuals identifying themselves as a member of another race or ethnicity[4].

17. Similar to the earlier time period, it is important to evaluate changes over time rather than looking at the aggregate numbers. I focused on six data points starting with the midterm election of 1970, which was two years after Amendment 6 went into effect and progressing in 10-year increments with the exception of 2018, which is the latest year for which data are available.

% Denials Based on Crime Involving Moral Turpitude	1970	1980	1990	2000	2010	2018	% Overall Population
Black	39%	38%	34%	32%	29%	25%	14%
White	51%	51%	54%	57%	61%	63%	80%
Other race and/or ethnicity	10%	11%	12%	11%	10%	12%	6%

18. During this time period, 1968–2018, the racial demographics in the State of Moot remained essentially static: 80% white, 14% Black, and the remaining 6% were members of another race or ethnicity.

19. It appears that the 1968 amendment had two significant impacts.

20. One, there were fewer prospective voters denied on the basis of "crime involving moral turpitude." Specifically, that proportion dropped from 23% to 15% of the total denials.

---

4 "Black" corresponds to the census category "Black or African American alone"; "white" corresponds to "White alone, not including Hispanic or Latino" whereas "Other race and/or ethnicity" captures all of the remaining categories, including but not limited to Latinx, Native American, Pacific Islander, Asian, and individuals of two or more races.

21. Second, the amendment had an immediate albeit minor impact on the racial breakdown of "crime involving moral turpitude" denials; the gap between Black and white denials narrowed. During the time period, 1970 to 2018, the gap has continued to narrow but remains significant to this day.

22. I also reviewed publicly available information in regards to unpaid LFOs (legal financial obligations) in regards to persons convicted of a felony.

23. In regards to persons convicted of a felony, 70% of them had outstanding LFOs. Of those with outstanding LFOs, 74% of them had balances in excess of $1,000. And 42% had balances in excess of $5,000 that were unpaid.

24. The State of Moot also provides yearly information on the collection rate of LFO's. Over the past five years, the collection rate has averaged 24.5%. The Clerk of Court also states that two greatest factors that impacted collectability were indigency (30%) and incarceration (25%).

25. I also reviewed relevant statistics and information about the state's collection of restitution surcharges.

26. Based on my review of publicly available information and statistics, the state has collected $1,561,560.43 in restitution surcharges since 2005, when it began collecting those surcharges.

27. Of that total, $978,450.13 has been distributed to non-profit organizations that work with individuals recently released from incarceration. It appears those organizations provide housing, meals, job training, and mentoring to individuals that have recently been released or paroled.

28. Based on my review of publicly available information and statistics, the state has distributed approximately $583,110.30 of that to various state departments and agencies. That amount represents 37.3% of the collected amount of restitution fees.

I declare under penalty of perjury that the foregoing is true and correct.

Executed on: <u>July 20, 2020</u>   */s/Dr. Kelly Williams*
                                        Kelly Williams, Ph.D.

United States District Court
District of Moot

Drew Smith, on behalf of Plaintiff Group One, and Logan Blake, on behalf of Plaintiff Group Two, Plaintiffs, v. Secretary of State Parker Willis, Governor Taylor Apple, Defendants.	Court File No. 20-CV-00878 Judge: Jordan Packard **Memorandum Opinion and Order Granting Defendants' Motion to Dismiss**

This matter comes before the Court on Defendants' Motion to Dismiss the Complaint.

Order

Based upon the files and evidence, the briefs and arguments of counsel, and the accompanying Memorandum, the Court hereby orders that:

1. Defendants' motion is granted; and

2. Plaintiffs' Complaint is dismissed in its entirety.

Let judgment be entered accordingly.

Dated: <u>November 20, 2020</u>   <u>/s/ Jordan Packard</u>
                                       Jordan Packard
                                       Judge United States District Court

Memorandum Opinion

I.   Facts

Since becoming a state in 1829, the Moot state constitution has permitted disenfranchisement of citizens for certain crimes. In 1895, the State of Moot modified Section 6 of the state constitution. The amended Section 6 added a number of additional crimes resulting in disenfranchisement. The amended Section 6 also permitted disenfranchisement for "crime involving moral turpitude."

Over the next seventy years, twenty-three percent (23%) of prospective voters were denied on the grounds of having been convicted of a "crime involving moral turpitude." Based on the state's own public records, of those discretionary denials, forty-seven percent (47%) were Black, forty-four percent (44%) were white, and nine percent (9%) were individuals of another race and/or ethnicity[5]. During this time period, 1895–1968, the demographics of Moot remained essentially static: 80% white, 14% Black, and the remaining 6% were members of another race or ethnicity.

In 1968, the state of Moot amended Section 6. The legislative record from that session makes clear that the impetus behind the change was to ensure that the laws of the State of Moot apply equally to all people. There is conflicting information about how the legislature intended to achieve that goal. Ultimately, the amended Section 6 was approved by the citizens of Moot during a general election. Section 6 was amended in two ways. One, "lesser" crimes were removed. Two, additional felony-level crimes were added. Section 6 still permitted, and continues to permit, disenfranchisement for "crime involving moral turpitude."

Between 1968–2018, fifteen percent (15%) of voting registration denials listed the stated reason as "crime involving moral turpitude." Of prospective voters subject to those discretionary denials, fifty-eight percent (58%) were white, thirty-two percent (32%) were Black, and ten percent (10%) were individuals identifying themselves as a member of another race or ethnicity. During this time period, 1968–2018, the State of Moot's population remained fairly static, 80% white, 14% Black, and the remaining 6% were members of another race or ethnicity.

In 2005, the state of Moot added a restitution surcharge to Moot Stat. § 550.611. That surcharge adds a 5% surcharge based on the total of restitution. That surcharge is payable to the state, although the state is obligated to designate a majority of those funds to non-profit organizations that provide rehabilitation services to persons convicted of a felony in an effort to prevent recidivism. Since the introduction of the surcharge, the state has provided 62.7% of the collected amounts to those organizations,

---

[5]   It appears that one of Plaintiff's experts, Dr. Kelly Williams, went to great lengths to convert the publicly available information to correspond with current census categories. For the purposes of this memorandum, this Court will adopt Dr. Williams findings.

whereas the remainder has gone to the general fund. It is unclear if this portion will be allocated to non-profit organizations at some future date.

In 2018, the state of Moot passed a new law, Moot Stat. § 680.95, that provided a statutory mechanism for disenfranchised individuals to regain their voting rights. Upon completion of all terms of a sentence, which includes both durational terms—incarceration, probation, and/or parole— as well as monetary terms—court-ordered fines and restitution—an individual may register to vote.

II. Procedural Background

Plaintiffs commenced this action against Defendants alleging that Section 6 of the Moot Constitution is racially discriminatory and therefore unconstitutional under the Fourteenth Amendment. Plaintiffs also allege that the recently enacted re-enfranchisement statute, § 680.95, (with reference to Moot Stat. § 550.611) is unconstitutional for two reasons: impermissible wealth discrimination under the Fourteenth Amendment and an improper tax in violation of the Twenty-Fourth Amendment. Plaintiffs seek declaratory judgment that the above-cited provisions are unconstitutional.

Defendants have collectively moved for dismissal of the Complaint pursuant to Fed. R. Civ. P. 12, contending that Moot State's felony disenfranchisement provision as currently on the books does not, as a matter of law, violate the Fourteenth Amendment. Defendants assert that the provision does not discriminate in effect, and the state has gone to great lengths to remove any discriminatory taint that may have attached to it previously.

Defendants further assert that Moot Stat. § 680.95 does not violate the Fourteenth Amendment as a matter of law because it is rationally related to the state's interest in having persons convicted of a felony complete the terms of their sentence, including repaying their debt to society. Lastly, Defendants assert as a matter of law that Moot Stat. § 680.95 does not require payment of an impermissible poll tax because the LFOs are not taxes; they consist of criminal penalties and restitution—both of which categories are inextricably linked to the criminal act and part and parcel of the sentencing.

III. Legal Analysis

A. Standard for Motion to Dismiss

To survive a motion to dismiss, a pleading must contain enough facts to state a claim for relief that is "plausible on its face" and the court should accept all well-pleaded factual allegations as true. *Ashcroft v. Iqbal,* 556 U.S. 662, 678 (2009) *(citing Bell Atl. Corp. v. Twombly,* 550 U.S. 544, 570 (2007)). When examining motions to dismiss, a court has discretion to consider many types of evidence, even hearsay, if it feels that it is substantive and comprehensive enough to facilitate disposition of action. *Holmes v. TV-3, Inc.*, 141 F.R.D. 692 (W.D. La. 1991). A copy of a written instrument that is an exhibit to a pleading is a part of the pleading for all purposes. Fed. R. Civ. P. 10(c).

B. Racial Discrimination Claim

The disenfranchisement of persons convicted of a felony "has an affirmative sanction in § 2 of the Fourteenth Amendment" and does not, in itself, deny Equal Protection. *Richardson v. Ramirez*, 418 U.S. 24, 54, 94 S.Ct. 2655, 2671 (1974). However, Section 2 of the Fourteenth Amendment does not give a state *carte blanche* to engage in "purposeful racial discrimination" when enacting and enforcing disenfranchisement laws. *Hunter v. Underwood*, 471 U.S. 222, 233 (1985).

In order to prevail on a claim of racial discrimination, a plaintiff must first establish that a facially neutral statute has a disproportionate impact on the basis of race. *Id.* at 225 (*citing Vill. of Arlington Heights v. Metro. Hous. Dev. Corp.*, 429 U.S. 252, 270 (1977)). If the plaintiff can meet that burden, the inquiry does not end; the plaintiff must also establish that the challenged provision was motivated by racial animus at the time it was enacted. *Id.* If the plaintiff can meet that burden the defendant then has the burden of establishing that the challenged provision would have been enacted in any event. *Id.* However, the burden-shifting is an evidentiary standard and not relevant to a 12(b)(6) analysis. *See Hayden v. Paterson*, 594 F.3d 150, 163 n.11 (2d Cir. 2010).

In light of this precedent, the question is whether Plaintiffs have alleged facts that, if taken as true, would satisfy those two prongs—that is, disproportionate impact and racial animus as a motivating factor. Here, Plaintiffs have made a showing that barely nudges their claim "across the line from conceivable to plausible" for the first prong, but cannot—as a threshold matter of law—satisfy the second one. *See Twombly* 550 U.S. at 570.

Plaintiffs sufficiently allege that Section 6 has a disparate impact on Black voters, based on the demographics of the state. However, Section 6 was amended in 1968 with the express intent to remove any alleged racial taint. Since the 1968 amendment, prospective Black voters have been disenfranchised at rates more comparable to the overall population of the state. In other words: the amended Section 6 has blunted, and appears on its way towards curing, the alleged disproportionate impact on prospective Black voters. The court is not convinced Plaintiffs could meet their burden of proof at trial. Nevertheless, at this stage the court must accept well-pled factual allegations as true. As a result, Plaintiffs have made a sufficient showing on this prong at this stage.

Under the second prong, Plaintiffs allege sufficient facts to establish racial animus as a key motivation behind the changes wrought by the 1892 constitutional convention. The argument, however, falls apart when analyzing the impetus and motivations behind the 1968 amendment. The legislative history makes it clear that the original sponsor of the amended Section 6 wanted to "clean the slate." Quite simply, the State made an overt and conscious effort to revise Section 6 to remove any racial animus.

Two of our sister circuits have held that subsequent changes—no matter if they restrict or broaden the categories of crimes subject to disenfranchisement—remove any racial taint that originally may have existed. *Compare Johnson v. Governor of Florida*, 405 F.3d 1214, 1223 (11th Cir. 2005) (holding that a substantial 1968 amendment to Florida's disenfranchisement laws, which restricted the class of felons barred from voting and was enacted with no evidence of racial bias, removed the taint as a matter of law) *with Cotton v. Fordice*, 157 F.3d 388, 391 (5th Cir. 1998) (holding that subsequent changes to Mississippi's disenfranchisement statute, which broadened it by adding additional crimes in an effort to remove any historical bias, removed the racial taint associated with the original version).

Plaintiff repeatedly asserts that "crime involving moral turpitude" is a vague term and perhaps carries a nefarious intent. The Supreme Court, however, has expressly declared otherwise. "No case has been decided holding that the phrase is vague, nor are we able to find any trace of judicial expression which hints that the phrase is so meaningless as to be a deprivation of due process." *Jordan v. De George*, 341 U.S. 223, 230 (1951).

In addition, the State recently enacted a re-enfranchisement provision designed to provide persons convicted of a felony a clear avenue to regain their voting rights. The court notes that Plaintiff provides a rather detailed explanation of the justifications for the 1968 amendment. Even accepting all reasonable inferences based on some potentially curious statements (and perhaps non-statements), the state removed any and all original taint in the enactment of the provision. As a result, this claim fails as a matter of law.

C. Proper Level of Scrutiny in Regards to Alleged Wealth Discrimination

"No state shall . . . deny to any person within its jurisdiction the equal protection of the laws." U.S. Const. amend. XIV, § 1. The Supreme Court has only required a rational basis justification, in deference to the legislature, when reviewing most state classifications. *See Romer v. Evans*, 517 U.S. 620, 631 (1996). When a law classifies either in a suspect way, or in a manner that burdens fundamental rights, those classifications are subject to more heightened scrutiny. *See Loving v. Virginia*, 388 U.S. 1, 11 (1967).

Plaintiffs urge us to apply heightened scrutiny to the matter at hand. Plaintiffs rely on a limited number of decisions where the Supreme Court applied heightened scrutiny to wealth discrimination. *See Harper v. Virginia Bd. of Elections*, 383 U.S. 663 (1966) (applying heightened scrutiny to a poll tax; *see also Griffin v. Illinois*, 351 U.S. 12 (1956) (applying heightened scrutiny to access to a criminal appeal); *see also Bearden v. Georgia*, 461 U.S. 660 (1983) (applying heightened scrutiny to poverty-based imprisonment). Notably, neither the Supreme Court, nor any of our sister circuits, have applied heightened scrutiny in this particular context.

Defendants, on the other hand, make the case for rational scrutiny. Defendants have the better argument by far. Plaintiff is indeed walking down a lonely road, and one that this Court is not inclined to go down. It is abundantly clear that persons convicted of a felony do not have a fundamental right to vote. *See Richardson*, 94 S. Ct. at 2671. *See also Wesley v. Collins*, 791 F.2d 1255, 1261 (6th Cir. 1986) (holding that the right to vote of persons convicted of a felony is not fundamental.). It is equally clear that "wealth" is not a suspect classification and thus not subject to heightened scrutiny. *See San Antonio Indep. Sch. Dist. v. Rodriguez*, 411 U.S. 1, 29 (1973).

Both the Sixth and Eleventh Circuits have examined this particular issue, and applied rational basis scrutiny to the statutes at issue. *See Johnson v. Bredesen*, 624 F.3d 742, 746–50 (6th Cir. 2010); *see also Jones v. Gov. of Fla.*, 975 F.3d 1016 (11th Cir. 2020).

Plaintiffs argue that the novel line of reasoning in the now overruled panel decision in *Jones* (and the dissent in the *en banc* decision) should embolden this Court to blaze a new trail. *See Jones v. Gov. of Fla.*, 950 F.3d 795 (11th Cir. 2020), *overruled by Jones v. Gov. of Fla.*, 975 F.3d 1016 (11th Cir. 2020). The court is admittedly impressed with the novelty and creativity of the 11th Circuit's panel reasoning in *Jones*—particularly the "open the door" argument. However, intellectual admiration is insignificant grounds for trailblazing uncharted territory. And in addition, the 11th Circuit's initial decision in *Jones* only applied heightened scrutiny to some of the plaintiffs who were genuinely unable to pay, not the entire class of persons convicted of a felony. *Jones*, 950 F.3d at 795.

In sum, this Court is not inclined to disregard the body of caselaw on this issue and chooses to base its decisions on settled Supreme Court precedent directly germane to the issue of disenfranchisement and the well-reasoned decisions of our sister circuits. Creative analogies have their place in our jurisprudence, for sure, but here *Richardson* and *San Antonio Independent School District* speak directly to the questions at issue. There is no fundamental right to vote and wealth is not a suspect classification. This Court will apply rational basis review.

Wealth Discrimination Claim

To survive rational basis scrutiny, a re-enfranchisement statute must only be rationally related to legitimate government interests. *See Johnson*, 624 F.3d 742; *see also Jones*, 975 F.3d 1016. Traditional rational basis review is highly deferential to government action. *F.C.C. v. Beach Commc'ns, Inc.*, 508 U.S. 307, 313 (1993). In fact, "a legislative choice is not subject to courtroom fact-finding and may be based on rational speculation unsupported by evidence or empirical data." *Id.*

The parties similarly disagree as to the scope of the review. Plaintiffs have pursued an "as-applied" claim and believe the law should be evaluated as to them. Defendants have argued, and persuasively, that rationality should be applied to the "typical" person convicted of a felony who is impacted by the re-enfranchisement statute.

Here, it is a close call as to whether Plaintiffs' group of indigent prospective voters is actually representative of the typical person convicted of a felony that is impacted by the re-enfranchisement statute. Plaintiffs have presented evidence that indicates perhaps they are representative, and this indeed may be the case. For example, 70% of persons convicted of a felony had unpaid and outstanding LFOs. Of that group, 74% had balances in excess of $1,000 and 42% had balances that were in excess of $5,000. The state has also disclosed that the collection rate from persons convicted of a felony is only 24.5%.[6]

On the other hand, while 70% of persons who have a felony on their record have unpaid LFOs, 25% of that group is currently incarcerated, paroled, or on probation. These individuals are ineligible to vote irrespective of LFO status as they have not yet completed the durational terms of their sentences. In other words, regardless of whether the person convicted of a felony paid their LFO, they would still be ineligible to vote because they are still serving their sentence. Removing that group of individuals from the 70% firmly brings that group into the "toss-up" categorization and it is far from obvious whether the indigent plaintiffs represent the "mine run" case of a felon with LFOs. As a result, this Court believes that Plaintiffs' group of persons convicted of a felony is not representative of the "typical" person impacted by the statute.

To be clear, this Court's application of rational basis is to the group at large—all persons convicted of a felony. When applied to this group, the statute is rationally related to a legitimate government interest.

The state has presented three main rationales behind the enactment of Moot Stat. § 680.95: making sure that victims of crimes receive restitution, ensuring persons convicted of a felony repay their debt to

---

[6]   This tends to indicate that a large proportion of persons of felonies were ordered to pay large amounts of restitution, based on the financial damage caused by their individual acts.

society, and helping persons convicted of a felony reintegrate into society by collecting a surcharge that pays for support programs. The first two rationales have repeatedly survived rational basis review by other courts. That is true for one clear reason: they are laudable and prudent goals. Incentivizing restitution, for example, serves the dual purpose of making the victim of a crime whole while deterring would-be criminals. The reintegration program provides for rehabilitation. This Court is concerned about the third rationale. Those concerns, however, are more fully addressed later in this opinion.

Even with that concern, however, the third goal does not undercut the state's main rationale here, and ultimately, the statute does not discriminate on the basis of wealth as to all persons convicted of a felony.

D. Poll Tax Claim

The Twenty-Fourth Amendment provides that a citizen's right to vote "shall not be denied or abridged by the United States or any State by reason of failure to pay any poll tax or other tax." U.S. Const. amend. XXIV, § 1. At least three circuit courts have considered whether financial obligations that are part of a criminal sentence are a poll tax. *See, e.g., Johnson,* 624 F.3d at 751; *Jones,* 975 F.3d at 1039; *Harvey v. Brewer,* 605 F.3d 1067, 1080 (9th Cir. 2010). All three courts emphatically decided the answer was no. *Johnson* 624 F.3d at 751; *Jones* 975 F.3d at 1039; *Harvey* 605 F.3d at 1080.

Defendants point to those decisions, along with a recently dismissed claim in Alabama, and say there is simply no need to engage in a rigorous analysis. Plaintiffs, however, direct the court again to *Jones*. Plaintiffs argue that while the 11th Circuit cited the proper legal test in *Jones*, it failed to completely apply the test properly, and as a result reached the wrong result. *See Jones,* 975 F.3d at 1038, applying *Nat'l Fed'n of Indep. Bus. v. Sebelius,* 567 U.S. 519, 565–66 (2012). The court agrees that the functional approach from *National Federation of Independent Business v. Sebelius* in regards to a Twenty-Fourth Amendment claim is sound and will apply it to the matter at hand. That approach requires a close examination of three key factors to determine whether an exaction is a penalty or a tax: (1) the size of the exaction; (2) the scienter requirement; and (3) the enforcer of the exaction. *Nat'l Fed'n of Indep. Bus. v. Sebelius,* 567 U.S. 519, 565–66 (2012).

Before turning to that analysis, it is important to note that the Twenty-Fourth Amendment makes an important distinction between "poll" taxes—that is, a fixed sum payable by everyone—and "other" taxes. The majority opinion in *Jones* dismisses the relevance of legislative history of the amendment. The dissent in *Jones* does not, and its examination of the legislative history bolsters the argument that the "other tax" provision is one of broad applicability. The payment of money, Representative Dante Fascell told his colleagues in the House when the soon-to-become amendment was debated in 1962, "whether directly or indirectly, whether in a small amount or in a large amount should never be permitted to reign as a criterion of democracy." 108 Cong. Rec. at 1765 (remarks by Rep Fascell).

That said, applying the functional test to the restitution requirements of a criminal sentence can only lead to one conclusion: not a tax. Applying the test to the surcharge, on the other hand, calls for a more rigorous analysis.

The larger the exaction the less likely it is to be a tax, and the presence of a scienter requirement suggests a penalty rather than a tax. *See Nat'l Fed'n of Indep. Bus.* 567 U.S. at 565–566. Here, the size, or amount, of the surcharge straddles the line between tax and non-tax territory. Depending on the overall amount of restitution, five percent could represent a significant balance. The court does not believe this factor weighs strongly in favor for either side, and turns to the remaining two factors.

In terms of scienter, the restitution surcharge does not appear to be a tax. Judicial officers devote significant time and reasoning into determining the restitution element of a sentence.

The enforcer of the exaction and the recipient of the recouped surcharge bear additional scrutiny. The state says that the surcharge is collected to fund agencies and entities that provide services to assist persons recently released from incarceration to rehabilitate themselves as they rejoin society. That is indeed a worthy and rational goal. However, in *National Federation of Independent Business*, the court reasoned that the recipient of the funds/fees is an important element. Here, the majority of the funds do go to non-state organizations. A portion of the fee does go to the state. Plaintiffs argue that this fact alone is sufficient to establish the restitution surcharge as a tax. This indeed is a valid concern. However, the majority of the surcharge is passed along to other entities. And although this Court admits that another court may feel differently, this Court does not believe that the fee can, as a threshold matter of law, be considered a tax.

In sum, the exaction is neutral. The scienter requirement weighs in favor of the state. And the final factor, while admittedly concerning, also weighs in favor of the state. As a result, the restitution surcharge is a penalty, not a tax.

For all of the foregoing reasons, Defendants' motion is granted and Plaintiffs' complaint is dismissed in its entirety.

Dated: <u>November 20, 2020</u>   */s/Jordan Packard*
                                        Jordan Packard
                                        Judge United States District Court

1829 Moot State Constitution Article VII, Section 6

The elections shall be forever free and fair and no property qualification for eligibility to office, or for the right of suffrage, shall ever be required in Moot. Every white male citizen of the United States, of the age of twenty-one years, who shall have been a resident of Moot six months preceding the election, shall be entitled to vote at any and all elections.

However, the General Assembly shall exclude from suffrage those convicted of bribery, perjury, forgery, or other high crimes or misdemeanors.

1895 Moot State Constitution Article VII, Section 6

The elections shall be forever free and fair and no property qualification for eligibility to office, or for the right of suffrage, shall ever be required in Moot. Every male citizen of the United States, of the age of twenty-one years, who shall have been a resident of Moot six months preceding the election, shall be entitled to vote at any and all elections.

However, those who shall be convicted of the following crimes shall be disqualified from registering and from voting: treason against the state, perjury, embezzlement of public funds, malfeasance in office, larceny or receipt of stolen property, assault and spousal battery, adultery, crimes against nature, rape, or any crime involving moral turpitude. Furthermore, any person who shall be convicted of being a vagabond or tramp, or of violating any State election law, shall be similarly disqualified.

1969 Moot State Constitution Article VII, Section 6

The elections shall be forever free and fair and no property qualification for eligibility to office, or for the right of suffrage, shall ever be required in Moot. Every citizen of the United States, of the age of eighteen years, who shall have been a resident of Moot three months preceding the election, shall be entitled to vote at any and all elections.

However, those who shall be convicted of the following crimes shall be disqualified from registering to vote and from voting: murder in the first and second degrees, felony sex offenses, burglary, robbery, grand larceny, and any felony crime involving moral turpitude.

Partial Legislative History for Moot State
Statute § 550.001
(1968 Legislature Senate Bill 68–42)

MINUTES OF THE FLOOR DEBATE ON SB 68–42 IN
THE SENATE ON THURSDAY, OCTOBER 10, 1968.

<u>Remarks of Senator T.L. Brixton, sponsor of the proposed bill</u>:

The purpose of this bill is to amend Section 6 of the Moot Constitution to remove its racial taint. This matter will ultimately require a vote of the citizens of Moot as a Constitutional amendment, but the first step in the process is for this body to pass legislation proposing the change. The House has already passed the companion bill by a vote of 65 in favor, and 35 opposed.

I will briefly summarize the history that has led us to this moment.

The State of Moot has a sad history of discriminating against its Black citizens both in terms of crime-conviction rate and in terms of voting rights.

At the time of our statehood in 1829, the Moot Constitution excluded from "suffrage those convicted of bribery, perjury, forgery, or other high crimes or misdemeanors."

In 1894, after an all-white constitutional convention, the list of crimes that barred individuals from the ballot box was dramatically increased. Article VII, Section 6 ("Section 6") of the Moot Constitution provided:

> those who shall be convicted of the following crimes shall be disqualified from registering and from voting: treason against the state, perjury, embezzlement of public funds, malfeasance in office, larceny or receipt of stolen property, assault and spousal battery, adultery, crimes against nature, rape, or *any crime involving moral turpitude* (emphasis added). Furthermore, any person who shall be convicted of being a vagabond or tramp, or of violating any State election law, shall be similarly disqualified.

The express purpose of Section 6 was to disenfranchise Black citizens of Moot. William F. Johnston, who chaired the 1894 convention, told the delegates that the change was needed to thwart the 15th Amendment to the U.S. Constitution without running afoul of it. "We are," he told the delegates, "not discriminating on account of race per se . . . we all know what moral turpitude means."

They added catch-all categories, such as crimes which could be described as "involving moral turpitude" (CIMT). The vagueness of such categories, which were never defined by statute (because "we all know what moral turpitude means"), allowed election officials to deny applications of Black citizens convicted of a felony to register and vote while allowing white citizens convicted of a felony to register and vote.

On top of that, the new provision also included crimes that fell far outside of the historical idea of "high crimes." Given Johnston's thinly veiled statement, it is clear that some of those crimes were included for the express purpose of disproportionately disenfranchising our Black citizens. For example, we know that white citizens of Moot were rarely, if ever, prosecuted for vagrancy.

Voters ratified the new constitution in November 1895. In *State v. Smith*, 100 Moot 26 (1896), our Supreme Court upheld Section 6 and its enforcement as valid and non-discriminatory. Yet, the racially discriminatory impact soon became apparent.

Between 1895 when Section 6 was ratified, and now in 1968, tens of thousands of individuals have been convicted of felonies. During this time period, voting registration was conducted in person by a voting registrar. As part of the voting eligibility determination, voting registrars had to determine, and indicate, the race and/or ethnicity of the applicant. The voting registrar then would check the criminal records and if the individual had been charged with a felony, the registrar compared the charges to those expressly listed in Section 6 of the state constitution. If there was no match with an expressly denominated crime, the registrar could still make a discretionary determination that the crime was one involving moral turpitude. Although there were multiple reasons why an individual could be denied, only one reason required a discretionary decision by a voting registrar: whether an individual committed a crime involving moral turpitude.

Because "crime involving moral turpitude" was neither defined in the Moot Constitution nor by statute, that determination was made solely by voting registrars on an individual evaluation of each registration ("We all know what moral turpitude means.") During this time period, from 1895 to now, twenty-three percent (23%) of voting registration denials listed the stated reason as "crime involving moral turpitude." I have been repeatedly told by the Secretary of State that compared to the overall population, prospective Black voters are disenfranchised at a much higher rate compared to prospective white voters. That is resoundly unjust.

Our Governor has recently stated "it is long overdue that we rewrite our history, our Constitution, and our criminal code, to ensure that all of our citizens are subject to both the same laws and same penalties." Now I say, "it is time to clean the slate." Given the lengthy, and disturbing history of moral turpitude as a thinly veiled phrase to justify discrimination against our Black citizens, I propose to amend Section 6 of the Moot Constitution in its entirety by striking all its previous language and by identifying the voter disqualifying offenses as only murder in the first and second degrees, felony sex offenses, burglary, robbery, and grand larceny.

I therefore propose that Section 6 read as follows:

> Those who shall be convicted of the following crimes shall be disqualified from registering to vote and from voting: murder in the first and second degrees, felony sex offenses, burglary, robbery, and grand larceny.

I yield the balance of my speaking time.

Remarks of Senator F.T.B Me:

Mr. Speaker, may I be heard in support of Senate Bill 68–42?

The Speaker: Yes, you may Senator Me.

Senator Me: I rise in support of Senate Bill 68–42. "Moral turpitude" has never had a proper place in our constitutional language. It means whatever its beholder has in mind. We know that our predecessors in the legislature, and I frankly suspect some of our colleagues still today, would have in mind the use of the phrase to punish persons based on the color of their skin and not on the nature of their actions. That has no place in our law.

. . . .

Remarks of Senator J.P. LeBlanc:

Mr. Speaker, may I be heard for purposes of an amendment to Senate Bill 68–42?

The Speaker: Yes, you may, Senator LeBlanc.

Senator Le Blanc: There is nothing inherently discriminatory about the phrase "moral turpitude", which has long been used in immigration law. It is also used by the American Bar Association in its Model Rules of Professional Conduct.

The phrase 'moral turpitude' has no racial taint. Some crimes that in 1895 were thought to involve moral turpitude may not even exist today for all I know. And some might only develop in the future. And some might be committed primarily by white citizens. How do we know? We need flexibility. What if future developments in telephony and computing will allow our citizens to vote fraudulently by pushing a button multiple times from the comforts of their home? What if a citizen is working with the Russians to interfere with our election processes? Would that conduct constitute one of the felonies identified in Senator Brixton's proposed language? Would a citizen convicted of those activities be allowed to register and vote in the future just because the conduct is not one of Senator Brixton's enumerated felonies? Yet, we could certainly say such conduct would be reprehensible and morally turpitudinous. We must have a catchall phrase that allows some flexibility to voting registrars.

I propose amending Senate Bill 68–42 to read as follows:

> Those who shall be convicted of the following crimes shall be disqualified from registering to vote and from voting: murder in

the first and second degrees, felony sex offenses, burglary, robbery, grand larceny, and any felony crime involving moral turpitude.

. . . .

The Speaker: Senator LeBlanc has offered an amendment to Senate Bill 68–42. Does anyone wish to speak for or against the amendment?

. . . .

Remarks of Senator A.L. Post:

Mr. Speaker, may I be heard in support of Senator LeBlanc's amendment?

The Speaker: Yes, you may Senator Post.

Senator Post: I rise in support of Senator LeBlanc's amendment. I see no reason to expansively give persons convicted of a felony the right to vote. Voting registrars need to have the ability to make case-by-case determinations whether a person convicted of a felony should be able to exercise an important constitutional right even after they have served their time.

Remarks of Senator T. L. Brixton:

Mr. Speaker, may I be heard in opposition to Senator LeBlanc's amendment?

The Speaker: Yes, you may Senator Brixton.

Senator Brixton: I vehemently oppose Senator LeBlanc's amendment. It restores the very language that is problematic. I personally assume that the restoration of the language about moral turpitude just puts us back again in 1894.

. . . .

. . . .

VOTING ON SB 68–42

A vote was first taken in the Senate on Senator LeBlanc's amendment to the Senator Brixton bill. The LeBlanc amendment passed with a vote of 51 in favor, 47 against, and 2 abstentions.

A vote was then taken in the Senate on Senate Bill 68–42 as amended by the LeBlanc Amendment. Senate Bill 68–42 was then passed with a vote of 54 in favor, 42 against, and 4 abstentions.

A vote was then taken in the House on Senate Bill 68–42, substituting for the prior companion legislation passed in the House. The House passed Senate Bill 68–42 in its final form by a vote of 58 in favor, and 42 against.

The citizens of Moot then voted in the general election for a constitutional amendment adopting the language of Senate Bill 68–42. The amendment received 52% of the popular vote and the constitutional amendment became effective.

The following is an excerpt from a news bulletin distributed by the Mootville chapter of the NAACP during the 1968 legislative session

———

Update on the Most Recent Legislative Session—Please Review and Vote!

The state legislature has passed a proposed constitutional amendment in regard to Section 6.

Like many of you, we believe this amendment falls far short of what is needed. Quite simply, better is not good enough. We are committed to push for future changes to ensure Section 6 is equally applied to all.

However, the proposed amendment is an improvement over the current version. With that in mind, we encourage you to support, and vote, in favor of this amendment.

The following is an excerpt from a memorandum sent from the Governor of Moot to the Secretary of State in April 1970

———

To: Secretary of State Paris

From: Governor Dell

April 4, 1970

Dear Secretary of State Paris,

As you are well aware, Section 6 of our state constitution has recently been amended.

You are expressly charged with overseeing the transparency and validity of elections in the state of Moot.

As a result, you are hereby authorized, and duly charged, to interpret and provide guidance as to the meaning of "crime involving moral turpitude" as it pertains to Section 6.

Regards,

Governor Dell

The following is an excerpt from a memorandum sent from Secretary of State Paris to current, and future, voting registrars.

————

To: Voting registrars

From: Secretary of State Paris

April 15, 1970

Dear Voting Registrars:

Each individual registrar shall determine the meaning of "crime involving moral turpitude" on a case-by-case basis to allow for a comprehensive determination. If unclear, registrars are tasked with reviewing the legislative history for additional guidance.

Regards,

Secretary of State Paris

2020 Moot Statutes

§ 550.611 Restitution (all criminal convictions and nolo contendere pleas)

   (a) Compensation in full, which may include uninsured property loss, lost wages, uninsured medical expenses, or other losses as determined by the court, as specified in the criminal sentence;

   (b) a surcharge equal to five (5) percent of the total amount determined in (a). The state shall designate a majority of the surcharges to be allocated to non-profit organizations that provide rehabilitation services to persons convicted of a felony in an effort to prevent recidivism.

   The sum of these amounts comprises the restitution for each individual case and shall be payable to the clerk of court.

   (last revised 2005).

§ 680.95 Re-enfranchisement

   (a) Re-enfranchisement. Any person convicted of a felony automatically regains their individual voting rights once they have completed all terms of their sentence, as defined in (b).

   (b) All terms of sentence. (1) incarceration, probation, and/or parole; and (2) payment of all restitution, (pursuant to Moot State Stat. § 550.611), along with any additional financial obligations or penalties/fines ordered by the court as part of the sentence (collectively referred to as "legal financial obligations" or "LFOs").

   (last revised 2005).

APPENDIX C

MODEL BRIEF

■ ■ ■

Note: The following are excerpts from a sample appellate brief. You may find it helpful to review the brief in conjunction with the mock oral argument in Appendix D, which relates to the same problem.

STATE OF MOOT

COURT OF APPEALS

NO. 21–XXXX

MILLBROOK TAYLOR,

    Appellant,

vs.

MOOT STATE DEPARTMENT
OF SOCIAL SERVICES,

    Appellee.

BRIEF OF MOOT STATE DEPARTMENT OF SOCIAL SERVICES.

[NAME OF FIRM] Christopher Soper # Andrew Prunty #	[NAME OF FIRM] Randall P. Ryder # Bradley G. Clary # Evan Nelson #
Main Street Moot Telephone: Email:	Main Street Moot Telephone: Email:
ATTORNEYS FOR APPELLANT	**ATTORNEYS FOR APPELLEE MOOT STATE DEPARTMENT OF SOCIAL SERVICES**

SUMMARY OF THE CASE

This case involves Millbrook Taylor, a private daycare in the State of Moot. Taylor's only claim is that Moot Health and Safety Code § 159 is an invalid exercise of the State of Moot's police power under the Tenth Amendment.

The State of Moot has broad police powers to protect the health and wellbeing of its citizens. In *Jacobson v. Massachusetts* and in *Zucht v. King*, the U.S. Supreme Court ruled that states have broad discretion to protect public health so long as they do not act arbitrarily or unreasonably. The State of Moot acted purposefully and reasonably in enacting Moot Health and Safety Code § 159, a mandatory vaccination law for all daycares. The State's interest in protecting the public from communicable diseases outweighs any alleged personal privacy interest asserted by the Taylor Daycare. The District Court correctly weighed those interests in holding that § 159 is a permissible use of state police power under well-settled precedent.

The state police power ruling in this case is entirely straight forward. An allotment of five minutes to each party would be sufficient time within which to address the issue.

. . .

TABLE OF CONTENTS

TABLE OF AUTHORITIES

Page No.

CASES

CONSTITUTION

STATUTES AND RULES

PRELIMINARY STATEMENT

This is an appeal, insofar as Taylor is concerned, from an Order dated September 27, 2020, of the Honorable Ethan P. Schulman of the Moot Superior Court, County of Mootville. In its order, the Superior Court granted summary judgment in favor of the Appellee, holding that Moot Health and Safety Code § 159 does not violate the Tenth Amendment of the United States Constitution.

Jurisdiction of this Court on appeal is invoked pursuant to Moot Rules of Appellate Procedure.

STATEMENT OF ISSUE

Whether Moot Health and Safety Code § 159 is a reasonable exercise of the State of Moot's inherent power police to protect the health and safety of its citizens under the Tenth Amendment?

The District Court correctly held yes.

Most apposite cases and statutory provisions:

U.S. Const., amend. X

Jacobson v. Massachusetts, 197 U.S. 11 (1905)

Zucht v. King, 260 U.S. 174 (1922)

STATEMENT OF THE CASE

A. Overview.

Appellant brought this action seeking to invalidate Moot Health and Safety Code § 159 on the grounds it was an unconstitutional exercise of Moot State's police power under the Tenth Amendment.

In 2011 and 2015, there were two significant measles outbreaks in Moot. In response, the Moot State legislature, in conjunction with the Moot State Department of Health, drafted and enacted Moot Safety and Health Code § 159. Section 159 requires that "a person shall not be employed or volunteer at a daycare center if he or she has not been immunized against influenza, pertussis, and measles." Section 159 contains an exemption for individuals determined by a physician to be medically unfit for the vaccine.

Millbrook Taylor is the sole proprietor and operator of a daycare facility in Stillwater Bay since 2017. At the beginning of the 2017 school year, Millbrook Taylor ("Taylor") hired Parker Jordan ("Jordan") to serve as Director of Early Childhood Development. Jordan has a fear of needles that is rooted in a family member's reaction to a childhood vaccine. Based on Jordan's representations, but without a physician's determination that Jordan was medically unfit to receive the vaccine, Taylor granted Jordan an exemption to the vaccination policy.

In January 2018, the Moot Department of Social Services ("MDSS") conducted a routine inspection of Millbrook Taylor Daycare. As a result of the inspection, MDSS notified Taylor that Jordan was unvaccinated and, thus, Millbrook Taylor Daycare was in violation of § 159. As a result, MDSS acted on its statutory authority and began assessing daily civil penalties against the Daycare, which it paid.

In response, Taylor filed the present lawsuit. The parties filed cross motions for summary judgment at the trial court. Taylor's position was that § 159 was an arbitrary and unreasonable exercise of the State of Moot's police power for two reasons. First, § 159 is arbitrary because it only applies to individuals employed at daycares. Second, § 159 is unreasonable because it fines Taylor for refusing to infringe on Jordan's liberty interest in personal privacy.

The State's position was that it has a duty to protect the health of its citizens and § 159 is a permissible exercise of its power under the Tenth Amendment for three reasons. First, mandatory vaccination statutes like § 159 have been upheld since the U.S. Supreme Court decided *Jacobson v. Massachusetts*, 197 U.S. 11 (1905) over a hundred years ago. Second, § 159 was enacted in response to two recent disease outbreaks in Moot. Section 159 was drafted and passed after close consultation with the State Department of Health. Third, Jordan's alleged harm is speculative, at best. Even assuming Jordan suffers minor side effects, the State's interest in public health outweighs Jordan's personal liberty interest.

The Honorable Ethan P. Schulman of the Moot Superior Court granted judgment in favor of MDSS on September 27, 2020. The trial court relied on *Jacobson* in holding that Section 159 was a permissible exercise of Moot's police power in an effort to protect the health and wellbeing of its citizens.

B. Facts*

1. Widespread Usage of Vaccines Has Eradicated Dangerous Diseases.

The widescale implementation and acceptance of vaccines has transformed public health and led to a significant reduction of communicable diseases. (R. at 16.) In the early 20th Century, parts of the country were overtaken by a lethal virus called smallpox. (R. at 19.) To combat this epidemic, states enacted mandatory vaccination laws and courts upheld those laws due to the great risks our communities would face without such protection. (R. at 14.) Since this epidemic, states have continued to use vaccines to protect their communities from both smallpox and other communicable diseases. (R. at 55.) Diseases are becoming rare because of vaccinations. (R. at 35.) Experts suggest that vaccines have caused the complete disappearance of targeted diseases. (R. at 24.)

2. School and Daycare Vaccinations Prevent Outbreaks

According to medical professionals, school vaccination requirements are critical to preventing outbreaks of communicable diseases. (R. at 13.) All 50 states, the District of Columbia, and Puerto Rico require proof of immunization for public schools and childcare facilities. (R. at 71.) Studies indicate that where there is legislation requiring immunization for school participation, immunization rates increase, and the incidence of vaccine-preventable diseases decreases dramatically. (R. at 73.) In states with progressive mandatory vaccination requirements, outbreaks occur at a much lower rate, compared to states with less progressive requirements. (R. at 76.)

---

* The proper citation form depends on which appellate courts you are in. For example, some of the formats include: (R. at ___.); (Joint Appendix at ___.); (R. at ___., Complaint ¶ ___.) For the purposes of this model brief, we have adopted (R. ___.)

3. Broad Vaccination Exemption Requirements Pose a Risk to Herd Immunity.

Herd immunity is a critical companion to mandatory vaccination statutes in the fight against dangerous diseases. (R. at 69.) Despite their general effectiveness, vaccines can be unsafe or ineffective for certain individuals. (R. at 70.) Herd immunity is a critical way to protect those who cannot be vaccinated for medical reasons. (R. at 71.) Herd immunity occurs when "nearly all [medically qualified] individuals" have received proper immunization. (R. at 72.) School immunization requirements are designed to protect children by building high community immunity. (R. at 70.) Population immunization rates of at least 90% are required to achieve community immunity (and at least 95% for highly contagious diseases, e.g. pertussis and measles). (R. at 71.)

Where local laws permit broader non-medical exemptions immunization rates decrease and disease rates increase. (R. at 72.) A substantial portion of the medical community supports eliminating non-medical exemptions and regard them as an unnecessary risk to public health since outbreaks are linked to under-immunized communities. (R. at 70.)

4. In Response to Two Dangerous Measles Outbreaks, Moot Enacted a Vaccination Statute to Protect Children in Daycare Centers.

In 2011, an unvaccinated child was exposed to measles and, upon returning to the community, the child caused 20 additional cases and 14 hospitalizations in Moot. (R. at 14.) Shortly thereafter, in 2015, a widely publicized measles outbreak occurred at a Happy Funland, a popular amusement park in Moot. (R. at 16.) The 2015 outbreak was more severe than the 2011 outbreak. (R. at 18.) The outbreak resulted in fifty additional cases and twenty-four hospitalizations. (R. at 19.)

In response, the Moot legislature considered additional vaccination requirements to prevent a future outbreak. (R. at 26.) The state legislature worked closely with the State Health Department to determine the most effective and reasonable solution. (R. at 28.) Ultimately, the consensus was clear: a mandatory vaccination statute with limited exceptions for medical necessity only. (R. at 29.) Section 159 requires that "a person shall not be employed or volunteer at a daycare center if he or she has not been immunized against influenza, pertussis, and measles." (R. at 33.) Section 159 also contains an exemption, for any individual that is deemed medically unfit by a physician. (*Id.*) Because of the nature of the vaccine, pre-school children cannot receive the vaccine. (*Id.*) In passing § 159, the legislature stated that § 159 was "one of many protective measures by the State to prevent harmful outbreaks of vaccine-preventable diseases." (R. at 39.)

Following enactment of § 159, the State Health Department provided guidance on administration of the statutory requirements. (R. at 42.) Similarly, the State Health Department has vigorously enforced the statute for years. (R. at 44.)

5. Millbrook Taylor Hired Parker Jordan Without a Vaccine

Millbrook Taylor ("Taylor"), operates an independent elementary school in Stillwater Bay (R. at 9.) Millbrook Taylor has a school policy to enforce[e] all Moot vaccination laws. (R. at 14.) Taylor recommends that all enrolled students receive the vaccinations required by Moot law and recommended by the CDC. (R. at 8.)

At the beginning of that 2017 school year, Millbrook Taylor hired Parker Jordan ("Jordan") to serve as Director of Early Childhood Development. (R. at 14.) At the time of her hiring, Jordan was discussing a number of employment opportunities with other schools and non-profit organizations. (*Id.*). Jordan has a fear of needles based on her brother's adverse reaction to a chickenpox vaccination as a child. (R. at 15.) Jordan alleges that her brother suffered a severe headache and significant arm pain after receiving the vaccination. (*Id.*) Since that experience, Jordan has refused any medical treatment, including vaccinations, that involve a needle. (*Id.*) Jordan has neither sought, nor received a medical-based exemption from vaccinations. (*Id.*) Based solely on Jordan's statements, Taylor granted Jordan an exemption to the vaccination policy. (*Id.*) This is the first and only accommodation Millbrook Taylor has granted where there is a risk of physical harm to others due directly to the exemption. (R. at 14.)

In January of 2018, the Moot Department of Social Services ("MDSS") conducted a routine inspection of Millbrook Taylor consistent with MDSS's policies. (R. at 29.) This inspection revealed that Jordan was unvaccinated and, thus, Millbrook Taylor Daycare was in clear violation of § 159. (R. at 31.) MDSS notified Millbrook Taylor of its violation and gave it a period to rectify the deficiency and become compliant. (R. at 32.) Millbrook Taylor failed to become compliant and retained Jordan as an employee, disregarding Moot law. (R. at 34.) As a result, MDSS acted on its statutory authority and began assessing daily civil penalties against Millbrook Taylor, which the daycare paid. (R. at 31.)

6

II. SUMMARY OF ARGUMENT

This case is about a state's duty to protect and preserve public health through a reasonable and necessary vaccination requirement for persons who work with children in daycare centers. In enacting and enforcing § 159, the State of Moot rationally and reasonably exercised its police power. This court should affirm the District Court's grant of summary judgment and hold that § 159 should be enforced against the Appellant for three reasons.

First, since deciding *Jacobson* over a hundred years ago, the Supreme Court has repeatedly upheld mandatory vaccination laws that advance the public health and safety, so long as they are not arbitrary or unreasonable. *Jacobson v. Massachusetts,* 197 U.S. 11 (1905). Here, Section 159 was enacted under similar circumstances to *Jacobson* and for the same purpose: to protect its citizens against a dangerous disease.

Second, § 159 is neither arbitrary nor unreasonable. The State of Moot enacted a narrow vaccination requirement for daycare centers in direct response to two significant public health emergencies. Because pre-school children cannot receive this particular vaccine, § 159 is designed to protect teachers entrusted with their care. Notably, Section 159 also contains an exemption for those deemed medically unfit to receive the vaccine.

Third, the State's interest in preventing communicable diseases outweighs the Appellant's individual liberty interest. Mandatory vaccination laws have been upheld even when there is a minor infringement on an individual liberty interest. Here, Appellant's claimed interest is speculative, at best. Section 159 is narrow, reasonable, and designed to protect the most vulnerable members of the population: children. This court should affirm the district court's grant of summary judgment and hold that § 159 should be enforced against the Appellant.

III. ARGUMENT

A. Standard of Review.

A grant of summary judgment is reviewed *de novo. Sandoval v. County of Sonoma,* 912 F.3d 509, 515 (9th Cir. 2018). "[V]iewing the evidence in the light most favorable to the nonmoving party," the Court must determine "whether there are any genuine issues of material fact and whether the [lower] court correctly applied the relevant substantive law." *Wallis v. Princess Cruises, Inc.,* 306 F.3d 827, 832 (9th Cir. 2002).

When *de novo* review is required, the Court reviews the issues with fresh eyes and does not defer to lower court judgments. *Salve Regina College v. Russell*, 499 U.S. 225, 238 (1991).

B.   Section 159 is a Valid and Reasonable Exercise of Moot's Police Power.

1.   Rational Basis Is the Appropriate Level of Scrutiny to Apply to Mandatory Vaccination Laws.

The state police power is a broad right reserved to the states granting them authority to enact regulations to "promote the health, peace, morals, education, and good order of the people." *Barbier v. Connolly*, 113 U.S. 27 (1884). Under the police power, states are authorized to restrict, within limits, the rights and liberties of their citizens for the "general good." *Id.* at 32. Restrictions imposed by states under the police power are judged by their reasonableness and must be directed at carrying out a public purpose. *Id.*

2.   Section 159 Is Rationally Related to Its Stated Goals.

Under rational basis scrutiny, a statute must only be rationally related to a legitimate state interest. *Heller v. Doe by Doe*, 509 U.S. 312, 319–20 (1993). The enacting legislature need not choose the least restrictive means for achieving the regulation's purpose. *Id.* at 330. A legislature is not required to articulate its rationale for a regulation analyzed under rational basis, and courts must accept a generalized statement "even when there is an imperfect fit between means and ends." *Id.* at 321.

Here, the express purpose of § 159 is to prevent outbreaks of communicable diseases in Moot. A sensible way of putting that goal into practice, as determined by the State, is to require all those who enter daycare premises be vaccinated. By prohibiting unvaccinated persons from entering facilities, the state can efficiently and reliably reduce the likelihood of passing any vaccine-preventable diseases along to children. Section 159 also furthers the State's goal in maintaining herd immunity. Herd immunity is an important method of protecting individuals, like the children of Moot, that are unable to receive certain vaccinations.

In the alternative, Jordan's position that § 159 could be less restrictive is not persuasive in light of the court's rationale in *Heller*. First, § 159 only applies to a valuable group in society—those entrusted with caring for children. Second, any further reduction of § 159's already narrow focus would reduce its effectiveness. As noted in a recent study, states with the most progressive vaccination statutes have the greatest success in preventing outbreaks. The State's actions were not only rational, they were grounded in widely-accepted findings in the medical community.

3. Courts Have Consistently Upheld Mandatory Vaccination Laws in the Face of Personal Privacy Rights.

The State's enactment of § 159 follows well-settled precedent in regards to mandatory vaccination laws. For over a hundred years, courts have consistently recognized the validity of mandatory vaccination laws for the purpose of protecting public health, safety, and welfare. *See Jacobson v. Massachusetts,* 197 U.S. 11 (1905)*; see also Zucht v. King,* 260 U.S. 174 (1922). The Supreme Court has repeatedly held that the public interest in health and safety, specifically with regard to mandatory vaccinations, is superior to personal privacy rights.[1] *Jacobson,* 197 U.S. 11; *Zucht,* 260 U.S. 174.

In *Jacobson,* the Supreme Court upheld a mandatory vaccination statute amid a smallpox outbreak. *See Jacobson,* 197 U.S. at 12. The vaccination statute in *Jacobson* was imposed on all residents of Cambridge, MA. *Id.* The Court held that there are certain circumstances under which exemptions should be permitted: arbitrary, oppressive, or unreasonable applications of the law which go beyond what is reasonably required for the safety of the public. *Id.* at 28. The Court specifically recognized a medical exemption in situations where a person is unfit for vaccination and it would be "cruel and inhuman in the last degree" to require. *Id.* at 38. Ultimately, the Court determined that the defendant fell outside any of the permissible exemptions and had to submit to vaccination despite expressing concerns based on past adverse reactions to vaccine treatments. *Id.* at 37. The Court's ruling was unequivocal: mandatory vaccination laws are not only constitutional, but also desirable to protect public health and subject to only very narrow exemptions. *Id.*

This court should follow the Court's reasoning in *Jacobson* and find that § 159 is not arbitrary, unreasonable, or oppressive. Similar to *Jacobson,* § 159 was enacted in response to a significant public health event. The State has taken proactive steps to protect against a foreseeable and preventable disease outbreak. And like *Jacobson,* § 159 does not require vaccinations of those who are medically unfit.

---

[1] The Supreme Court's per curiam majority opinion in Roman Catholic Diocese v. Cuomo, 141 S.Ct 63 (2020) does nothing to undo these fundamental principles as it focused on the potential conflict between public safety and free exercise of religion. There is no free exercise issue in the present case.

There are two notable factual differences from *Jacobson* that support the State's actions here. First, unlike the defendant in *Jacobson*, Jordan only presents speculative evidence that she would suffer a negative medical reaction from a vaccination. Jordan's fear of needles, while understandable, does not rise to the level of evidence of physical harm or being medically unfit. Unlike the defendant in *Jacobson*, Jordan has only alleged an adverse reaction for a family member—not herself. Second, Moot has enacted a narrow vaccination statute. Section 159 only applies to individuals that choose to work in the daycare industry. The mandatory vaccination statute in *Jacobson* was much broader—a blanket vaccination requirement based on residency. Jordan is required to be vaccinated only because of her decision to seek employment in the daycare industry, one of many areas of employment available to her.

4. States Can Enact Mandatory Vaccinations Even Without a Public Health Emergency

Even if this court holds that the two recent measles outbreaks were not a public health emergency, the State's enactment of § 159 is a permissible proactive effort to protect the community. In *Zucht*, the Court upheld an ordinance which operated to exclude Plaintiff from attending both public and private schools for refusing vaccinations. *Zucht*, 260 U.S. at 175. In its ruling, the Court made no mention of any emergency, immediacy, urgency, or the like. *Id. at* 174. Nonetheless, the Court upheld the ordinance based on the state's "broad discretion required for protection of the public health." *Id.* at 177.

Zucht demonstrates that mandatory vaccination laws do not depend on a *Jacobson*-like "emergency," i.e. enacted in response to an active outbreak. Further, the law at issue in *Zucht* established a prerequisite for attending school, versus for accepting employment in the daycare industry. Requiring vaccination for school attendance is a much harsher restriction than requiring it for employment in a discrete professional field. School attendance is much more fundamental to our notions of individual rights compared to unfettered employment autonomy.

The law upheld in *Zucht*, similar to that in *Jacobson*, is far more restrictive than § 159 and, as such, should guide this court in upholding § 159. Here, Jordan has numerous employment opportunities available to her. Working in a physical daycare facility is not the only job available and applicable to her area of expertise. By refusing to comply with the vaccination requirement, Taylor and Jordan are not simply placing their own health at risk—they are risking the health and safety of the children entrusted to their care. And indirectly, they are also putting any child they encounter in harm's way.

This is exactly what § 159 and the laws in *Jacobson* and *Zucht* are designed to protect against. It is the duty of the State of Moot "primarily to keep in view the welfare, comfort, and safety of the many, and not permit the interests of the many to be subordinated to the wishes or convenience of the few," which is precisely what Taylor and Jordan would cause to occur if they are not required to comply with § 159 is allowed. *Jacobson,* 197 U.S. at 29.

5. Plaintiffs' Purported Contra Authority is Distinguishable.

Plaintiff erroneously relies on *Cruzan* to argue that Jordan's personal liberty interest outweighs the State's interest in preserving public health. *Cruzan v. Missouri,* 497 U.S. 261 (1990). In *Cruzan,* the Court weighed a state's interest in preserving life versus a guardians' rights to end life support for a patient in a vegetative state. *Id.* Plaintiff's reliance on *Cruzan* is misplaced for two reasons.

First, in *Cruzan,* the individual had a more significant liberty interest—the right to live. *Id.* at 262. Here, Jordan's interest is not comparable—a fear of needles and a speculative fear of potential side effects from a vaccine. Second, even so, the Court ruled in favor of the state in *Cruzan,* holding that the state's interest outweighed the individual liberty interest. This Court should engage in the same weighing of interests and reach the similar result: the State's interest is more compelling.

CONCLUSION

In enacting § 159, the State of Moot followed over a hundred years of well-settled precedent. States have a clear and established power to protect their citizens, so long as the state's use of that power is neither arbitrary nor unreasonable.

Here, the State took purposeful and reasonable action. The State acted in response to two outbreaks of a dangerous disease. The State conferred with the State Department of Health and relied on well-accepted data about the impact of vaccines and the importance of herd immunity. Section 159 was enacted to protect children by requiring vaccinations for a small subset of the population. And for individuals who are medically unable to receive the vaccination, they can request an exemption.

The historical impact of vaccinations is clear: fewer outbreaks of communicable diseases and enhanced public health. Current events demonstrate the devastating impact when a vaccine is not available for a communicable disease.

Section 159 is rational, reasonable, and specifically designed to protect the most vulnerable members of the population. The State of Moot has a duty to protect its citizens and has done so in a way that only has a minor, and permissible, impact on individual privacy. This court should uphold the District Court's ruling that validated § 159 as a valid and reasonable exercise of the State's police power.

Respectfully submitted,

Date:

[NAME OF FIRM]

By _____
Randall P. Ryder, #
Main Street
Utopia
Telephone:
Email:

[NAME OF FIRM]
Bradley G. Clary #
Main Street
Utopia
Telephone:
Email:

Evan Nelson, #
Main Street
Utopia
Telephone:
Email:

ATTORNEYS FOR APPELLEE

APPENDIX D

MOCK ORAL ARGUMENT

■ ■ ■

Note: This mock oral argument is based upon the model brief in Appendix C for ease of student use. The argument has been fictionalized and condensed to try to illustrate succinctly certain oral argument techniques. Before you study the argument, review the presentation guidelines and typical questions identified in Part 3—Oral Argument. Then look for examples in the mock argument.

Oral Argument in *Taylor v. Moot State Dep't of Soc. Serv.*
By counsel for Appellee Moot State Dep't of Soc. Serv.

[Counsel] May it please the Court.	The traditional opening for a court of appeals argument.
I am Brad Clary. I am here today on behalf of [alternatively: I represent] Appellee the State of Moot Department of Social Services.	Especially if appearances have not already been entered, but even if they have been, you should remind the court who you are and whom you represent. Do not use an abbreviation such as SMDSS without first using the full name.
[Alternatively: I am Brad Clary. My co-counsel, Randall Ryder, and I are here today on behalf of Appellee the State of Moot Department of Social Services.]	[Re-introduce co-counsel if you are splitting argument time.] Give the court a thematic anchor for the argument. Keep this short. However you frame the theme (because you may have several potential choices), plan to work it into the rest of the argument.
This case is about preserving public health through a reasonable and necessary vaccination requirement for persons who work with children in daycare centers.	

Moot Health and Safety Code § 159.7 says that, "a person shall not be employed or volunteer at a daycare center if he or she has not been immunized against influenza, pertussis, and measles."	Introduce the key legal provision(s).
The Tenth Amendment to the U.S. Constitution says that, "The powers not delegated to the United States by the Constitution, nor prohibited by it to the States, are reserved to the States respectively, or to the people."	Identify the key specific legal issue(s) the court must decide to resolve the appeal. Note how the framing of the issue connects it with the identified theme.
The issue in the case is whether Code Section 159.7 is a valid exercise of Moot's police power under the Tenth Amendment to protect children in daycare from dangerous childhood diseases.

The answer is yes, and you should affirm the district court's grant of summary judgment for three reasons:

    1.   The U.S. Supreme Court in *Jacobson v. Massachusetts* and in *Zucht v. King* has specifically ruled that the States have broad discretion to protect public health if they do not act arbitrarily or unreasonably.

    2.   Moot's mandatory vaccination law is neither arbitrary nor unreasonable.

    3.   The U.S. Supreme Court has never ruled that a worker has a | Answer your own issue statement. Tell the court what you want it to do and why. Give the court a road map of the one, two, or three key reasons for doing what you want it to do. Tell the court up front if you have three reasons to list; telling the court you have three reasons increases the chances the court will listen for all three before it interrupts with a question. Notice that now the court knows everything it needs to know to rule in your favor. If questions now re-arrange the order or focus on only one piece of the argument, so be it. |

fundamental right to avoid a vaccination when balanced against a State's reasonable public health interest.

[Court] Counsel, before you begin discussing the State's police power, can you tell me if there is any question as to how to interpret the relevant Moot Code section?

Expect and welcome questions. You are engaged in a dialogue, not a speech. Questions give you insight into what the court is thinking. Questions will typically probe the definitional parameters of the relevant legal test.

[Counsel] No, there is no real dispute in the present case as to statutory interpretation, your Honor. The statute's plain language requires daycare volunteers and employees to be vaccinated against the three named diseases. The legislature's conference committee reports and floor debates considered and expressly rejected exceptions. The same reports and debates evidence a widely shared consensus in a broad public health purpose for the statute. The State Health Department's regulations explain how the statutory requirement is to be administered, and the Health Department has been rigorously enforcing the statute and the Department's regulations for years. Plaintiff's argument is solely that the statute infringes on Plaintiff's individual liberty interest in bodily autonomy.

Give simple, direct answers. If the question calls for a yes or a no, then try first to say yes or no, and then give the explanation. Here, briefly describe the standard statutory interpretation analysis and then move on. Of course, if there were a material dispute over the meaning of the statute, the response to the question would have to be more detailed.

[Court] All right. So let's move to the issue of the police power of the State under the Constitution. First, what is our standard of review on appeal of the summary judgment decision? Second, are

These are typical kinds of questions: What is our standard of review? Are there any material fact disputes? What about the legal merits?

there any material fact disputes that preclude summary judgment? Third, on the merits, how broad is the State's police power?

[Counsel] First, your Honor, the standard of review on appeal is de novo on the legal question of the State's constitutional power.

Second, the material facts giving rise to this case are essentially uncontradicted. We insist that the Plaintiff's worker be vaccinated to work in daycare; Plaintiff's worker flatly refuses; Plaintiff is suing us to invalidate the statute; the data is clear regarding the relevant diseases and vaccine; the Court can evaluate the balance of interests as a matter of law.

Third, the State's police power in the public health and safety arena is very broad, if it is reasonably exercised.

[Court] But you lose if it is not?

[Counsel] No. We lose if the exercise of the power is <u>both</u> unreasonable <u>and</u> so unreasonable as to be arbitrary. Here it is neither.

Pay attention to the standards that will apply to the procedural posture on appeal. In the hypothetical, the appeal is from the grant of a summary judgment motion. The rules of procedure require that there be no material fact disputes for summary judgment to be granted as a matter of law. A respondent in such a setting will almost invariably in one way or another be asked if there are any material fact disputes.

Again, give simple, direct answers.

Let's take the measles vaccine part of the statutory provision, for example. The measles data in the record at page (R. at 68.) shows that before there was a measles vaccine in 1963, approximately ninety percent of American children were infected with the measles virus by age fifteen. The record (R. at 70.) also shows that roughly twenty-eight percent of children under age five who contract measles require hospitalization. The record (R. at 71.) shows that children who do not get a measles vaccine are thirty-five more times likely to contract measles. But the record (R. at 75.) shows children of pre-school age are too young to safely receive the vaccine. Therefore Plaintiff's argument fails when Plaintiff suggests we should just vaccinate the children themselves. We need the *adults* who work with those children in daycare to be vaccinated. That is neither arbitrary nor unreasonable.

[Court] What is your authority for the reasonableness test?

[Counsel] The State chiefly relies on the U.S. Supreme Court's decisions in *Jacobson v. Massachusetts* and in *Zucht v. King*.

In *Jacobson*, the Massachusetts Board of Health had passed a regulation requiring all inhabitants of Cambridge to be

Figure out in advance of the oral argument whether there are questions you must concede, and then concede them. Here you have offered a two-part test. You concede only if you lose under both parts. Then expand on the "why" of your argument.

You have stated a form of two-pronged "even if" test in the present case. ("We win for reason number one. Even if we do not win for reason number one, we win for reason number two.") So, another way to answer the Court's question could be: "No, your Honor, we do not, because the test is not mere unreasonableness. *Even if* the Court thought the statute unreasonable in some way, the statute is still valid unless it is so far beyond what is reasonably required for the health of children that it is both unreasonable and arbitrary."

Cite to specifics in the record. Specifics tend to be more persuasive than generalities.

If you are in an opportune position to do so, especially when you are respondent, consider including a reference to the adversary's argument and identifying the true focal point of debate.

Expect the "what is/are your best case(s)" question. Be prepared to identify one or more, and to succinctly explain its/their application to your case.

immunized against smallpox. Jacobson challenged the mandate on the ground that it infringed his liberty interests. The Court ruled that a mere infringement on an individual liberty interest is not automatically unconstitutional, but only when the infringement is unreasonable. The Court upheld the Massachusetts regulation under the State's police power.

In *Zucht*, a San Antonio ordinance required mandatory vaccination of public and private school children as a prerequisite for attending school. The petitioner challenged the ordinance as a deprivation of liberty, but the Supreme Court ruled that "broad discretion [is] required for the protection of public health."

The same logic applies in this case.

[Court] Aren't those cases old?

[Counsel] Yes, your Honor, 1905 and 1922, respectively. But they have not been overruled and are still the law. They have been guiding the States for a century.

[Court] But at the time *Jacobson* was decided, wasn't there a serious smallpox problem in Cambridge? The necessity of the mandatory vaccination regulation was clearer in that case than it is in the present case, wouldn't you say?

If there are one or more truly landmark cases, do not be afraid to get into their facts. You can usually explain those in one succinct paragraph if you have prepared in advance.

Be prepared to give a cite for the quote if the Court wants one: 260 U.S. at 177.

Be prepared to explain why any key case you are citing is not problematic. If a case is a landmark one, do not shy away from it just because it is old, if it still makes sense in the present. *Stare decisis* is an important and useful principle. We need predictability in the law.

Again, be prepared to explain why any key case you are citing is not materially distinguishable.

[Counsel] Yes, in part, and no in part, your Honor. I agree that the presence of a smallpox outbreak in *Jacobson* demonstrated the urgency of the regulation there. But the mere fact that we do not have an outbreak in the present case does not mean the State should ignore precautions to *prevent* an outbreak. Turning again to measles, for example, the data is clear that measles outbreaks are back on the rise. And of course, influenza and pertussis remain serious problems.

[Court] Are there Supreme Court cases where the Court has upheld an individual liberty interest as against forcible injection of medication? I am thinking of decisions such as *Cruzan v. Director, Mo. Dep't of Health* in 1990. How do you balance the individual interest of the worker and the public interest in children's health in the present case?

[Counsel] Yes, your Honor, there is another line of cases. But in cases like *Cruzan*, the Court was addressing the right of an individual to refuse hydration and nutrition, even where the refusal would lead to death of that individual, in circumstances where the only effect would be on the relevant individual. Even in that setting, the Court upheld the right of the state to define the evidentiary factors applicable to the individual right. The Court

The Court is now moving into the third point you made in your opening introduction. You must be ready to discuss a balancing test.

Expect the Court to ask you to address the other side's key authorities. You must be ready to directly address any contrary authority that might be on the Court's mind. Often, this might involve a slippery slope argument. Much appellate argument comes down to slippery slope problems: "Look at the consequences, Court, of adopting the other side's legal position in comparison to mine." Ideally, you are advocating a legal test which will allow your client to prevail when applied in the present case and yet also will not put the court on a slippery slope in other cases. Here, you are not telling the Court that another line of cases is wrongly decided, but instead that the line's extension will create bad law in third party injury scenarios.

Note the use of the theme: The State's duty is to protect the health of children.

ruled in favor of the State on the factors in that case and I am not aware of any Supreme Court case rejecting something like a vaccination requirement where the public safety of thousands of third persons (here, children) is at stake.

[Court] But how should we weigh the balance if, for example, Plaintiff's worker in this case has already had the measles as a child? What if Plaintiff could establish that (1) a person who has already had and recovered from measles cannot pass the disease on to a child, and (2) this worker personally has already had measles long ago? Would that make application of the mandatory vaccination statute arbitrary as applied to the Plaintiff's worker in this case in that the public safety of third persons would not truly be at stake?

Try to anticipate hypothetical line-drawing questions. Courts will often suggest alternative scenarios to test the limits of a lawyer's proposed legal solution for a case and thereby to test whether there are slippery slopes involved.

[Counsel] In theory, yes that could be a different equation, your Honor. But here the Plaintiff has not argued that the relevant worker has already had measles. So the issue is not before the Court. Moreover, we know that influenza, for example, comes in many seasonal variations. So just because the worker may have recovered from a prior case of flu, for example, does not mean the worker could not pass along flu to a child presently. The vaccination statute speaks to influenza, pertussis, *and* measles.

The Court is still testing the line. Be ready for that.

[Court] So let's test out your logic. Suppose the State of Moot passes a statute that requires all persons to wear a face mask when in public to prevent transmission of the coronavirus. And suppose an individual challenges that statute as a violation of the individual's liberty interest. Would that statute be valid?	
[Counsel] Absolutely, your Honor, as long it is reasonable and not arbitrary. So, in your hypothetical, as long as the State was concerned about the health of the public, and there was reasonable scientific evidence that wearing a mask would help prevent spread of coronavirus, and the State did not act arbitrarily, the statute would be valid and enforceable.	Still more line testing.
[Court] What about a statute mandating a coronavirus vaccine for daycare workers?	
[Counsel] Yes, that statute would be valid, but the same legal test applies. A vaccine is more intrusive than a mask. But let's suppose the data indicates the vaccine is effective in adults. Let's suppose the vaccine is not effective in young children. Let's suppose there are serious side effects from coronavirus in children of daycare age. Let's suppose we need to keep daycares open so that parents can drop their children off and return to places of employment to keep the economy functioning. Requiring	

the daycare workers to be vaccinated in that scenario would be neither unreasonable nor arbitrary in the public interest.

[Court] What's your view about the applicability of the Supreme Court's per curiam majority opinion in *Roman Catholic Diocese v. Cuomo*?

[Counsel] That opinion was on a temporary injunction procedural issue in a case where New York set limits on the number of attendees at religious services. But there is no issue of free exercise of religion in Taylor Daycare's case.

[Court] So, in the end, what do you want us to rule?

[Counsel] You should rule as a matter of constitutional law that States have broad discretion to protect public health if they do not act arbitrarily or unreasonably. Moot's mandatory vaccination law is neither arbitrary nor unreasonable. Therefore the law is valid and may be enforced against Plaintiff.

Thank you.

Be ready to tell the Court in the end exactly what ruling you want, and then, if you have said everything that really needs to be said, say thank you and sit down! An oral argument is not an exercise in filling up time.

APPENDIX E

GOLDILOCKS FACT
DEVELOPMENT EXERCISE

■ ■ ■

Developing facts is a critical part of advocacy. In the following chart, read the facts on the left, and then consider the available tools in the middle column. Now decide if you represent Goldilocks, or the Three Bears, and use the tools to re-characterize facts in a manner that is favorable to your client. Use the right column to indicate which tool(s) you used and write your new fact(s).

Facts

10 year old Goldilocks ran away from her parents after being grounded, and got lost in the woods.

After awhile, she became hungry, and smelled food. She came upon a house and could see three bowls of fresh porridge just inside the kitchen. She could also see a pot of porridge on the stove.

The front door was open. Goldilocks hesitated to see if anyone was home. Not seeing anyone, she dashed inside and grabbed a bowl.

As she grabbed the bowl, she tripped. When she tripped, it caused a chair to fall over and crack one of its legs.

She then ran out of the house, ate the porridge, and placed the empty bowl on the front step before leaving.

The occupants of the house—papa bear, mama bear, and baby bear—were very sad. While they were outside playing, an intruder had entered their house during baby bear's first birthday. The intruder had eaten his porridge, and broken his new chair made by Grandma bear.

Tools

Re-order the facts

Create new facts by combining/ summarizing

Add/change adjectives

Add/change adverbs

Re-characterize within reason

Minimize "bad" facts

Start with a theme

Add headings

Create new fact (something missing)

Repeat an important fact

Emphasize or highlight a particular fact

"Hide" a bad fact

Tool:

New Fact:

Tool:

New Fact:

Tool:

New Fact:

Here are two examples of how attorneys representing Goldilocks and the Three Bears might reframe the facts.

Facts	Goldilocks Facts	Three Bears Facts
10 year old Goldilocks ran away from her parents after being grounded, and got lost in the woods.	A young girl found herself isolated in an unknown place, and took necessary measures to protect her well being.	A family's special celebration was ruined, and an irreplaceable gift was ruined, by an unwelcome trespasser.
After awhile, she became hungry, and smelled food. She came upon a house and could see three bowls of fresh porridge just inside the kitchen. She could also see a pot of porridge on the stove.	After a disagreement with her parents, Goldilocks sought refuge in a nearby forest. After a considerable amount of time, and realizing she could not find her way home, Goldilocks needed to take steps to sustain herself.	The bear family was about to celebrate Baby Bear's first birthday. They had prepared porridge, set the table, and were going to give him his first chair. The chair had been hand-made by Grandma bear.
The front door was open. Goldilocks hesitated to see if anyone was home. Not seeing anyone, she dashed inside and grabbed a bowl.	Drawn in by the smell of sustenance, she was lured to a welcoming house. She then saw an abundance of food, but nobody was eating it. In fact, she could not even see anyone in the house.	Instead of celebrating, it was a day of infamy.
As she grabbed the bowl, she tripped. When she tripped, it caused a chair to fall over and crack one of its legs.	After realizing the front door was open, she carefully checked to see if the house was indeed vacant.	While they were outside, an intruder snuck into their house. The intruder ate the birthday meal, and destroyed baby bear's first chair.
She then ran out of the house, ate the porridge, and placed the empty bowl on the front step before leaving.	Upon confirmation, she obtained a small portion of the available food— enough to sustain her hunger. Mindful of her actions, she carefully returned her used utensils to the house.	The cold-hearted vandal even left the empty bowl on the front step as a callous reminder of their destructive and disruptive visit.
The occupants of the house—papa bear, mama bear, and baby bear— were very sad. While they were outside playing, an intruder had entered their house during baby bear's first birthday. The intruder had eaten his porridge, and broken his new chair made by Grandma bear.	There was still an entire table of food, along with a bowl of unused hot porridge for the occupants. Although a chair was knocked over, the damage was very minor.	

APPENDIX F

USE OF UNPUBLISHED OPINIONS

■ ■ ■

In April 2005, the Advisory Committee on the Federal Appellate Rules of Practice and Procedure of the Judicial Conference, chaired by then-Third Circuit Judge and now-Supreme Court Justice Samuel Alito, recommended the adoption of a new rule, Federal Rule of Appellate Procedure 32.1, that requires federal appellate courts to permit citation of unpublished judicial opinions and orders. A year later, in April 2006, the U.S. Supreme Court adopted the Committee's recommended rule change and the new rule became effective on January 1, 2007.

The rule applies only to unpublished opinions issued after January 1, 2007. Accordingly, local circuit court rules may continue to restrict or prohibit the citation of unpublished opinions issued before that date. The rule does not address whether attorneys are allowed to cite these unpublished opinions as binding precedent or merely persuasive authority. The rule requires parties that cite unpublished opinions to file and serve copies of these opinions unless they are available in publicly-accessible electronic databases, such as Westlaw. The new rule does not provide guidance as to which opinions should be unpublished. In fact, the recent debate over unpublished opinions has focused principally on whether parties can legitimately use such opinions and the value of such opinions and not on whether appellate courts should issue them.

Even before the Supreme Court amended Rule 32 of the Federal Rules of Appellate Procedure, there was a trend in the state appellate courts toward abandoning the prohibition on the use of unpublished opinions.[1] In those courts where prohibitions on the use of unpublished opinions are still in effect, parties may consider petitioning the court for a designation change—to make the opinion published.

Notwithstanding the liberalization of appellate court rules regarding the use of unpublished opinions, appellate litigants still need to consider that such opinions may be given little weight by appellate courts.[2] Accordingly, some legal commentators advise that lawyers cite

---

[1] *See* Stephen Barnett, *No-Citation Rules Under Seige: A Battlefield Report and Analysis*, 5 J. App. PRAC. & PROCESS 473 (2004).

[2] Seventh Circuit Judge Ilana Rovner stated that she is "fairly certain that unpublished opinions will be given very little weight" by appellate courts. Helen W. Gunnarsson, *New rule allows citation of unpublished federal opinions*, ILL. B. J. (Feb. 1, 2007).

unpublished opinions only when the opinion is directly on point and there is no published authority on the subject. Another circumstance in which an appellate litigant might consider citing unpublished opinions is when they demonstrate that other panels are in accord with a principle enunciated in a published opinion that has not yet been widely cited and therefore may not yet appear to be settled law.

INDEX

References are to Pages